Holt McDougal
Algebra 1

Pre-AP Resources

HOLT McDOUGAL

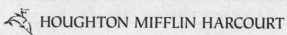

HOUGHTON MIFFLIN HARCOURT

Contents

Introduction

The Pre-AP* course is designed for students who want to be better prepared to take Advanced Placement courses while still in high school so that they may start in higher level courses upon entering college. The standard Algebra 1 course has been enhanced with additional materials and teaching tips that promote a deeper mathematical understanding of the topics, extend the topics past what is given in the standard course, and present new topics that are not typically included in a high school curriculum. The new and extended topics are specifically chosen to prepare the student for AP courses in terms of both their algebra and geometry skills and their understanding of the underlying concepts.

Pre-AP Students

Students pursuing an Advanced Placement course of study may be motivated by a variety of reasons.

- Their tentative career choices
- Their love or aptitude for the subject matter
- Their parents' desire to have them excel
- The academic prestige brought to them by enrolling in the course

Some students may be pursuing this course of study for the wrong reasons; schools should carefully screen students to determine which students should enroll in the Pre-AP course. Students enrolling in the course and their parents should be fully informed of the expectations and demands of the Pre-AP course. It is also highly recommended that a system be in place whereby students enrolled in the Pre-AP course may be re-enrolled into a section of the standard course in the event that the teacher, the student, or the parents feel that the student is not well suited for the Pre-AP course once the course has begun.

Grades are not the only indicator of who is likely to excel in the Pre-AP program. Motivation and a willingness to work hard are two important factors for success that are very difficult to measure. Certain learning preferences and styles may also be more compatible with the Pre-AP course than others. So, be prepared to consider a variety of factors as your school develops its Pre-AP screening process.

Students who have earned high grades in previous mathematics courses are certainly candidates for admittance into the Pre-AP course. To determine whether these students should be admitted into the course, first determine whether there is any desire on the part of the student to follow the Pre-AP course of study. This may involve questioning the student about tentative career plans, enjoyment of mathematics, and general academic goals. Students who are motivated more by attaining high grades than by learning the material may not be the best fit for the Pre-AP course. Such students, as well as their parents, may become dissatisfied with the class, the teacher, or the school if they perceive that the student could be earning a higher grade in a standard course.

Consider as well that a student may have been able to maintain high grades in previous mathematics courses without developing a conceptual understanding of the mathematics. This could happen in situations where the concepts were presented but were never assessed as such. The student may have earned high grades by successfully learning how to work the exercises with limited understanding of the reasons for the processes. A student who does not pay attention while the teacher is developing the conceptual

*Pre-AP is a registered trademark of the College Entrance Examination Board, which was not involved in the production of and does not endorse this product.

understanding, but pays attention when the teacher starts demonstrating how to work the exercises, may not be a good candidate for the Pre-AP course because of the level of conceptual understanding expected in the course. This level of conceptual understanding is necessary in order to pass the Advanced Placement exams. Watch out for the student whose attitude is along the lines of "just show me how to do the problem." Even though that student may maintain high grades, he or she may become defensive when challenged to justify the mathematical processes used to solve a problem and overall be uncomfortable in the Pre-AP classroom.

Be warned that students who have high expectations of themselves because of a history of high grades in mathematics courses may become frustrated when placed in a new environment where they do not perform as well as they did in the old environment. These problems can potentially be disruptive to the entire class if not handled properly by the teacher. These students may not accept their own responsibility, and may blame the teacher, the school, or the curriculum. Such students would be much happier in the standard course which would be more compatible with their learning preferences.

While there are definite benefits to screening students who have maintained high grades, do not overlook students with average grades who may benefit from the Pre-AP course. In some situations, a student's learning style may not have been compatible with the teaching style in previous courses causing the student's learning and, consequently, grades to suffer.

Among average grade earners, look for students who are highly motivated to learn and have a desire to understand the mathematical concepts and not just work problems. These students may not have learned as much as they could have in previous courses because the conceptual justifications for the mathematical methods were missing from the classroom. For these students, the Pre-AP classroom may be the perfect environment in which to thrive academically. Even if the student maintains the same grade level in the Pre-AP level as in previous courses, the student could be learning mathematics with a deeper understanding. Remember that it will take some time to make up for the learning missed in the past. If such students display a continued desire to learn and maintain a good attitude in the Pre-AP course, they should remain in the program and be encouraged to do their best.

However, some minimal level of past academic achievement must be set as a cut off point for admission to the Pre-AP course. Students should not be encouraged to get in over their heads where they are likely to fail. The goal is to have every student in the mathematics course that is the best fit for that student. The screening process will certainly need to be fine-tuned from time to time as you learn what works for your classroom and what does not.

In the Pre-AP classroom, students will need to be highly motivated to learn the subject matter. Try to learn what motivates each of the students in the Pre-AP course and build on that motivation whenever possible.

- If a student is motivated by a particular career possibility, point out in class how the material may be used in that career or in other courses that lead up to that career.
- For students who enjoy learning mathematics, be sure to include challenging problems, some of which may be games or puzzles, and present them as being fun.

- For students who have an aptitude in mathematics, be sure that they clearly see their successes in the course and their potential for continued success; this group may need the most encouragement during challenging topics because they are accustomed to mathematics being easy for them. Encourage such students to participate in mathematics competitions.

- Students who are in the class because of parental expectations may be seeking the approval of authority in general; praise these students as much as possible and find ways to acknowledge their accomplishments.

Personality traits will also differ from student to student, even in a Pre-AP classroom. Some students will be extremely independent and prefer working alone, while others will be more social and prefer to work in a group where they can exchange ideas with others. Some students may tend to take a leadership role in the classroom, while others prefer to participate in a more discreet manner. Some students will want to figure everything out in a way that makes sense to them, while others are more willing to accept the teacher's explanations. Some students will be more intimidated by peer pressure than others, being concerned about giving a wrong answer when participating in class. Some students may not know when to stop struggling with a challenging problem and ask for help, while others may give up too soon and look for someone else to show them the solution. The Pre-AP classroom should be an environment that meets the needs of all students, giving each student the opportunity to be himself or herself while providing an atmosphere for learning.

Remember that treating your students fairly may not mean treating them all the same. Treat each student in the manner that will most effectively encourage that student to work hard and succeed in the course.

While most students in the Pre-AP classroom will want to be there, there may be the occasional student who really doesn't want to learn mathematics at the Pre-AP level. They may have appeared to meet all the criteria for the course and may have answered the screening questions correctly. These students may know how to play the academic game; rather than put their efforts into learning the subject matter, they put their efforts into working the system. These students may not be comfortable with open-ended assignments because they are looking for a formulaic method for success. Rather than doing their best, they want to do the minimal amount of work to earn the desired grade. In fact, they may actually ask the teacher *What do I need to do to get an A in this class?* They do not accept general answers such as *Participate in class discussions and do your best on the assignments.* As long as these students do not adversely affect other students, let them stay in the Pre-AP classroom and try to work with them, as best you can, to see that learning and understanding are the goals.

Pre-AP Parents

Whenever possible, you should inform parents, at least in writing if not in person, of the increased expectations and demands on the student in the Pre-AP course. Parents should be aware that the Pre-AP course may have more homework than the standard course and that some of the material in the course may seem quite different than the material they may have seen in high school courses before. Though it is not always possible, encourage parents to take an active role in the students' learning. Parents who understand the goals of the course are more likely to be supportive of the course and encourage their student to excel.

Pre-AP Content

The Pre-AP course includes the content of the standard Algebra I course as well as additional content that brings the course to the Pre-AP level. The additional materials include more proofs and justifications for selected methods, further examples of applications for some of the topics, extensions of some methods to cover more cases, explanations of the connections between various topics, alternative methods of solving some problems, and some new topics with an emphasis on building the reasoning skills for calculus.

Some of the additional content may make more sense once students have started taking a calculus course. The goal is to introduce additional content in order to give students exposure but not necessarily to expect full comprehension and mastery of the additional topics.

Time for the additional content is carved out of the schedule by combining similar lessons into one lesson, especially where topics from previous mathematics courses are reviewed. Although review topics are included, you should be able to review material more quickly with Pre-AP level students.

Some themes are developed through the text and additional materials. Look for opportunities to reinforce these themes, which include logic and logical reasoning, geometric interpretations of algebra, graphing calculator solutions, undefined expressions, special cases, and exceptions to rules.

Pre-AP Course

The Pre-AP course utilizes the text and special features within the text as well as supplemental materials found in this Pre-AP Resources book. Within the text, the Pre-AP course makes full use of the Investigating Algebra Activities, Graphing Calculator Activities, Mixed Problem Solving pages, and lesson Extensions. In this Pre-AP Resources book, you will find, Best Practices for each chapter, as well as copymasters that may be reproduced and distributed to the students. All of these products are an integral part of the Pre-AP course.

The Best Practices for each chapter provide additional background on some of the topics and suggestions on how to use the Math Background Notes from the Differentiated Instruction book in the Pre-AP classroom. This background material is essential to the level of understanding that we are striving for in the Pre-AP course. The Best Practices also suggest further activities or examples that may be helpful in introducing a new topic. In some cases, the Best Practices describe the level of understanding that the student is expected to achieve for a particular topic. Descriptions of the copymasters and how they fit into the courses are also provided in the Best Practices.

The copymasters contain the additional lessons that supplement those in the book. Some copymasters are full-day, stand-alone lessons, while others provide an additional example or special case to supplement a lesson. Copymasters include Key Concepts, Examples, and Activities similar to those in the text, so that the student's experience with the copymasters will be similar to that with the text. Some of the copymasters will be covered in class like a regular lesson, while others may be given as independent activity or as part of the daily homework assignment.

The copymasters build on the material in the text as well as on each other. Some copymasters may assume that previous copymasters have been utilized. If you skip one or more copymasters, be careful when using later copymasters that you have not missed a prerequisite. Of course, the previous material can be included in the current lesson if need be.

Pre-AP Assessment

The existing end-of-chapter assessment materials should be modified for the Pre-AP course to reflect both the additional topics that are covered as well as the depth at which the material is to be learned. Since it is difficult to assess understanding on a written test, some assessment should include the student presenting a solution to the teacher and explaining the methods used and why they work.

Ongoing assessment may be the best way to assess understanding and motivate students to work diligently on a daily basis. Students should know that all work may be assessed, so that no assignment is seen as unimportant or optional (unless it truly is optional). Assessment must go further than just determining whether the student can work the problems; it must include a component for mathematical understanding.

Pre-AP Classroom

The Pre-AP classroom should be an environment that inspires learning. Since learning styles differ even among Pre-AP students, it is important that the environment allows for a variety of learning styles. The in-class experience should set the example for the students' out-of-class work. Use a mixture of techniques such as class discussion, small group work, and individual work. In class, be involved in guiding students on how to use each of these techniques effectively. Then outside the classroom, when you are not present, the students will know your expectations of them as they complete assignments. Always set the example in class and encourage students to develop study habits that they can apply throughout their academic careers.

The class should be structured to allow students to express their ideas and talk through their thought processes as they make conjectures about new topics. All students need to be respectful of others' ideas, even when those ideas may seem farfetched. As the teacher, you must quickly deal with students who ridicule others for making mistakes or bad suggestions. Emphasize that many great mathematicians have gone done the wrong road many times before taking the right one.

The classroom also needs to be free from distractions that would keep students from being able to think deeply. Remember that you want the students to understand the mathematics behind the methods, which means that need to pay attention to logical arguments and follow the steps. This is hard to do in an environment where there may be other things attracting the students' attentions. Set guidelines for appropriate classroom behavior. Do not allow students to do work for other classes or write notes or text messages during the vital classroom discussions of the Pre-AP class.

Encourage students to come to class prepared to learn. If you never express your expectations of the students, they may assume that your expectations are low. Thus, tell them that you expect them to be ready for class to begin when the bell rings, which might include having all necessary materials on the desktop and materials put away. (Since classroom time is usually limited, don't let students waste doing what they should have done before class starts.) Tell them that they are expected to participate in all classroom activities whether those activities involve class discussion, small group work, or individual work. If you expect them to take notes or work along on their own calculators as you work an example on yours, you will need to tell them to do so. In order to prepare students for Advanced Placement courses, you are teaching more than mathematics in your classroom; you are teaching the work ethic that is necessary to succeed. The example you set of how you structure your classroom and use your time will reach far beyond your students' high school years.

Conclusion

Once you begin your Pre-AP course, remember to be flexible. You may need to adjust the pace or classroom procedures along the way. You may also find that the students are not responding as well as you had expected. Do not be discouraged. Modify the materials and suggestions to fit your needs. Even if you are not able to cover all the additional material in the Pre-AP course, if you emphasize mathematical understanding of the covered material, the students will still benefit greatly.

Remember that the students' goal is to be better prepared for AP courses, not to be perfect.

Pre-AP Copymaster List

Each copymaster can be used with the indicated textbook lesson.
Some items are designed to look more deeply at lesson content, while
others go beyond lesson content into a related topic. A few items can
be treated as additional lessons.

Chapter 5

Chapter 6

Chapter 7

Chapter 8

Chapter 9

Chapter 10

Chapter 11

Pre-AP Overview

CHAPTER 1

Best Practices

Lessons 1.1–1.2

Evaluating Expressions These lessons can be taught together as one lesson, as Lesson 1.2 discusses the content of Lesson 1.1 at a more advanced level. Approach the lessons together as learning how to simplify an algebraic expression after the variables have been replaced by numbers. The Graphing Calculator Activity with Lesson 1.2 shows how to evaluate such expressions using a calculator. In many cases, expressions may be entered into a calculator exactly as they appear on the page, since graphing and scientific calculators use the same order of operations presented in the text. However, the activity stresses that a numerator or denominator consisting of more than one term needs to be enclosed in parentheses when it is entered into a calculator. Have the students evaluate expressions such as $\frac{3^2 + 1}{2^3 - 3}$ with and without using the necessary parentheses to see that the results are different. In the end, be sure to emphasize the correct way to evaluate the expression.

Lessons 1.3–1.5

Writing Expressions Learning to write expressions in Lesson 1.3 is the first step to writing equations and inequalities in Lesson 1.4 and then solving problems using equations in Lesson 1.5. Emphasize the importance throughout these lessons of reading the verbal descriptions carefully to identify important information and to look for key words. Asking the students to identify everyday situations where an equation might be used to solve a problem will help them see the practicality of algebra. The problem solving process can be practiced using the Mixed Review of Problem Solving, the Problem Solving Workshop, and the copymaster entitled *Extended Problem Solving*. This copymaster presents some types of problems that can be solved using the Division Algorithm for integers.

Lesson 1.6

Precision Students may believe that if a measurement system is precise then the system produces technically correct answers. This would be a good time to challenge that idea. Ask students if they can think of a reason why a measurement tool that produces the same results under unchanged conditions may not provide technically correct answers.

Have students consider the simple task of weighing oneself on a basic analog bathroom scale. Ask those students who have experience with an analog scale if they have ever noticed that the pointer was not actually aligned on the 0-pound mark. Whenever a person repeatedly steps on and off the scale, the weights shown on the scale should all be the same, which means that the results are precise. But if the scale was not correctly set to 0 before beginning the measurements, the results would not be technically correct. If you have access to such a scale, bringing it for a demonstration will be beneficial for those students who are only familiar with a digital scale. Point out that analog scales have a dial or some other means for adjusting the pointer so it starts at 0 pounds.

Challenge students to think of other examples where the results of repeated measurements under unchanged conditions are precise but not technically correct.

Lessons 1.7–1.8

Functions Be sure that the students understand that functions may be represented by rules, tables, graphs, or sets of ordered pairs. The rules that define functions may be given as equations or as verbal descriptions. Have students suggest their own possible real-world functions, such as those on the copymasters entitled *Identifying Functions* and *Real-World Functions*. Have the class discuss whether each suggestion meets the criteria for being a function. The students can also discuss the best representations for their functions and whether more than one representation is suitable. Be sure that students are familiar with the table feature of their graphing calculators by covering the Graphing Calculator Activity with Lesson 1.7.

Lesson 2.1

Real and Irrational Numbers The copymaster entitled *Counting Sets of Rational Numbers* will challenge students to think about the rational numbers as being infinite both in the sense that they continue forever without bound and in the sense that there are infinitely many rational numbers between any two distinct rational numbers.

The copymaster entitled *Building a Number System* introduces the students to closure of sets of numbers. Closure is used to demonstrate the necessity of extending the whole numbers to the integers and the integers to the rational numbers. The development follows a natural course that roughly parallels the sequence in which students were introduced to these number systems in their childhood. The goal is to emphasize the relationship between sets of numbers and operations on those sets.

The copymaster entitled *The Need for Irrational Numbers* demonstrates both the geometrical and algebraic reasons for irrational numbers. Some irrational numbers, such as the square roots of positive rational numbers that are not perfect squares, can be motivated through the lack of closure of the positive rational numbers under taking square roots. Taking square roots should also be presented as the inverse operation of squaring. Develop the theme of inverse operations whenever applicable, so that later in their mathematical studies the concept of inverse functions will seem very natural to the students.

The Investigating Algebra Activity with Lesson 2.1, the Extension *Use Real and Rational Numbers*, and the copymaster entitled *More Logical Reasoning* continue the development of logic begun in Lesson 2.1.

Lessons 2.2–2.3

One- and Two-Step Equations These lessons may be easily combined. You may skip the application example for Lesson 2.2 since you will be covering the application example in

Lesson 2.3 the skills developed in these lessons are fundamental to solving all types of equations. Do not spend too much time focusing on the fact that these are linear equations; focus on the fact that you can add or subtract the same quantity or multiply or divide by the same nonzero quantity on both sides of an equation without changing the solutions of the equation.

For class discussion, ask your students why you can only multiply or divide both sides of an equation by a *nonzero* quantity. Have them experiment with multiplying and dividing by zero. They should realize right away that division by zero is undefined, so that dividing both sides by zero is meaningless. Multiplying by zero always results in the equation $0 = 0$, which is typically not equivalent to the original equation, so that multiplying by zero does not lead to a solution of the equation.

Lessons 2.4–2.5

Multi-Step Equations These lessons introduce more equation-solving techniques, which include simplifying one or both sides of an equation and adding the same variable expression to both sides of an equation. When solving an equation, you can add or subtract the same quantity on both sides, regardless of whether that quantity is a number, a variable, or an algebraic expression, without changing the solutions of the equation.

In Lesson 2.5, you should also note that you may not always multiply or divide both sides of an equation by a variable expression because the value of the variable expression may be zero. Starting with the equation $x = 1$ and multiplying both sides by x results in the equation $x^2 = x$. The number 0 is a solution of the second equation, but it is not a solution of the original equation. (You can check this by substitution.) Multiplying by x changed the solutions of the equation.

The copymaster entitled *Writing Repeating Decimals as Fractions* provides an additional application of solving equations. This is an excellent opportunity to review the multiple representations of rational numbers and the differences between the decimal forms of rational and irrational numbers.

Lessons 2.6–2.7

Solving Proportions These lessons introduce two ways to solve proportions: multiplying each side by an appropriate real number and using cross products. The proportions in Lesson 2.6 have denominators containing only real numbers and no variables, so that you can avoid the problem of multiplying each side of the equation by a variable expression. However, in Lesson 2.7, some proportions contain variables in the denominators. Challenge your students to think about whether these proportions with variables in denominators can be solved by the methods of Lesson 2.6. Can they reach the conclusion by themselves that cross multiplying is equivalent to multiplying both sides of the proportion by one denominator and then multiplying both sides by the other denominator? Ask students to explain whether 3 could be a solution of the proportion $\frac{5}{t-3} = \frac{10}{24}$. Then ask whether they see any need to check their solutions in the original proportion.

The copymaster entitled *Unit Rates and Dimensional Analysis* provides additional material on ratios and how they are used as well as practice multiplying and simplifying ratios. The copymaster entitled *Deciding When to Use Cross Products* helps students distinguish equations that can be solved using cross products from those that can not.

Lesson 2.8

Functions and Formulas In this lesson, the techniques for solving equations in one variable are used to rewrite functions and formulas containing two or more variables in different forms. Note that multiplying or dividing both sides of an equation by a variable is sometimes required. Ask students why the assumption that $a \neq 0$ is included in step 1 of Example 1. The copymaster entitled *Identifying the Domain of a Variable in a Formula* will help students recognize the natural restrictions on the values of variables in many real-world formulas. For many formulas, the values of the variables are limited in such a way that division by zero will not occur.

The copymaster entitled *Solving Linear Equations with a Graphing Calculator* extends the chapter by showing how many of the equations solved throughout the chapter can be solved with a graphing calculator. Using the calculator will help students relate equations to their graphs.

Pre-AP Best Practices

Lesson 3.1

Plotting Points The material in this lesson is mostly review for the students. The students have plotted points in the plane before and have worked with graphs that consist of a set of points. In fact, students graphed functions as sets of points in Lesson 1.8. The copymaster entitled *Scatter Plots* provides an additional application of plotting points. Emphasize the difference between scatter plots and graphs of functions to help prepare the students for graphing linear equations.

Lesson 3.2

Graphing Linear Equations In this lesson, we move from graphing an equation as a set of points to connecting those points to produce the graph of the equation. While the main technique in this lesson is to plot several points and then draw the line through them, more efficient methods will be developed in subsequent lessons. Now is the appropriate time to emphasize that the equations under consideration are linear, so that the students will make the connection between linear equations and graphs that are lines.

The Graphing Calculator Activity with Lesson 3.2 can be easily extended by applying the techniques of Lesson 2.8 to solve each of the equations in Exercises 11–18 in Lesson 3.2 for y and then graphing each equation with a graphing calculator. This is an excellent way for students to check their own work as they learn to recognize that their hand-drawn graph and the graph produced by their graphing calculators represent the same equation.

The Extension *Identify Discrete and Continuous Functions* and the copymaster entitled *Distinguishing between Discrete and Continuous Variables* will help to make the distinction between the graphs in Lesson 3.1 and those in Lesson 3.2 clearer. The graphs in Lesson 3.1 are not necessarily "unfinished" graphs because the points were not connected by a line; some variables in real-life situations can only have whole number or integer values, so that the corresponding graphs will only contain points corresponding to those whole numbers or integers. Encourage the students to think about whether it makes sense to draw a line through their points when graphing an equation from a real-life situation.

Lesson 3.3

Intercepts Begin this lesson by reviewing some basics of geometry about lines in the plane, especially that two points determine a line. Discuss how we've been plotting more points than we actually need before we draw our lines. Then present the intercepts as two convenient points to use to graph a line. Extend the lesson by discussing that not all lines have two intercepts. Horizontal and vertical lines are two cases of this that are covered on the copymaster entitled *Intercepts of Horizontal and Vertical Lines*. You can further discuss lines where the x-intercept and the y-intercept are actually the same point, $(0, 0)$. Challenge the students to think about the intercepts of the graphs of $x = 0$ and $y = 0$.

Lesson 3.4

Slope and Rate of Change As you present the formula for calculating slope, be sure to emphasize equally the interpretation of slope as rate of change. Students should be able to explain the derivation of the slope formula.

Example 4 picks up the theme once again that division by zero is undefined. If any students are still struggling with this concept, here is another opportunity to show them that division by zero is meaningless. By interpreting slope as the change in y corresponding to a change of 1 in x, we can see that a vertical line has an undefined slope because there is never a change of 1 in x. This case corresponds to a denominator of zero when you attempt to use the slope formula.

The copymaster entitled *Integer Solutions of Linear Equations* provides an additional application of slope. For some linear equations in two variables, only ordered pair solutions where both coordinates are integers have any useful interpretation. Once one such solution is found, the slope can be used to find other solutions. This process parallels the method of graphing a line using the slope and *y*-intercept presented in the following lesson.

Lesson 3.5

Slope-Intercept Form Emphasize that the slope-intercept form of a line is perhaps the most important form because it is the function form, the form that may be entered into a graphing calculator. Besides this, it is an extremely useful form because you can easily read the slope and the *y*-intercept of the line from the equation.

Have students verify that 5 is indeed the *y*-intercept of the graph of $y = 3x + 5$ by substituting 0 for *x* and simplifying. Then have them verify that the slope is 3 by finding one other point on the line and using that point and (0, 5) in the slope formula.

Encourage the students to use their graphing calculators to experiment with lines of different slopes but the same *y*-intercept and lines with different *y*-intercepts but the same slope.

You can omit Example 3 and assign the copymaster entitled *Interpreting the Slope and y-Intercept* in its place. These additional examples help the student to understand what the slope and *y*-intercept mean in some real-life situations.

Lesson 3.6

Direct Variation As you present this lesson, make sure that you do not lose the intuitive meaning of direct variation in all of the writing of equations. The copymaster entitled *Distinguishing between Direct Variation and Other Linear Models* will help you establish the differences in real-life situations.

Lesson 3.7

Linear Functions This lesson reframes the development of linear equations so far in this chapter in terms of functions. The function notation introduced at the beginning of the lesson may be new to some students and you may need to spend some time familiarizing them with it. The rest of the lesson is just a recap of what has already been done in the chapter using the new notation. Stress that the graphing calculator graphs functions.

Pre-AP Best Practices

Lessons 4.1–4.5

Writing Linear Equations In these lessons, emphasize the geometric fact that two distinct points in the plane determine one and only one line in the plane. It is true in three-dimensional space as well that two distinct points determine a line but equations of lines in space are not as simple to write because the concept of "slope" is not as straightforward. You may challenge students to attempt to define the "slope" of a line in space by looking at the diagonal of a rectangular box, which could be the interior of your classroom. Starting at one endpoint of the diagonal and moving along the diagonal toward the other endpoint, compare the change of distance from one side of the box to the changes of distances from the adjacent side and bottom of the box. The students should easily be able to describe two different slopes, one describing the rate of change for the distance from the adjacent side and the other describing the rate of change for the distance from the bottom of the box. Can these two slopes somehow be combined into one expression for the "slope" of the line? The difficulty of finding a simple way to describe the "slope" of a line in space will help the students appreciate the beautiful simplicity of the slope of a line in the plane.

Having established that two distinct points in the plane determine a unique line in the plane, we may conclude that those two points contain all the information we need to find out all there is to know about the line. We have already seen how to move from the two points to the slope of the line. In these lessons, we move from the two points or one point and the slope to an equation for the line. An equation for the line describes all the points on the line, not just the original points given. The Math Background Notes for the chapter show the derivations of the different formulas for writing an equation for a line. At the Pre-AP level, students should understand and be able to demonstrate the origins of these formulas. For example, a student should be able to explain that the point-slope form is derived from the slope formula by assuming that the slope m and one

point (x_1, y_1) are known. The arbitrary point (x, y) replaces (x_2, y_2) in the slope formula, and the point-slope formula is found by multiplying each side by the denominator $x - x_1$, as shown below.

Slope formula: $m = \dfrac{y_2 - y_1}{x_2 - x_1}$

Replace x_2 with x and y_2 with y: $m = \dfrac{y - y_1}{x - x_1}$

Multiply by the denominator: $m(x - x_1) = y - y_1$

The final form may then be found by interchanging the sides of the equations. See the Math Background Notes for details on deriving the other formulas.

Students should also understand how the point-slope form simplifies to the slope-intercept form when the point given is the y-intercept $(0, b)$. Replace (x_1, y_1) with $(0, b)$ in the point-slope formula, simplify, and add b to both sides, as shown below.

Point-slope form: $y - y_1 = m(x - x_1)$

Replace x_1 with 0 and y_1 with b: $y - b = m(x - 0)$

Simplify: $y - b = mx$

Add b to both sides: $y = mx + b$

This last line is the slope-intercept formula.

The Pre-AP level copymaster entitled *Representations of Lines* reinforces the idea that a line can be represented by two points, a point and a slope, an equation in any of the forms described in this chapter, or a graph. Students should be able to easily convert from one representation to another and be able to establish the coordinates of any point on a line.

Besides knowing the formulas and their derivations, the students also need to be able to determine which formula is necessary or even most convenient in a given situation. Students should also know some of the advantages and disadvantages of writing equations in different forms. The Pre-AP level copymaster entitled *Unique Representations* will help in one of these areas. The point-slope form of an equation for a line is not unique. While the slope m of the line is constant, any point on the line may be chosen as the point (x_1, y_1) for the formula. Since there are infinitely many different points on a line, there are infinitely many different point-slope equations for the line. It is important to point out that all of these equations are equivalent, meaning that they all have exactly the same solutions so that they describe the same line. One difficulty then is recognizing that two different equations actually represent the same line. Given two points, ask students to calculate the slope of the line passing through the points and then write two point-slope equations, one with each given point. Then challenge the students to use their equation-solving skills to rewrite one or both equations until the two equations are identical.

The standard form also suffers from a lack of uniqueness. However, this is often remedied by placing certain conditions on the coefficients in the equation. Assuming that the coefficients are rational numbers and that A is not zero, the equation $Ax + By = C$ can be rewritten so that A, B, and C are integers, the coefficient of x is positive, and A, B, and C are relatively prime (share no common factors). This is accomplished by multiplying both sides of the equation by an appropriate rational number. When the coefficients satisfy the conditions above, the standard form is unique.

The standard form has two advantages over the other forms. Every line in the plane has an equation in standard form. This is not true of either form that depends on the slope. Since a vertical line has an undefined slope, the equation of a vertical line cannot have either a point-slope or a slope-intercept form. The x- and y-intercepts of a line are easily determined from the standard form by first replacing y with 0 and dividing both sides by the coefficient of x and then replacing x with 0 and dividing both sides by the coefficient of y.

The slope-intercept equation for a line is unique. Students should understand that this means if two different people write an equation for a line in slope-intercept form the equations will be the same. Of course, the representation of the slope and y-intercept may differ; one person may choose to write a slope as a fraction $\frac{1}{2}$ while another may choose the decimal representation 0.5 for the same slope.

The slope-intercept form has the advantage that one may determine the slope and y-intercept of the line by simple observation. Being solved for y, the slope-intercept form also has the advantage of being in *function* form. It is easy to substitute values for x and find the corresponding values of y. This is also the form that is necessary for graphing a line on a graphing calculator. Given an equation of a line in any form, it is imperative that students be able to rewrite the equation in slope-intercept form in order to use their graphing calculators effectively.

Lessons 4.6–4.7

Modeling Data Writing equations that model data is an important application of algebra. Lesson 4.6 and the Graphing Calculator Activity that follows demonstrate two ways to find a linear equation that models a set of data. Emphasize that the goal of writing such models is to make predictions as in Lesson 4.7. Also point out the importance of drawing a scatter plot for the data to determine whether a linear model is a good fit. If the points in the scatter plot do not fall on or near a straight line, any predictions made using a linear model will be of limited or no value.

Best Practices

Lessons 5.1–5.3

Solving Linear Inequalities The steps for solving linear inequalities are nearly identical to those for solving linear equations, with one important difference: When multiplying or dividing both sides of a linear equation by a negative number, it is necessary to reverse the inequality symbol. At the Pre-AP level, this process need not be mysterious to the student. As with many concepts involving inequalities, an understanding of why the inequality symbol is reversed lies in an understanding of how numbers are ordered on the number line.

Students should never lose sight of the fact that $a < b$ means that a lies to the left of b on the number line. While students rarely have difficulty comparing two positive numbers and only sometimes have difficulty comparing a positive and a negative number, many struggle with the fact that $-2 < -1$. The number line is the best way to visualize the ordering of the real numbers. It is important that you help any struggling students visualize the ordering of the numbers so that they understand the processes for solving inequalities and interpreting their solutions.

In order to remember why we reverse the inequality symbol when we multiply by a negative number, have the students memorize a simple example. No student will have difficulty accepting that $1 < 2$. On the number line, this means that 1 is to the left of 2. When the numbers are each multiplied by -1, we have -1 and -2. A quick glance at the number line reveals that -2 is to the left of -1, so that $-2 < -1$ or, equivalently, $-1 > -2$. By comparing $1 < 2$ and $-1 > -2$, we see that when the numbers are made negative the inequality symbol is reversed. If students will memorize a simple example like this and recall it at the appropriate time, the rule for reversing the inequality when multiplying or dividing by a negative number need not be mysterious to them.

While there is little difference in the processes of solving linear equations and linear inequalities, there is a huge difference in the solution sets. Pre-AP level students should be expected to recall that a linear equation may have no solution, one solution, or all real numbers as solutions. While a linear inequality may also have no solution ($x + 1 < x$) or all real numbers as solutions ($x + 1 > x$), the typical case we will study has solution sets that are ranges of numbers, such as all the numbers greater than or equal to some fixed number. These ranges of numbers for inequalities correspond to the one-solution case for equations.

Throughout this process, do not lose sight of the fact that ranges of numbers have real-world interpretations. Most Algebra I students are looking forward to such privileges as driving a car and voting; they understand that in most states you need to be at least 16 years old to get a driver's license and that you must be at least 18 years old to vote. These correspond to ranges of numbers that can be represented by the inequalities $a \geq 16$ and $a \geq 18$. They also understand that to get children's prices at many amusement parks and restaurants you can be at most 12 years old, which corresponds to the inequality $a \leq 12$. Through examples such as these, you can reinforce the interpretation of inequalities as limitations or constraints. As most students understand financial constraints, money problems are also excellent examples for illustrating real-life inequalities.

Lesson 5.4

Compound Inequalities With the Pre-AP level copymasters entitled *The Meanings of* And *and* Or *in Logic* and *Graphing Calculators and Logic*, we continue to develop our logic theme in the Pre-AP level course. The key to understanding the solutions of compound inequalities is to correctly interpret the words *and* and *or*. Do not assume that your students fully understand the implications of these simple words. Take some time to develop an intuitive understanding of their meanings.

To return to our example of ages, the students will intuitively understand that to be old enough to both drive and vote they will need to satisfy the stricter age requirement, that is, be at least 18 years old ($a \geq 18$). However, to be old enough to drive or vote, they must satisfy the looser requirement of being at least 16 years old ($a \geq 16$). In this second case, point out that the statement *If you are at least 16 old years old, then you are old enough to drive or to vote* does not imply that you have the choice of driving or voting. The statement merely implies that you are old enough to do at least one of them; in this case, you are old enough to drive.

The copymaster entitled *Compound Inequalities with No Solution or All Real Numbers as Solutions* will further help to distinguish between the cases of *and* and *or*. Consider the statement *Guests who are at most 12 years old and at least 65 years old receive a 25% discount on admission.* The compound inequality $a \leq 12$ *and* $a \geq 65$ has no solution; no one is both at most 12 years old and at least 65 years old. Though we understand the intent of the statement, it should be properly stated as *Guests who are at most 12 years old or at least 65 years old receive a 25% discount on admission* if anyone is to receive the discount.

Lessons 5.5–5.6

Absolute Value Every time absolute value comes up is an excellent opportunity to remind the students that the absolute value of a number is the distance of the number from 0 on the number line. At the Pre-AP level, no student should be holding onto a *drop-the-negative-sign-if-the-number-is-negative* definition of absolute value. This way of thinking does not demonstrate an understanding of absolute value and merely shows that a student is going through the motions of mathematics. The copymaster entitled *A Closer Look at Absolute Value* will help you make this point.

The copymaster entitled *Solving Absolute Value Equations by Graphing* and the Extension *Graph Absolute Value Functions* provide a two-dimensional graphical representation of a linear inequality in one variable. Students need to understand that numbers can be ordered vertically as well as horizontally. Whereas $a < b$ means that a is to the left of b on a horizontal number line (x-axis), $a < b$ means that a is below b on a vertical number line (y-axis). Practically speaking then, the value of one algebraic expression is less than the value of a second algebraic expression where the graph of the equation formed from the first expression is lower than the graph of the equation formed from the second expression. In particular, the value of an expression is negative where the graph is below the x-axis and positive where the graph is above the x-axis.

The properties of the number line and the plane cannot be overemphasized when working with inequalities.

The copymaster entitled *Margins of Error* provides an additional example of applications of absolute value inequalities. While explaining the process for solving an inequality of the form $|x - 9| < 0.2$, remember that this statement may be read *x is within 0.2 unit of 9.* Emphasize the interpretation as distance on the number line.

Lesson 6.1

Lines in the Plane This chapter provides an excellent opportunity to review and present new concepts from plane geometry. The copymaster entitled *Graph Systems of Two Equations and Three Equations* presents the important facts from geometry that will enhance your students' understanding of systems of linear equations. The copymaster will also contrast some properties in the plane with corresponding properties in space. Students may be surprised by the differences.

Of course, the most important property of lines for the present lesson is that two distinct lines in the plane that intersect do so in exactly one point. The cases for lines that are not distinct or that do not intersect are discussed in Lesson 6.5, where it will be appropriate to talk about whether two lines intersect in terms of their slopes.

Solving Systems by Graphing The Graphing Calculator Activity can be extended using the copymaster entitled *Exploring Systems of Three Linear Equations* in which solutions to equations with three variables are explored using a graphing calculator. While the geometric aspect of the solution may be lost, students will be exposed to larger systems of equations and to more of the terminology and methods of matrix algebra.

As you move on to the algebraic methods of solving systems of linear equations, emphasize that the graphing method (particularly by hand) is not an efficient method of solving systems. The problem with extending this method to systems with three or more variables is just one of the difficulties. The necessity of drawing neat and precise graphs in order to estimate the solution is perhaps a greater problem.

Lesson 6.2

The Substitution Method The copymaster entitled *The Symmetric, Reflexive, and Transitive Properties of Equality* reviews the properties of equality of real numbers that make the substitution method possible:

$a = a$ Reflexivity

$a = b$ if and only if $b = a$ Symmetry

If $a = b$ and $b = c$, then $a = c$.   Transitivity

The substitution method of solving linear systems relies upon the fact that the solution of the system

$$ax + by = e$$
$$cx + dy = f$$

is a single ordered pair (x_0, y_0) that satisfies both equations. Since the values of x_0 and y_0 are the same in the equations $ax_0 + by_0 = e$ and $cx_0 + dy_0 = f$, the expressions $y_0 = \dfrac{e - ax_0}{b}$ and $y_0 = \dfrac{f - cx_0}{d}$ represent the same value of y_0. Therefore, the two expressions can be equated to form the equation $\dfrac{e - ax_0}{b} = \dfrac{f - cx_0}{d}$, where the two occurrences of x_0 represent the same number.

Through this process, the two equations with two variables are simplified to one equation with one variable, which we know how to solve. This is an example of a common mathematical theme: simplifying a new problem to a problem that we already know how to solve.

Lessons 6.3–6.4

The Addition Method The copymaster entitled *Adding Equals to Equals* reviews the property of equality of real numbers that makes the addition method of solving linear systems possible:

If $a = b$ and $c = d$, then $a + c = b + d$.

The addition method also relies upon the fact that the solution of the system

$$ax + by = e$$
$$cx + dy = f$$

is a single ordered pair (x_0, y_0) that satisfies both equations. Since the values of x_0 and y_0 are the same in the equations $ax_0 + by_0 = e$ and $cx_0 + dy_0 = f$, we can write the equation

$$(ax_0 + by_0) + (cx_0 + dy_0) = e + f.$$

The goal is to add the equations in such a way that one of the variables is eliminated.

Like the substitution method, the addition method simplifies a system of two equations with two variables to one equation in one variable.

Comparing the Substitution and Addition Methods

Each of these algebraic methods of solving systems of equations has its advantages and disadvantages. Encourage students to become proficient with both methods of solution. The substitution method can easily be extended to solve a system of two equations where one or both of the equations are nonlinear. The addition method can easily be extended to systems of three or more linear equations.

The copymaster entitled *Solving Systems of Linear Equations Using Cramer's Rule* presents another method for solving systems of linear equations. This copymaster introduces the students to determinants and their relationship to systems of equations. This method also extends easily to solve systems of three or more linear equations. Determinants can be evaluated using a graphing calculator.

Lesson 6.5

Systems with No Solutions or Infinitely Many Solutions

Emphasize the relationship between slope and whether two lines intersect or not. All students should be readily able to reproduce the three graphs in the Concept Summary box as examples of the three possible situations for intersections of two lines. Encourage students to examine the equations given in a system before attempting to solve the system. Many times a student will be able to identify equivalent equations or distinct lines with the same slope by examining the coefficients of x and y and the constant. While solving the system will lead to the correct conclusion, an intuitive understanding of the situations is very important at the Pre-AP level.

Lesson 6.6

Systems of Inequalities

The copymaster entitled *Describing Polygons with Systems of Inequalities* extends the lesson to include graphing systems of three or more linear inequalities that determine a polygonal region of the plane. Then students are challenged to write a system of inequalities that describe a given polygonal region. This process will give the students practice in determining the equation of a line from two points on the line.

CHAPTER 7

Best Practices

Lessons 7.1–7.3

Properties of Exponents The fact that exponential expressions represent repeated multiplication means that products, quotients, and powers of exponential expressions are relatively easy to handle. The copymaster entitled *Adding and Subtracting Exponential Expressions* contrasts the case of multiplication where any two exponential expressions with the same base can be combined with the case of addition and subtraction where like terms are necessary.

The copymaster entitled *Simplifying Rational Expressions* builds upon the previous copymaster and Lessons 7.1 and 7.2, demonstrating how exponential expressions involving the four basic operations as well as exponentiation are simplified.

Students at the Pre-AP level should be able to justify the Product and Quotient Properties as well as the definitions of negative and zero exponents. You can use one or both of the alternative explanations of negative and zero exponents that are presented in the Math Background Notes for this chapter. Give students an opportunity to explain to you or the class why it is natural that a negative exponent should indicate a reciprocal and why a nonzero base with a zero exponent equals 1.

At this level, you can also explain to the class why 0 cannot be raised to a negative or zero power, but first you may want to challenge your students to evaluate 0^0. Students may try to satisfy both "rules" that $0^n = 0$ and $a^0 = 1$, or they may try to justify that one rule takes precedence over the other in this situation. In the end, students should add 0^0 to their mental list of undefined expressions.

The Extension *Define and Use Fractional Exponents* and the copymaster entitled *Exploring Non-Integer Exponents with a Graphing Calculator* lay the ground work for accepting that the exponential functions presented later in the chapter are indeed defined for all real numbers. Encourage the students to experiment with all types of exponents on their calculators, including fractions, decimals, and irrational numbers such as π.

Lessons 7.4–7.5

Exponential Functions Exponential functions can be distinguished from the functions studied so far by the variable in the exponent rather than the base. However, there are many other features of these fascinating functions that set them apart. The copymaster entitled *Average Rates of Change* will help make the distinction between exponential functions and linear functions. By experimenting with the slope formula and different points on the graph of an exponential function, the students will quickly come to the conclusion that different pairs of points lead to different "slopes." This is a great time to emphasize once again that linear functions are characterized by their constant rates of change, or slopes.

While on the topic of rates of change, point out that exponential functions have steeper graphs than other types of functions. You might have students graph several different basic functions, such as $y = x$, $y = 2x$, $y = x^2$, $y = x^3$, and $y = 2^x$, with a graphing calculator and compare the graphs to see which one climbs faster.

The previous supplemental material defining non-integer exponents sets the stage for the copymaster entitled *Exponential Functions: Continuous or Noncontinuous*. Students should understand that if exponential expressions were only defined for integer exponents then the graph of an exponential function would be a set of points with one point corresponding to each integer value of the input variable x. However, since exponential functions are continuous, those points may be connected by a smooth continuous curve.

At the Pre-AP level, students should learn to identify the domain and the range of a function. See the Math Background Notes for this chapter for an explanation of the domain and range of an exponential function.

The graph of an exponential has other important characteristics. If the base is greater than 1, the values of the output variable y approach 0 as the graph continues to the left. The graph approaches but never touches the x-axis; we say that the x-axis is a **horizontal asymptote to the left.** Furthermore, the graph is always moving upward as you look at it from left to right; we say that the function is **increasing** for all real numbers x.

Similarly, if the base of an exponential function is greater than 0 and less than 1, the values of the output variable y approach 0 as the graph continues to the right. The graph approaches but never touches the x-axis; we say that the x-axis is a **horizontal asymptote to the right.** Furthermore, the graph is always moving downward as you look at it from left to right; we say that the function is **decreasing** for all real numbers x.

When a function is either increasing for all real numbers or decreasing for all real numbers, no horizontal line will intersect the graph in more than one point. (Have students investigate this fact in the graph of an exponential function.) It follows that there is exactly one value in the domain corresponding to each value in the range. When a function has this property, it is said to be **one-to-one.** One-to-one functions form a very special class of functions, the functions that have **inverses.** Thus, it is possible to "undo" the action of an exponential function. The copymaster entitled *Solving Exponential Equations* demonstrate how this can be done *informally*.

Growth and Decay Models

The exponential growth and decay models presented in these lessons have very important applications. Emphasize that growth occurs when the base of the exponential expression $1 + r$ is greater than 1 and that decay occurs when the base of the exponential expression $1 - r$ is less than 1. Discuss the origins of the model using the discussion in the Math Background Notes for this chapter.

Encourage students to find data in the media and then evaluate it to see whether changes in the data over time follow either an exponential growth or decay pattern. If they do, write a model for the data by choosing the value for the first time period to be the initial value and using the quotient of two consecutive data to determine r. The copymaster entitled *Model Limitations* will demonstrate that such models are best used to make predictions close to the actual data rather than in the distant future or the distant past.

Pre-AP Best Practices

Lessons 8.1–8.3

Operations on Polynomials In these lessons, we look at the operations of polynomial addition, subtraction, and multiplication. In the Pre-AP level copymasters, we have previously developed the concept of closure of a number system under an operation. To review, a set is **closed** under an operation if whenever the operation is performed on elements from the set the result is also a member of the set. The set of polynomials is closed under the operations of addition, subtraction, and multiplication. Thus, when we add two polynomials the result is a polynomial, when we subtract one polynomial from another the result is a polynomial, and when we multiply two polynomials the result is a polynomial. However, the set of polynomials is not closed under division.

Furthermore, polynomial addition is commutative and associative, the zero polynomial, 0, is an additive identity, and every polynomial has an additive inverse formed by changing the signs of the polynomial's coefficients. Polynomial multiplication is commutative and associative, and 1 is a multiplicative identity. Polynomial multiplication distributes over polynomial addition. It is no surprise that polynomial addition and multiplication have these properties when you remember that the variable in a polynomial represents a real number and the real numbers have these properties.

Notice that we did not mention a multiplicative inverse in the discussion above. Remember that the multiplicative inverse represents division and we have already stated that the set of polynomials is not closed under division. The reciprocal of a polynomial may not be a polynomial.

Pre-AP level students should be able to look at the set of polynomials as a number system in itself with many of the properties of the real numbers as stated above.

Amid all the special forms for multiplication, do not forget that there is a general algorithm, based on the distributive property for real numbers, which always works for multiplying polynomial: Every term of the first polynomial gets multiplied by every term of the second polynomial exactly once, and then like terms are combined. The Pre-AP level copymaster entitled *A Multiplication Strategy* illustrates this process in more detail. The special product formulas are special cases of the general algorithm where a pattern occurs that helps the student keep track of the individual products (FOIL) or saves steps in the multiplication process (square of a binomial). Though students can multiply polynomials effectively using only the general strategy, the special forms save time and work and are the basis for many of the factoring rules presented later in the chapter. The copymaster entitled *More with Special Products* presents additional forms of special products that are appropriate for Pre-AP level students.

Students can discover some of the special forms on their own by multiplying polynomials that satisfy certain conditions and observing patterns in the products. Encourage students to go beyond the special forms in the text and copymaster and find some of their own.

Lesson 8.4

Polynomial Equations As you present the material in this lesson, remember that you are motivating the material in the rest of the chapter. Our main reason for learning to factor polynomials is to solve polynomial equations. By emphasizing the real-life application of solving equations and factoring's role in that solution process, the student will see that factoring is more than just the tedious inverse of polynomial multiplication.

It is also appropriate at this level to mention the Factor Theorem which states that r is a solution of a polynomial equation if and only if $x - r$ is a factor of the polynomial. Thus, solving a polynomial equation is equivalent to factoring the polynomial. Geometrically, the solutions of a polynomial function are the x-intercepts of the graph of the corresponding polynomial function. Students could solve an equation such as $(3x - 2)(2x + 5) = 0$ and then graph $y = (3x - 2)(2x + 5)$ to verify that the solutions of the equation are indeed the x-intercepts of the graph. Never miss an opportunity to point out the geometric interpretation of an algebraic process.

Pre-AP level students need to thoroughly understand the zero-product property and its application. They should also be able to explain why the property does not hold if 0 is replaced by other numbers. The skills in this section are generalized and built upon throughout mathematics.

Lessons 8.5–8.8

Factoring Polynomials While the text focuses on polynomials that will factor, the Pre-AP level copymasters entitled *Prime Polynomials of the Form $x^2 + bx + c$* and *Prime Polynomials of the Form $ax^2 + bx + c$* focus on polynomials that do not factor over the integers. While an easier method to determine whether a trinomial in one of these forms will factor, the determinant, is presented in Chapter 9, it is instructive for the student to show that a polynomial is prime by exhausting the possibilities while trying to factor it. This process will enhance a student's ability to count the number of ways something can occur, to eliminate unreasonable answers, and to work in an organized manner. All the while, the process of factoring is being practiced in each unsuccessful factorization attempt. The patterns observed in showing that a trinomial is prime will help the student become a better factorer.

Since factoring polynomials is the inverse process of polynomial multiplication, the multiplication rules for the special products can be turned around to establish special forms for factoring. Emphasize that the special forms can be verified by multiplying out the factored form to check that both sides of the equation are indeed equal. None of the special forms for multiplication or factoring needs to be mysterious to a Pre-AP level student. Every rule is within the grasp of understanding.

Be sure to emphasize solving polynomial equations throughout the lessons on factoring as the main reason for learning to factor. In Lesson 8.8, ask the students to apply the zero-product property to a polynomial equation that is not completely factored. What do they observe? Do they think that the solutions of the original equation will be preserved if they finish the factoring process after applying the zero-product property once? Can the zero-product property be used more than once in the solution of an equation? Challenge the students with some of these questions and discuss their results in class.

Best Practices

Lessons 9.1–9.3

Graphs of Quadratic Equations As we introduce a new class of equations in two variables, it is very important that the students learn to distinguish quadratic equations from other types of equations by both their equations and by their graphs. Both the equations and the graphs of quadratic functions are distinctively different than the equations and graphs of linear and exponential equations previously studied. The Pre-AP level copymaster entitled *Features of the Graph of* $y = x^2$ will emphasize the distinctive features of the graphs of quadratic equations. The copymaster entitled *Compare Linear, Exponential, and Quadratic Graphs* presented later in the chapter will explore the difference between the graphs of quadratic equations and other types of equations in the language of functions.

The shape of the graph of a quadratic equation is called a **parabola**. At the Pre-AP level, you should present the geometric definition of a parabola as presented in the Math Background Notes for this chapter as well as the verification that the equation for a parabola is indeed a quadratic equation. The students should be able to follow the steps but it may be beyond their abilities to reproduce the verification.

Students also need to distinguish between quadratic functions whose graphs open upward and those whose graphs open downward and be able to determine whether the graph opens upward or downward by inspecting the equation.

Another important feature of the graph of a quadratic function is its vertex. The vertex of a parabola is either the lowest point on the graph or the highest point on the graph depending on whether the parabola opens upward or downward. Neither linear nor exponential equations have such an extreme point. Students should be able to find the coordinates of the vertex of a parabola by both algebraic and graphical methods and understand that quadratic equations are often used to model real-life situations where a maximum or a minimum value occurs.

Classes of equations are also distinguished from one another by rates of change. Recall that linear equations are characterized by their constant rates of change, and exponential growth models are characterized by their rapid rate of increase. The copymaster entitled *Average Rates of Change of Quadratic Functions* explores rates of change for quadratic functions and shows the growth rate of a quadratic function to be between that of a linear function and that of an exponential function. As such, quadratic functions will be used to model entirely different situations than linear and exponential functions are used to model. This will also be studied more closely later in the chapter.

The copymaster entitled *Area under a Graph* hints at a Calculus application, finding the areas of irregular regions, such as the area bounded by the graph of $y = 4 - x^2$ above and the x-axis below. The copymaster presents the idea of approximating the area by computing the areas of simpler regions, such as rectangles, for which we use area formulas. The copymaster concludes by introducing the student to the definite integral function of the graphing calculator, which computes the area of such a region.

In solving quadratic equations of the form $ax^2 + bx + c = 0$, the student must understand that the solutions of this equation are the x-intercepts of the graph of $y = ax^2 + bx + c$. This is the basis for one method of solving quadratic equations on a graphing calculator: Graph the equation and use the ZERO function to locate the x-intercepts. Graphs of quadratic equations also very clearly demonstrate that a quadratic equation may have 0, 1, or 2 solutions, as shown in the Key Concept box on page 644. Emphasize the importance of visualizing the solutions, or lack thereof, for a quadratic equation. Such geometric interpretations of solutions are very important in the copymaster entitled *Systems of Equations with at Least One Nonlinear Equation*, where students are asked to find the solution of such a system. A quick sketch of the equations may reveal the number of solutions we are seeking, if any.

The copymaster entitled *Solving Quadratic Inequalities by Graphing* reinforces these geometric ideas once again by relating the solutions of the inequality $ax^2 + bx + c < 0$ to the values of x where the graph of $y = ax^2 + bx + c$ lies below the x-axis and the solutions of the inequality $ax^2 + bx + c > 0$ to the values of x where the graph of $y = ax^2 + bx + c$ lies above the x-axis. You may recall that we solved linear inequalities similarly in Chapter 6.

Lessons 9.4–9.6

Solving Quadratic Equations These lessons present three more methods for solving quadratic equations. As more methods are presented, it becomes more important to recognize the distinctive features of each one that makes it the most desirable method to use in a specific instance. For example, the two methods presented so far, factoring and graphing, both have serious limitations. Many quadratic equations have solutions but the trinomial will not factor over the integers, and it is difficult to determine exact values from graphs. The first of the three new methods only works when the coefficient of the x-term is zero. The last two methods work for any quadratic equation but can be quite cumbersome. Solving a quadratic equation is more than just knowing several methods; it is also knowing which method to use.

Although the algebraic process of completing the square of a quadratic expression has many important uses, the main reason for presenting it here as a method of solving quadratic equations is that it is used to derive the quadratic formula. The student can easily see that the method works for all quadratic equations and consequently see that the quadratic formula will also work for all quadratic equations.

Throughout the process of learning all these methods, do not forget the geometrical interpretation of the solutions or the relationship to the factors of the quadratic expression.

Lesson 9.7

Systems of Equations In preparation for the many applications found in calculus, where

coefficients and solutions may not be integral and an appropriate viewing window is not always easy to determine, students should encounter problems that demonstrate these challenges.

Ask students to write and solve their own systems using randomly chosen coefficients. In most cases, the resulting solutions will not involve integers. Ask students to write and solve systems with non-integer coefficients. If they use larger numbers, the solutions are likely to be outside the standard viewing window of their graphing calculator.

Lesson 9.8

Regression Models Emphasize that choosing the correct model to represent data is just as important as calculating the regression equation correctly. Scatter plots are a vital step in determining which type of regression model should be used. Patterns that may not be obvious in a table or list of data become obvious when the data is graphed. Recognizing characteristics of the graphs of the major classes of functions in the scatter plot will help to determine which type of function should be used to model the data. The copymaster entitled *Using Regression Models* and the Math Background Notes provide further insight to regression models, their use, and their limitations.

Lesson 9.9

Representing Functions This lesson lends itself to once again reinforcing the importance of the concept of functions in mathematics and, more importantly, in the real world. Have students identify real-world situations that can be modeled using either a linear, quadratic, or exponential function. Be sure to have students verify that each relationship identified is indeed a function. Discuss the domain and range of each function. For those relationships whose domain or range (or both) is restricted, ask students to give reasons for these restrictions. Ask students to identify the x- and y-intercepts, if they exist, and to interpret them in the real-world context of the situation. Lead students to identify where each function increases and decreases, and ask them to explain why this occurs.

CHAPTER 10

Best Practices

Lessons 10.1–10.5

Data Analysis As you present the material for these sections, keep in mind that the goal of data analysis is interpretation. While students need to learn the processes of data analysis, they must also learn to draw conclusions from the work they have done.

Pre-AP students should be able to describe the steps of data analysis, from collecting data to drawing conclusions, including what should be done at each step to insure the validity of their conclusions. The copymaster entitled *More Examples of Bias* looks more closely at how the validity of a conclusion may be jeopardized at the data collection stage.

Students should be able to select the appropriate measures of central tendency for a data set and the appropriate type of graph that should be used to display the data. Students should also be aware of how reporting the wrong measure of central tendency or displaying the data incorrectly can be misleading.

Lesson 10.3

Relative Frequency Tables Challenge your Pre-AP students to investigate relative frequency tables. These tables are constructed by dividing each data value in a two-way table by the total in the bottom right corner of the table. So, the relative frequency total for the table is 1.00. The marginal and joint frequencies are decimals between 0 and 1. Ask students to make a relative frequency table for the two-way table in Example 2. Then ask them to draw a stacked bar graph for the data with a bar for each language. Each bar consists of a component for boys and a component for girls. Ask students to compare the representations of the data.

Pre-AP Best Practices

Lessons 11.1–11.5

Basics of Probability A Pre-AP student needs a good understanding of the basics of probability, including interpretation of probabilities. The student should understand that a probability of 0 indicates that an event cannot occur and that a probability of 1 indicates that an event will definitely occur. The probabilities of all other events are numbers between 0 and 1. The sum of the individual probabilities of the possible outcomes must equal 1. The Pre-AP student should be able to identify and reject probabilities that are not valid and give a verbal description of the likelihood that an event will occur based on a valid probability for the event. The copymaster entitled *Probability Distributions and Expected Value* covers these topics.

Counting Outcomes Counting techniques are very important in the computation of theoretical probabilities. Students should be able to use the formulas for combinations and permutations as well as be able to count combinations and permutations by listing them (in simple cases). Pre-AP students should also be able to give an explanation of how the formulas work, including what the expressions in the numerators and denominators represent. The copymasters entitled *Permutations* and *Combinations* provide additional resources in this area.

Compound Events Lesson 13.4 is extended by several copymasters that give further practice in computing probabilities where more than one event is involved. In order to compute such probabilities effectively, students must be able to identify basic relationships among the events in question.

Students should first be able to identify whether two events *A* and *B* from the same sample space are **mutually exclusive** and correctly interpret how this affects the probabilities of the compound events *A or B* and *A and B*. In addition, students should be able to list the outcomes in the events *A or B* and *A and B* given the outcomes in the events *A* and *B*.

Students should also be able to explain how the sample space may change in a two-step experiment such as choosing one item from a bag and then choosing a second item without replacing the first. In these cases, the students should be able to describe the consecutive choices as either **independent** or **dependent** events and give an explanation of what these terms mean.

These topics are covered in more detail in the copymasters entitled *More Compound Events* and *Distinguishing between Mutually Exclusive and Independent Events*.

The copymaster entitled *Binomial Probabilities* looks at computing the probabilities of events composed of outcomes of a sequence of independent experiments where each experiment has exactly two possible outcomes. The typical experiment is similar to flipping three coins, a nickel, a dime, and a quarter, where there are two possibilities for each coin, heads or tails. Typical questions involve finding the probability of getting two or more heads. Students will learn how to work these problems by listing and counting outcomes and by using formulas.

The copymaster entitled *Conditional Probabilities* looks at how knowing that one event has occurred affects the probability of another event occurring. The typical problem involves a narrowing of the sample of space in question. For example, suppose one student is chosen at random from a school to receive a prize. Lisa and Alexander have the same probability of receiving the prize. However, if just before announcing the name of the winner the principal announces that the winner is a girl, then Alexander's probability of winning is now zero and Lisa's probability has increased since the sample space is smaller. Students will learn to work these problems by counting and by using formulas.

CHAPTER 1 # Extended Problem Solving

The Division Algorithm

Given any two integers a and b with $a > 0$, there are unique integers q and r such that $b = qa + r$, where $0 \leq r < a$. The integer a is the divisor, b is the dividend, q is the quotient, and r is the remainder. The remainder is less than the divisor.

For $a = 5$ and $b = 13$ in the division algorithm, we have $13 = 2 \cdot 5 + 3$, so that $q = 2$ and $r = 3$. Note the value of r, 3, is less than the value of a, 5.

If an integer is divided by 5, the possible remainders are 0, 1, 2, 3, and 4.

EXAMPLE 1 ## Find a divisor

The head of a political action committee has several volunteers who will call the offices of the 535 members of the U.S. Congress. When she tries to divide the 100 Senators evenly among the volunteers, she has four Senators left over. When she tries to divide the 435 House members evenly among the volunteers, she has three left over. What are the possible numbers of volunteers?

Solution:

Step 1 Read and Understand

The problem involves division with remainders. When the numbers 100 and 435 are both divided by the same unknown divisor, the remainders are 4 and 3, respectively. We want to find all possible values for the unknown divisor.

Step 2 Make a Plan

We will list all the divisors of 100 that result in a remainder of 4. Then we will check to see which of those divisors result in a remainder of 3 when divided into 435.

Step 3 Solve the Problem

We begin by listing all the divisors of 100 that result in a remainder of 4. Since the remainder, 4, is less than the unknown divisor, we can conclude that the divisor is at least 5. We can reason further that since the remainder is 4, the divisor divides evenly into $100 - 4 = 96$. So, we are looking for the divisors of 96 that are greater than or equal to 5. Those numbers are shown below.

6, 8, 12, 16, 24, 32, 48, 96

We could reason similarly about the divisors of 435 and find the common numbers in the two lists, but instead we will check these eight numbers by performing the divisions.

Extended Problem Solving *continued*

Divisor		Remainder
6	$435 = 72 \cdot 6 + 3$	3
8	$435 = 54 \cdot 8 + 3$	3
12	$435 = 36 \cdot 12 + 3$	3
16	$435 = 27 \cdot 16 + 3$	3
24	$435 = 18 \cdot 24 + 3$	3
32	$435 = 13 \cdot 32 + 19$	19
48	$435 = 9 \cdot 48 + 3$	3
96	$435 = 4 \cdot 96 + 51$	51

The divisors 6, 8, 12, 16, 24, and 48 of 435 result in a remainder of 3, so the political action committee has 6, 8, 12, 16, 24, or 48 volunteers.

Step 4 Look Back

None of the possible numbers of volunteers seems to be unreasonable. You can check the numbers by dividing them into both 100 and 435 and verifying that you get the correct remainders. ■

EXAMPLE 2 ## Find a dividend

When Coach Allen attempted to divide the Lettermen's Club into three equally sized groups, he had two athletes left over. When he attempted to divide the club into five equally sized groups, he also had two athletes left over. Assuming that the Letterman's Club has at least 20 members, what is the smallest number of members it could have?

Solution:

Step 1 Read and Understand

The problem involves division with remainders. When an unknown dividend is divided by both 3 and by 5, the remainder is 2. We want to find the smallest possible value of the dividend that is greater than or equal to 20.

Step 2 Make a Plan

We will use the division algorithm to list the possible dividends that result in a remainder of 2 for each divisor, 3 and 5. Then we will choose the least common dividend from the two lists that is greater than or equal to 20.

Extended Problem Solving *continued*

Step 3 Solve the Problem

We will list the dividends in tables.

Divisor: 3

Quotient		Dividend
1	$1 \cdot 3 + 2 = 5$	5
2	$2 \cdot 3 + 2 = 8$	8
3	$3 \cdot 3 + 2 = 11$	11
4	$4 \cdot 3 + 2 = 14$	14
5	$5 \cdot 3 + 2 = 17$	17
6	$6 \cdot 3 + 2 = 20$	20
7	$7 \cdot 3 + 2 = 23$	23
8	$8 \cdot 3 + 2 = 26$	26
9	$9 \cdot 3 + 2 = 29$	29
10	$10 \cdot 3 + 2 = 32$	32

Divisor: 5

Quotient		Dividend
1	$1 \cdot 5 + 2 = 7$	7
2	$2 \cdot 5 + 2 = 12$	12
3	$3 \cdot 5 + 2 = 17$	17
4	$4 \cdot 5 + 2 = 22$	22
5	$5 \cdot 5 + 2 = 27$	27
6	$6 \cdot 5 + 2 = 32$	32
7	$7 \cdot 5 + 2 = 37$	37
8	$8 \cdot 5 + 2 = 42$	42
9	$9 \cdot 5 + 2 = 47$	47
10	$10 \cdot 5 + 2 = 52$	52

The smallest dividend common to both lists is 17, but we know that the club has at least 20 members. The next common dividend is 32, which is greater than 20. The smallest number of members that the Lettermen's Club could have is 32.

Step 4 Look Back

The answer seems to be reasonable. You can check the answer by dividing 32 by both 3 and 5 and verifying that you get a remainder of 2 both times. You can also verify that this will not happen for the numbers between 20 and 31, inclusive. ■

Practice

1. Which letter represents the dividend in the equation $b = qa + r$?

2. What are the possible remainders when an integer is divided by 8?

3. If, in a division problem, the divisor is greater than the dividend, then what is the quotient? Assume that both the dividend and the divisor are positive.

4. When a number is divided by 9, the quotient is 7 and the remainder is 8. What is the number?

5. When one integer is divided by another, the remainder is 15. What is the smallest possible value of the divisor?

6. When 75 is divided by a number, the remainder is 3. What is the greatest possible value of the divisor?

CHAPTER 1 — Extended Problem Solving *continued*

7. When a number is divided by 18, the remainder is 5. What is the smallest possible value of the number?

8. When 52 is divided by a number, the remainder is 1. What are the possible values of the divisor?

Problem Solving

9. Halley has 15 CDs and 25 DVDs. When she divides the CDs evenly among her friends, she has three left over. When she divides the DVDs evenly among her friends, she has one left over. List the numbers of friends that Halley could have.

10. Jerome deals the cards in a game evenly to all the players. When there are 3 players, he has one card left over. When there are four players, he has two cards left over. If there are at least 50 cards in the game, what is the smallest possible number of cards?

11. Bella chooses a number between 1 and 100. If she divides her number by 10, the remainder is 8. If she divides her number by 11, the remainder is 1. What is her number?

12. Michael is given a box of baseball cards. If he divides the cards evenly among himself and seven of his friends, he will have six cards left over. If he divides the cards only among his seven friends, he will have five cards left over. What is the least number of baseball cards that could be in the box?

13. The owner of an auto shop has 23 cars waiting for an oil change and 17 cars waiting for a tire rotation. If he divides the oil changes evenly among his employees, he has three left over. If he divides the tire rotation evenly among his employees, he has two left over. How many employees does the auto shop have?

14. Vincente has 1000 paper clips, 500 rubber bands, and several small boxes. When he divides the paper clips evenly among the boxes, he has 16 left over. When he divides the rubber bands evenly among the boxes, he has 20 left over. What is the minimum number of boxes that Vincente could have?

15. **Challenge** Lance has a box of 100 candy bars. If he divides the candy bars evenly among the students in his math class, he will have four left over. If he divides them evenly among the students in his Spanish class, he will have 8 left over. If there is one more student in his math class than in his Spanish class, how many students are in each class?

16. **Challenge** Tana chooses a number between 1 and 200. If she divides her number by 10, the remainder is 9. If she divides her number by 8, the remainder is 7. If she divides her number by 6, the remainder is 5. What is her number?

CHAPTER 1 Identifying Functions

A function is often described by a rule that tells you how to assign each input its output value.

EXAMPLE 1 **Identify and use a description of a function**

When new students arrive for school orientation, they must get into a line to register and pick up their orientation packets. Each student is assigned a line according to the first letter of his or her last name as shown in the table at the right. Is the process of assigning each student to a line a function? To which lines will new students named Tom Carville and Leslie Yarborough be assigned?

Line Assignment by First Letter of Last Name

Letter	Line
A–F	1
G–L	2
M–S	3
T–Z	4

Solution:

In this situation, the domain is the set of new students and the range is the set of lines. The table describes a rule for assigning each new student to a line. The rule describes a function if each new student is assigned to exactly one line. Since every letter is represented in the table and no letter is assigned to more than one line, each new student will be assigned to exactly one line. This process is a function.

Since the first letter in Tom Carville's name is C, he will be assigned to Line 1. Since the first letter in Leslie Yarborough's last name is Y, she will be assigned to Line 4. ∎

KEY CONCEPT

Conditions for a Rule to Describe a Function

In order for a rule to describe a function, all of the following must be true:

- There must be a clearly defined domain (set of inputs).
- There must be a clearly defined range (set of outputs).
- The rule must clearly state how to assign an output to each input.
- The rule must assign only one output to each input.

Notice that the rule in Example 1 satisfies all four conditions stated in the Key Concept. Let's look at some rules that do not satisfy the conditions.

EXAMPLE 2 **Identify a rule that does not describe a function**

The legislature has decided that all families with children under 18 years old should receive a tax credit. Families with one child will receive a $500 credit, families with two children will receive a $900 tax credit, and families with three children will receive a $1200 tax credit. Does this rule for assigning tax credits define a function? Explain.

CHAPTER 1 **Identifying Functions** *continued*

Solution:

The domain is clearly stated in the first sentence as the set of all families with children under 18 years old. However, the rule only assigns a tax credit to families with one, two, or three children. It is not clear what tax credit a family with four or more children would receive. This rule does not fully describe a function. ■

Number of Children	Tax Credit
1	$500
2	$900
3	$1200
4	?
5	?

EXAMPLE 3 ## Identify a rule that does not describe a function

Mrs. Jenkins is using the following rule to assign research topics to the students in her class.

- If your first name begins with A–M, write a paper on photosynthesis.
- If your first name begins with N–Z, write a paper on paleontology.
- If you have blue eyes, write a paper on ontology.

Does this rule for assigning research topics describe a function? Explain.

Solution:

The domain is clearly stated as the set of students in Mrs. Jenkins's class. However, this rule is not a function because students with blue eyes will be assigned more than one topic. For example, if Ken is a student in the class and he has blue eyes, then according to the rule he is assigned two topics, photosynthesis and ontology. ■

Practice

Identify the domain and the range of each rule.

1. Mr. Brown is giving cash bonuses to his employees. Employees who have worked for him five years or less will receive $1000. Employees who have worked for him more than five years will receive $2000.

2. Candace is giving gifts to her friends. She is giving each male friend a video game and each female friend a CD.

3. The students at Woodruff High School are being assigned locations for their class meetings. All freshmen will go to the gymnasium, sophomores will go to the auditorium, juniors will go to the cafeteria, and seniors will go to the football field.

4. Mrs. Childress is assigning research topics to the students in her art classes. Students who have chosen to paint a portrait as their final project will research van Gogh. Students who have chosen to make a sculpture as their final project will research Rodin.

Problem Solving

5. When customers arrive at a buffet restaurant, they must pay for their meals as they enter. The price that a customer pays is determined by age as shown in the table at the right. Does this rule of assigning a price by age represent a function? Explain. If Jared is 16 years old, how much will he pay for his meal?

Price of Buffet

Age	Price
12 or under	$6.95
13–64	$12.95
65 or over	$8.95

CHAPTER
1

Identifying Functions *continued*

6. Mrs. Dietrich assigns each of the 20 students in her class to one of four groups for their laboratory experiment. The groups are named A, B, C, and D. She writes the letter A on five slips of paper, the letter B on five slips of paper, and so on. As the students enter the classroom, each one draws a slip of paper from a box. The student is assigned to the group designated by the letter on his or her slip of paper. Does this rule of assigning students to lab groups describe a function? Explain.

7. Patients who require a certain medication are prescribed dosages according to several factors as shown in the table at the right. Does this rule of assigning dosages to patients describe a function? Explain.

Dosage of a Medication	
Factor	**Dosage**
Under age 40	200 mg
Age 40 or older	300 mg
Over 150 pounds	400 mg

8. A congressman proposed a new tax plan where each individual taxpayer's deadline for filing an annual tax return will be his or her birthday. Does this rule for assigning a deadline to each taxpayer describe a function? Explain.

9. An auto insurance company has decided to give all of its customers a rebate. Each customer who drove no more than 5,000 miles in the past year will receive a $200 rebate, and each customer who drove more than 5,000 miles but no more than 10,000 miles will receive a $150 rebate. Does this rule for assigning a rebate to each customer describe a function? Explain.

10. Coach Johnson is using the following rule to divide the football team into four groups.

   - If a player was born in January, February, or March, then the player belongs to Group 1.
   - If a player was born in April, May, or June, then the player belongs to Group 2.
   - If a player was born in July, August, or September, then the player belongs to Group 3.
   - If a player was born in October, November, or December, then the player belongs to Group 4.

   Does this rule for assigning each football player to a group describe a function? Explain.

CHAPTER 1 Real-World Functions

In many real-world situations, one quantity depends upon two or more other quantities.

EXAMPLE ### Identify the variables in a function

Mr. Garrison is planning to fill his car with gasoline on his way to work tomorrow. What factors will determine how much he will spend?

Solution:

The amount that Mr. Garrison will spend depends upon both the number of gallons that he buys and the price per gallon. The cost of filling a car with gasoline is a function of two variables. ■

Practice

1. Apples are usually sold by the pound. What factors will determine the price of three apples?

2. At his part time job, Jose is paid by the hour. What factors will determine how much he earns this week?

3. Mrs. Kingsley is driving from her home to a friend's house in another town. What factors will determine how long her trip takes?

4. Mr. Waters is renting a car by the day. What factors will determine the cost of renting the car?

5. Greg is calculating the area of a triangle. What factors determine the area of a triangle?

6. Dina is calculating the area of a rectangle. What factors determine the area of a rectangle?

7. Cindy is finding the volume of a cylinder. What factors determine the volume of a cylinder?

8. Valerie is finding the volume of a cone. What factors determine the volume of a cone?

9. **Challenge** What factors determine the volume of a rectangular prism?

10. **Challenge** What factors determine the amount of money in a savings account?

Activity

11. Use the Internet or some other reliable source to find a quantity that depends upon at least four factors.

Counting Sets of Rational Numbers

CHAPTER 2

The number of objects in a set is called the cardinality of the set.

EXAMPLE 1 ### Find the cardinality of a set

The cardinality of the set $\{a, b, c, d, e\}$ is 5, because the set contains five letters: a, b, c, d, and e.

The cardinality of the set of positive integers less than 10 is 9, because there are nine positive integers less than 10: 1, 2, 3, 4, 5, 6, 7, 8, and 9. ■

To find the cardinality of a set, you may need to list the objects in the set as in Example 1. This is especially true when the set is expressed in set-builder notation as in Example 2.

EXAMPLE 2 ### Find the cardinality of a set expressed in set-builder notation

Find the cardinality of the set $\{x \mid x$ is an integer and $-6 \leq x < 1\}$.

Solution:

Notice that the set includes -6 but not 1. So, the set contains the numbers $-6, -5, -4, -3, -2, -1,$ and 0. Since there are seven numbers in the set, its cardinality is 7. ■

In the examples so far, we have been able to list the objects in the set. We can do this because the sets are small. Larger sets require different counting techniques.

EXAMPLE 3 ### Find the cardinality of a large set

Find the cardinality of the set $\{x \mid x$ is an integer and $-50 \leq x \leq 100\}$.

Solution:

Let's break the set up into smaller sets, count the smaller sets, and add the totals of the smaller sets. There 50 integers between -50 and -1, inclusive, 100 integers between 1 and 100, inclusive, and the number 0. The cardinality of the set $\{x \mid x$ is an integer and $-50 \leq x \leq 100\}$ is $50 + 100 + 1$ or 151. ■

Some sets have no limits or bounds; these sets are said to be **infinite**. The set of integers itself has no bounds. When we write the integers as $\ldots, -3, -2, -1, 0, 1, 2, 3, \ldots$, the three dots at each end indicate that the numbers continue without end in both directions. So, the set of integers is infinite.

The cardinality of an infinite set can not be described by any real number.

EXAMPLE 4 ### Identify an infinite set

Find the cardinality of the set $\{x \mid x$ is an integer and $x > 4\}$.

Solution:

This set contains the numbers 5, 6, 7, 8, 9, $\ldots$, which continue without end. The set $\{x \mid x$ is an integer and $x > 4\}$ is infinite. ■

Counting Sets of Rational Numbers *continued*

CHAPTER 2

Other sets are infinite but bounded. A set of numbers is **bounded** when there is some number that is less than or equal to every number in the set and another number that is greater than or equal to every number in the set.

EXAMPLE 5 ## Recognize a bounded infinite set

The set $\left\{ \frac{1}{2}, \frac{1}{3}, \frac{1}{4}, \frac{1}{5}, \frac{1}{6}, \ldots \right\}$ is infinite because the fractions of the form $\frac{1}{n}$ continue without end. However, all of the numbers in the set are greater than 0 and less than or equal to $\frac{1}{2}$. So, this set is *bounded below* by 0 and *bounded above* by $\frac{1}{2}$. The set $\left\{ \frac{1}{2}, \frac{1}{3}, \frac{1}{4}, \frac{1}{5}, \frac{1}{6}, \ldots \right\}$ is a bounded infinite set. ■

Example 5 illustrates that there are infinitely many rational numbers between 0 and $\frac{1}{2}$.

EXAMPLE 6 ## Determine whether an infinite set is bounded or unbounded

Determine whether each of the following infinite sets is bounded or unbounded.

  a. $\{x \mid x \text{ is a positive multiple of } 5\}$

  b. $\{\ldots, -10, -9.5, -9, -8.5, -8\}$

  c. $\{0.9, 0.99, 0.999, 0.9999, 0.99999, \ldots\}$

Solution:

  a. The set of positive multiples of 5 contains 5, 10, 15, 20, 25, ... There is no real number greater than every number in this set. Since this set is not bounded above, the set is unbounded.

  b. There is no number less than all of the numbers in the set $\{\ldots, -10, -9.5, -9, -8.5, -8\}$, so the set is unbounded.

  c. All of the numbers in the set $\{0.9, 0.99, 0.999, 0.9999, 0.99999, \ldots\}$ are greater than 0 and less than 1, so the set is bounded. ■

Practice

Find the cardinality of the set.

  1. $\{\blacktriangle, \blacksquare, \bullet, \blacktriangledown\}$ **2.** $\{f, g, k, l, t, y\}$

  3. $\{u, v, w, x, y, z\}$ **4.** $\{F, G, H, I, J\}$

  5. $\{A, B, C, \ldots, X, Y, Z\}$ **6.** $\{m, n, o, \ldots, r, s, t\}$

List the numbers in the set. Then find its cardinality.

  7. the set of positive integers less than 5   **8.** the set of positive integers less than or equal to 8

  9. $\{x \mid x \text{ is an integer and } 0 < x < 15\}$ **10.** $\{x \mid x \text{ is an integer and } 5 \le x \le 15\}$

  11. $\{x \mid x \text{ is an integer and } -9 \le x < -1\}$ **12.** $\{x \mid x \text{ is an integer and } -4 \le x \le 4\}$

| CHAPTER 2 | **Counting Sets of Rational Numbers** *continued* |

Find the cardinality of the set without listing the numbers in the set.

13. $\{x \mid x$ is an integer and $-10 \leq x \leq 10\}$

14. $\{x \mid x$ is an integer and $-100 \leq x \leq 100\}$

15. $\{x \mid x$ is an integer and $0 \leq x < 1000\}$

16. $\{x \mid x$ is an integer and $-500 < x \leq 0\}$

Find the cardinality of the set or state that the set is infinite.

17. $\{x \mid x$ is an integer and $x < 12\}$

18. $\{x \mid x$ is a positive integer and $x < 12\}$

19. $\{x \mid x$ is a negative integer and $x \geq -8\}$

20. $\{x \mid x$ is an integer and $x \geq -8\}$

Determine whether the infinite set is bounded or unbounded.

21. $\left\{1\frac{1}{2}, 2\frac{1}{2}, 3\frac{1}{2}, 4\frac{1}{2}, 5\frac{1}{2}, \ldots\right\}$

22. $\left\{3\frac{1}{2}, 3\frac{1}{3}, 3\frac{1}{4}, 3\frac{1}{5}, 3\frac{1}{6}, \ldots\right\}$

23. $\{0.1, 0.01, 0.001, 0.0001, 0.00001, \ldots\}$

24. $\{1, 10, 100, 1000, 10,000\}$

Problem Solving

25. Greg has listed the names of all the students in his Algebra class on a piece of paper. Is the set of names infinite? Explain.

26. Hannah recorded the ages, in years, of five hundred people attending a concert. Find one age that could reasonably be less than or equal to all the ages in the set. Then find another age that could reasonably be greater than or equal to all the ages in the set.

Building a Number System

CHAPTER 2

The set of numbers 0, 1, 2, 3, 4, 5, ... is the set of whole numbers. When you first learned to add, subtract, multiply, and divide, you worked exclusively with this set of numbers. The set of whole numbers has shortcomings as illustrated in Example 1.

EXAMPLE 1 ## Add, subtract, multiply, and divide whole numbers

The numbers 4 and 8 are both whole numbers. Observe what happens as we add, subtract, multiply, and divide these two numbers.

Add: $4 + 8 = 12$ and $8 + 4 = 12$ **Subtract:** $4 - 8 = -4$ and $8 - 4 = 4$

Multiply: $4 \times 8 = 32$ and $8 \times 4 = 32$ **Divide:** $4 \div 8 = \frac{1}{2}$ and $8 \div 4 = 2$

The results of the additions $4 + 8$ and $8 + 4$, multiplications 4×8 and 8×4, subtraction $8 - 4$, and the division $8 \div 2$ are whole numbers. The results of the subtraction $4 - 8$ and the division $4 \div 8$ are not whole numbers. When you subtract or divide two whole numbers, the result may not be a whole number. ■

A set of numbers is **closed** under an operation if whenever that operation is performed on elements of the set the result is also an element of the set.

KEY CONCEPT

Closure of the Whole Numbers under Addition and Multiplication

The set of whole numbers is closed under the operations of addition and multiplication.

The set of whole numbers is not closed under the operations of subtraction and division.

This means that whenever you add or multiply two whole numbers, you always get a whole number as your answer. However, when you subtract or divide two whole numbers, your answer may not be a whole number.

In an attempt to build a number system closed under the four operations of addition, subtraction, multiplication, and division, we expand the whole numbers by including additional numbers.

The set of numbers ..., $-3, -2, -1, 0, 1, 2, 3,$ ... is the set of integers. The set of integers contains the set of whole numbers as well as the opposites of the whole numbers. The set of integers does not have the same shortcomings as the set of whole numbers. This is illustrated in Example 2.

CHAPTER 2	**Building a Number System** *continued*

EXAMPLE 2 ## Subtract and divide integers

The numbers -5 and 9 are both integers. Observe what happens as we subtract and divide these two numbers.

Subtract: $-5 - 9 = -14$ and $9 - (-5) = 14$

Divide: $-5 \div 9 = -\dfrac{5}{9}$ and $9 \div (-5) = -\dfrac{9}{5}$

The results of the both subtractions are integers. The results of the divisions are not integers. When you divide two integers, the result may not be an integer. ■

KEY CONCEPT

> ## Closure of the Integers under Addition, Subtraction, and Multiplication
>
> The set of integers is closed under the operations of addition, subtraction, and multiplication.
>
> The set of integers is not closed under the operation of division.

This means that whenever you add, subtract, or multiply two integers, you always get an integer as your answer. However, when you divide two integers, your answer may not be an integer.

Now we expand the integers in an effort to build a number system that is also closed under division.

The set of rational numbers is the set of all numbers that can be written as the quotient of two integers. The set of rational numbers includes the set of integers because every integer can be written as the quotient of itself and 1.

EXAMPLE 3 ## Divide rational numbers

The numbers $-\dfrac{2}{3}$ and $\dfrac{1}{6}$ are both rational numbers. Observe what happens as we divide these two numbers.

$$-\dfrac{2}{3} \div \dfrac{1}{6} = -\dfrac{2}{3} \cdot \dfrac{6}{1} = -4 \text{ and } \dfrac{1}{6} \div \left(-\dfrac{2}{3}\right) = \dfrac{1}{6} \cdot \left(-\dfrac{3}{2}\right) = -\dfrac{1}{4}$$

The results of the both divisions are rational numbers. Note also that the results of the division problems in Examples 1 and 2 were also rational numbers. ■

KEY CONCEPT

> ## Closure of the Integers under Addition, Subtraction, Multiplication and Division
>
> The set of rational numbers is closed under the operations of addition, subtraction, and multiplication.
>
> With the exception of dividing by zero, the set of rational numbers is closed under division.

CHAPTER 2

Building a Number System *continued*

When you add, subtract, or multiply two rational numbers, your answer will always be a rational number. When you divide a rational number by any rational number except zero, your answer will be a rational number.

KEY CONCEPT

Division by Zero is Undefined

Dividing a number by zero has no meaning; the result is not a real number. Division by zero is undefined.

EXAMPLE 4

Divide by zero

Expressions of the form $\frac{-5}{0}$, $\frac{0}{0}$, and $\frac{3}{0}$ have no meaning. ■

So far in this lesson, you have seen the need to expand the whole numbers to the integers and then the rational numbers in order to have a number system closed under our four basic operations. In a later lesson, you will see the need for expanding the rational numbers to the real numbers.

EXAMPLE 5

Determine closure of other sets of numbers

Determine whether the set is closed under each of the four basic operations, addition, subtraction, multiplication, and division. If not, give an example.

a. $\{0, 1\}$

b. the set of positive rational numbers

Solution:

a. Addition: The set is not closed under addition because $1 + 1 = 2$ is not in the set.

Subtraction: The set is not closed under subtraction because $0 - 1 = -1$ is not in the set.

Multiplication: The set is closed under multiplication since $0 \times 0 = 0$, $0 \times 1 = 0$, $1 \times 0 = 0$, and $1 \times 1 = 1$ are all in the set.

Division: The set is closed under division, with the exception of dividing by zero, since $\frac{0}{1} = 0$ and $\frac{1}{1} = 1$ are in the set.

b. Addition, Multiplication, and Division: The set is closed under addition, multiplication, and division because the sum, product, or quotient of two positive rational numbers is also a positive rational number.

Subtraction: The set is not closed under subtraction because $\frac{1}{2}$ and $\frac{3}{4}$ are positive rational numbers but $\frac{1}{2} - \frac{3}{4} = -\frac{1}{4}$ is not a positive rational number. ■

Pre-AP Copymasters

| CHAPTER 2 | **Building a Number System** *continued* |

Practice

1. **Writing** Describe what it means for a set of numbers to be closed under the operation.

   a. addition   **b.** subtraction   **c.** multiplication   **d.** division

2. **Writing** Why is division by zero an exception to the closure of the rational numbers under division?

Perform each operation. Then determine whether your answer is a whole number.

3. $5 + 8$ 4. $16 + 35$ 5. $5 - 8$ 6. $16 - 35$

7. 8×5 8. 35×7 9. $8 \div 5$ 10. $35 \div 7$

11. $26 \div 26$ 12. $24 \div 72$ 13. $72 \div 24$ 14. $35 \div 14$

Perform each operation. Then determine whether your answer is an integer.

15. $-3 + 6$ 16. $-3 - 6$ 17. -3×6 18. $-3 \div 6$

19. $-5 + (-5)$ 20. $-5 - (-5)$ 21. $-5 \times (-5)$ 22. $-5 \div (-5)$

23. $20 + (-10)$ 24. $20 - (-10)$ 25. $20 \times (-10)$ 26. $20 \div (-10)$

Perform each operation. Then determine whether your answer is a rational number.

27. $-\frac{1}{2} + \frac{1}{2}$ 28. $-\frac{1}{2} - \frac{1}{2}$ 29. $-\frac{1}{2} \times \frac{1}{2}$ 30. $-\frac{1}{2} \div \frac{1}{2}$

31. $0 + \frac{8}{9}$ 32. $0 - \frac{8}{9}$ 33. $0 \times \frac{8}{9}$ 34. $0 \div \frac{8}{9}$

35. $37.2 + 1.2$ 36. $37.2 - 1.2$ 37. 37.2×1.2 38. $37.2 \div 1.2$

Determine whether the expression is undefined.

39. $-2 \div 0$ 40. $0 \div (-2)$ 41. $\frac{9}{0}$ 42. $\frac{0}{9}$

Determine whether the set is closed under each of the four basic operations: addition, subtraction, multiplication, and division. If not, give an example.

43. $\{-1, 1\}$ 44. $\{-1, 0, 1\}$ 45. $\{-2, 2\}$ 46. $\{-2, 0, 2\}$

47. the set of positive integers   48. the set of negative integers

49. the set of odd integers   50. the set of even integers

51. the set of prime numbers   52. the set of perfect square whole numbers

CHAPTER
2

Building a Number System *continued*

Problem Solving

53. Britt is planning a car wash. He has three teams of volunteers assigned to wash the cars. Can he guarantee that each team will wash the same number of cars? Explain.

54. Kendra invited an even number of her friends to her birthday party. An even number of the invitees could not attend. Did Kendra have an even number of friends at her party? Explain.

55. Lupe has an odd number of books and her friend Toni has an odd number of books. If they combine their books, will the total number of books be odd? Explain.

56. Jacob bought several books and his total before tax was $54.95. Is it possible that each of the books cost a whole number of dollars? Explain

57. Naomi has three whole number test scores in her science class. Will her average test score necessarily be a whole number? Explain.

58. The length and width of Yung's room are both expressed in terms of rational numbers. Can the area of the room also be expressed as a rational number? Explain.

CHAPTER 2

The Need for Irrational Numbers

The rational numbers are a convenient set of numbers because whenever you add, subtract, multiply, or divide two rational numbers (with the exception of dividing by zero), the result is also a rational number. So, why do we need irrational numbers?

The need for irrational numbers first arose in geometry as illustrated in Example 1.

EXAMPLE 1

Identify the need for irrational numbers in geometry

When the side of a square or the diameter of a circle has a rational measurement, neither the length of the diagonal of the square nor the circumference of the circle has an exact measurement that can be expressed as a rational number.

1 cm

1 cm

1 cm

The length of the diagonal in the square above is $\sqrt{2}$ centimeters, and the circumference of the circle is π centimeters. Both of these measurements are irrational. ∎

The need for irrational numbers also arises in algebra as illustrated in Example 2.

EXAMPLE 2

Identify the need for irrational numbers in algebra

There is no rational number x for which the statement $x^2 = 3$ is true. However, the statement is true for $-\sqrt{3}$ and $\sqrt{3}$, both of which are irrational. ∎

Practice Activity

Use the Internet or some other reliable source to help you with the following.

1. Write a brief summary of the history of irrational numbers.

2. Find examples of irrational numbers other than π and square roots.

Challenge

3. Are there more rational numbers than irrational numbers? Explain.

4. Are the irrational numbers closed under addition, subtraction, multiplication, and division? If not, give examples. (Recall that a set of numbers is **closed** under an operation if whenever that operation is performed on elements of the set the result is also an element of the set.)

CHAPTER 2 # More Logical Reasoning

In logic, a statement is either true or false. Also, every statement has a negation or opposite.

KEY CONCEPT

The Negation of a Statement

The negation of a statement expresses the opposite of the statement. The negation of a true statement is false, and the negation of a false statement is true.

EXAMPLE 1 ## Find the negation of a statement and its truth value

Find the negation of the statement *The Golden Gate Bridge is in New York City*. Then determine whether the statement and its negation are true or false.

Solution:

Since the Golden Gate Bridge is in San Francisco, the statement is false. Its negation is *The Golden Gate Bridge is not in New York City*. The negation of the statement is true. ■

EXAMPLE 2 ## Find the negation of a mathematical statement

Find the negation of the statement. Then determine whether the statement and its negation are true or false.

  a. $2 + 7 = 8$ **b.** $2 + 7 > 8$

Solution:

  a. Since $2 + 7 = 9$, the statement $2 + 7 = 8$ is false. The negation of the statement is $2 + 7 \neq 8$, where the symbol $\neq$ means *not equal to*. The negation of the statement is true.

  b. Since $2 + 7 = 9$ and $9 > 8$, the statement $2 + 7 > 8$ is true. The negation of *2 + 7 is greater than 8* is *2 + 7 is not greater than 8*. Logically then, the negation is equivalent to *2 + 7 is less than or equal to 8* or $2 + 7 \leq 8$. The negation is false. ■

Notice in Example 2a that the negation of the false statement $2 + 7 = 8$ is not the true statement $2 + 7 = 9$. The negation of $2 + 7 = 8$ simply asserts that $2 + 7$ is not 8 but does not tell us what $2 + 7$ does equal. However, in Example 2b we can logically conclude that if a real number is not greater 8 then it must be less than or equal to 8.

Some statements involve quantifiers such as *all, none,* or *some*.

EXAMPLE 3 ## Negate an *All* statement

Find the negation of the statement *All integers are even*. Then determine whether the statement and its negation are true or false. Provide a counterexample for the false statement.

More Logical Reasoning *continued*

Solution:

You may be tempted to think that the opposite of this statement would be something similar to *No integers are even,* but let's look at this more closely. The original statement *All integers are even* is false because there are definitely integers that are not even. The statement *No integers are even* is also false because there are integers that are even. Since the negation of a false statement must be true, the statement *No integers are even* cannot be the negation of *All integers are even.*

The negation of *All integers are even* is *Some integers are not even.* While asserting the existence of integers that are not even, this statement also allows for the existence of integers that are even.

The original statement is false, and its negation is true. The number 3 is an integer that is not even, so 3 is a counterexample for the false statement *All integers are even.* ■

In the statement *Some integers are not even,* the word *some* is correctly interpreted as at *least one;* it does not necessarily imply *more than one.*

EXAMPLE 4 **Negate a *None* statement**

Find the negation of the statement *No prime numbers are even.* Then determine whether the statement and its negation are true or false. Provide a counterexample for the false statement.

Solution:

In this statement, *none* is expressed by the word *no.*

Again, you may be tempted to think that the negation of *No prime numbers are even* is *All prime numbers are even,* but this cannot be because both statements are false.

The negation of *No prime numbers are even* is *Some prime numbers are even.* While asserting the existence of at least one prime number that is even, this statement also allows for the existence of prime numbers that are not even.

The original statement is false, and its negation is true. The number 2 is a prime number that is even, so 2 is a counterexample for the false statement *No prime numbers are even.* ■

Note that 2 is the only prime number that is even. So, in the statement *Some prime numbers are even* in Example 4, the word *some* should not be interpreted to mean more than one. If you choose, you may express the negation as *At least one prime number is even* or *There is an even prime number.* The second statement, while stating that there is one even prime number, also allows for more than one.

EXAMPLE 5 **Negate a *Some* statement**

Find the negation of the statement *Some rational numbers are integers.* Then determine whether the statement and its negation are true or false. Provide a counterexample for the false statement.

CHAPTER 2

More Logical Reasoning *continued*

Solution:

The negation of *Some rational numbers are integers* is *No rational numbers are integers*. The original statement is true, and its negation is false. The number −1 is a rational number that is an integer, so −1 is a counterexample for the false statement *No rational numbers are integers*. ■

KEY CONCEPT

The Negation of a Statement with a Quantifier

Statement	Negation
All are …	*Some are not …*
None are …	*Some are …*
Some are …	*None are …*

Practice

Find the negation of the statement. Then determine whether the statement and its negation are true or false.

1. The Grand Canyon is in Minnesota.
2. Niagara Falls is in Alabama.
3. One inch is longer than one centimeter.
4. One pound is heavier than one kilogram.
5. A triangle has five sides.
6. A trapezoid has four sides.
7. The day after Monday is Thursday.
8. The day before Wednesday is Tuesday.
9. Apples grow on trees.
10. Strawberries are blue.

Find the negation of the statement. Then determine whether the statement and its negation are true or false.

11. $5 + 6 = 13$
12. $4 + 8 = 12$
13. $5 \times 6 = 11$
14. $5 + 6 < 13$
15. $4 + 8 > 12$
16. $5 \times 6 \geq 13$
17. $3.2 \leq \pi$
18. $\sqrt{3} > 1.7$
19. $\sqrt{2} \geq 2$
20. $0.11 < 0.101$
21. $0.303 \leq 0.033$
22. $0.818 > 0.188$

Find the negation of the statement. Then determine whether the statement and its negation are true or false.

23. All cars are red.
24. All trucks are green.
25. All squares are rectangles.
26. All rectangles are squares.

27. All whole numbers are integers.

28. All negative numbers are less than zero.

29. No cars are red.

30. No trucks are green.

31. No squares are triangles.

32. No rectangles are squares.

33. No integers are irrational.

34. No positive numbers are less than zero.

35. Some cars are red.

36. Some trucks are green.

37. Some squares are triangles.

38. Some rectangles are squares.

39. Some integers are positive.

40. Some rational numbers are irrational.

Find the negation of the statement. Then determine whether the statement and its negation are true or false. Provide a counterexample for the false statement.

41. All integers are whole numbers.

42. All whole numbers are greater than zero.

43. All even numbers are prime.

44. All odd numbers are prime.

45. No integers are whole numbers.

46. No odd numbers are prime.

47. No odd numbers are positive.

48. No rational numbers are whole numbers.

49. Some integers are whole numbers.

50. Some odd numbers are prime.

51. Some positive real numbers are irrational.

52. Some negative real numbers are rational.

53. **Challenge** Find the negation of each statement.

   a. Some pianists are not singers.

   b. Some birds do not fly.

   c. At least one author is a poet.

   d. At least one athlete is a millionaire.

   e. At least one book is not a novel.

   f. At least one car is not red.

Name _____ Date _____

Writing Repeating Decimals as Fractions

You can rewrite a repeating decimal as a fraction by writing and solving a linear equation.

KEY CONCEPT

Representations of Rational Numbers

A rational number can be written both as a fraction, where the numerator and denominator are both integers, and as a decimal, where the decimal expansion either terminates or has a repeating block of digits.

EXAMPLE 1 ## Write a repeating decimal as a fraction

Write the repeating decimal 0.55555... in its fraction form.

Solution:

Let $x = 0.55555...$ Then we want to write x in fraction form. We start by multiplying each side of the equation by 10. We get $10x = 5.55555...$ Since the fives continue indefinitely, we can write as many as we want to the right of the decimal.

Now we line up the two equations in the paragraph above and subtract:

$$10x = 5.55555...$$
$$(-)\ \underline{x = 0.55555...}$$
$$9x = 5$$

We finish by dividing each side of the equation $9x = 5$ by 9:

$$\frac{9x}{9} = \frac{5}{9}$$
$$x = \frac{5}{9}$$

The repeating decimal 0.55555... is equivalent to the fraction $\frac{5}{9}$. ■

In Example 1, we multiplied each side of the equation $x = 0.55555...$ by 10 because the repeating block has just one digit, 5. In general, if the repeating block of the decimal form of a rational number has n digits, multiply each side of the equation by 10^n.

EXAMPLE 2 ## Write a repeating decimal as a mixed number

Write the repeating decimal $2.\overline{36}$ as a mixed number.

CHAPTER 2

Writing Repeating Decimals as Fractions *continued*

Solution:

Let $x = 2.\overline{36} = 2.363636\ldots$ We multiply each side of the equation by 10^2 or 100 because the repeating block has two digits. We get $100x = 236.363636\ldots$ Then we subtract equations and solve for x.

$$100x = 236.363636\ldots$$
$$(-)\quad x = \quad 2.363636\ldots$$
$$99x = 234$$

$$\frac{99x}{99} = \frac{234}{99}$$

$$x = \frac{234}{99}$$

$$x = \frac{26}{11} \quad \text{or} \quad 2\frac{4}{11}$$

The repeating decimal $2.\overline{36}\ldots$ is equivalent to the mixed number $2\frac{4}{11}$. ■

Practice

Write each repeating decimal as a fraction.

1. $0.22222\ldots$ **2.** $0.44444\ldots$ **3.** $0.\overline{7}$ **4.** $0.\overline{8}$

5. $0.171717\ldots$ **6.** $0.595959\ldots$ **7.** $0.\overline{26}$ **8.** $0.\overline{71}$

9. $0.636363\ldots$ **10.** $0.818181\ldots$ **11.** $0.\overline{205}$ **12.** $0.\overline{477}$

Write each repeating decimal as a mixed number.

13. $5.11111\ldots$ **14.** $3.55555\ldots$ **15.** $6.\overline{6}$ **16.** $7.\overline{92}$

17. $4.232323\ldots$ **18.** $9.191919\ldots$ **19.** $6.\overline{516}$ **20.** $9.\overline{755}$

21. Use the techniques of Example 1 to rewrite $0.99999\ldots$ What value do you get? Do you believe that your answer and $0.99999\ldots$ are equivalent? Explain.

22. Rewrite $8.515151\ldots$ as a mixed number two ways. First follow the method of Example 2. Then form a mixed number by taking 8 as the whole part and rewriting $0.515151\ldots$ as a fraction to get the fractional part. Do you get the same answer? Describe a method of rewriting a repeating decimal as a mixed number that is different than that in Example 2.

23. Suppose that a repeating decimal has a block of three repeating digits. Would the methods of this lesson still work if you multiplied by 10^6 instead of 10^3? Explain. You may want to try it for a few numbers such as $0.\overline{123}$, $0.\overline{456}$, and $0.\overline{789}$ before you answer.

24. Can the methods of this lesson be used to rewrite the decimal expansion of π as a fraction where both the numerator and the denominator are integers? Explain.

CHAPTER 2 Unit Rates and Dimensional Analysis

KEY CONCEPT

Unit Rate

A rate expressed with a denominator of 1 is called a unit rate. Any rate can be expressed as a unit rate.

A rate such as 50 miles per hour is already expressed as a unit rate: $\frac{50 \text{ miles}}{1 \text{ hour}}$. The following example shows how to rewrite other rates as unit rates.

EXAMPLE 1 Express a rate as a unit rate

Julian bought a 16-ounce bottle of soda for $1.20. In this situation, the unit rate is the price per ounce of soda. To find the price per ounce, divide the price of the whole bottle by the number of ounces in the bottle.

$$\frac{\$1.20}{16 \text{ oz.}} = \frac{\$1.20 \div 16}{16 \text{ oz.} \div 16} = \frac{\$0.075}{1 \text{ oz.}} \text{ or } \$0.075 \text{ per ounce}$$

The unit rate is 0.075 dollar per ounce, or equivalently, 7.5 cents per ounce. ∎

Unit rates are useful when making comparisons among different rates.

EXAMPLE 2 Compare rates

Mr. Nabors drove 460 miles in 8 hours, while Ms. Sanchez drove 560 miles in 10 hours. On average, who was driving faster?

Solution:

In order to compare the two speeds, we calculate the corresponding unit rates.

Mr. Nabors: $\frac{460 \text{ miles}}{8 \text{ hours}} = \frac{460 \text{ miles} \div 8}{8 \text{ hours} \div 8} = \frac{57.5 \text{ miles}}{1 \text{ hour}}$ or 57.5 miles per hour

Ms. Sanchez: $\frac{560 \text{ miles}}{10 \text{ hours}} = \frac{560 \text{ miles} \div 10}{10 \text{ hours} \div 10} = \frac{56 \text{ miles}}{1 \text{ hour}}$ or 56 miles per hour

On average, Mr. Nabors was driving faster than Ms. Sanchez. ∎

KEY CONCEPT

Dimensional Analysis

The units in which a rate is expressed can be changed using dimensional analysis.

EXAMPLE 3 Change the units in a rate

Miss Jenkins paid $42.75 per square yard to have new carpet installed in her house. Express the rate in dollars per square foot.

Solution:

To express the rate in square feet instead of square yards, we recognize that 1 square yard = 9 square feet and multiply by the appropriate ratio.

$$\frac{\$42.75}{1 \text{ yd}^2} \cdot \frac{1 \text{ yd}^2}{9 \text{ ft}^2} = \frac{\$42.75}{\cancel{1 \text{ yd}^2}} \cdot \frac{\cancel{1 \text{ yd}^2}}{9 \text{ ft}^2} = \frac{\$42.75}{9 \text{ ft}^2} = \frac{\$42.75 \div 9}{9 \text{ ft}^2 \div 9} = \frac{\$4.75}{1 \text{ ft}^2} \text{ or } \$4.75 \text{ per square foot}$$

The equivalent rate is $4.75 per square foot. ∎

CHAPTER 2 # Unit Rates and Dimensional Analysis *continued*

It is possible to change more than one unit at a time using dimensional analysis.

EXAMPLE 4 ## Change the units in a rate

Toby was traveling on his bicycle at a rate of 30 feet per second. Find his speed in miles per hour.

Solution:

In this example, we need to change feet to miles and seconds to hours. We will use 5280 feet = 1 mile, 60 seconds = 1 minute, and 60 minutes = 1 hour.

$$\frac{30 \text{ ft}}{1 \text{ sec}} \cdot \frac{1 \text{ mile}}{5280 \text{ ft}} \cdot \frac{60 \text{ sec}}{1 \text{ min}} \cdot \frac{60 \text{ min}}{1 \text{ hr}} = \frac{30 \text{ ft}}{1 \text{ sec}} \cdot \frac{1 \text{ mile}}{5280 \text{ ft}} \cdot \frac{60 \text{ sec}}{1 \text{ min}} \cdot \frac{60 \text{ min}}{1 \text{ hr}}$$

$$= \frac{30 \cdot 60 \cdot 60 \text{ miles}}{5280 \text{ hr}} = \frac{108{,}000 \text{ miles}}{5280 \text{ hr}}$$

$$\approx 20.5 \text{ miles per hour}$$

The equivalent rate is approximately 20.5 miles per hour. ∎

We can use dimensional analysis to compare rates expressed in different units.

EXAMPLE 5 ## Compare rates

A meter on one pipe indicated that water was flowing through the pipe at a rate of 50 gallons per minute. A meter on a second pipe indicated that water was flowing through that pipe at a rate of 2750 gallons per hour. Which pipe had water flowing through it at the faster rate?

Solution:

In order to compare the two rates, we must first express them in the same units. There is no need to change both rates. We will express the rate of water flowing through the first pipe in gallons per hour.

First pipe: $\frac{50 \text{ gal}}{1 \text{ min}} \cdot \frac{60 \text{ min}}{1 \text{ hour}} = \frac{50 \text{ gal}}{1 \text{ min}} \cdot \frac{60 \text{ min}}{1 \text{ hour}} = \frac{3000 \text{ gal}}{1 \text{ hour}}$ or 3000 gallons per hour

Water was flowing through the first pipe at the faster rate. ∎

Practice

Express each rate as a unit rate.

1. $1.26 for 12 ounces of orange juice
2. $1.59 for 2 liters of soda
3. $10.80 for 3 pounds of cheese
4. $35.70 for 6 pounds of roast beef
5. $52,500 raised for charity in 14 days
6. 18,600 customers served in 15 weeks
7. 215 miles traveled in 4 hours
8. 518 kilometers traveled in 8 hours
9. 90 pages read in $2\frac{1}{2}$ hours
10. 182 words typed in $3\frac{1}{2}$ minutes
11. $0.75 for 0.5 liter of water
12. $3.50 for 0.25 hour of internet service
13. Mia paid $6.32 for 8 candy bars at one store. Allison paid $5.25 for 7 candy bars at another store. How much did each girl pay per candy bar? Who paid the higher price per candy bar?

CHAPTER 2 # Unit Rates and Dimensional Analysis *continued*

14. Nat paid $4.75 for 50 minutes of long distance calling. Chi paid $6.75 for 75 minutes of long distance calling. How much did each boy pay per minute? Who paid the higher price per minute?

15. Mr. Lighthorse drove 580 miles in 10 hours. Mr. Lopez drove 660 miles in 12 hours. How fast was each man driving? On average, who was driving faster?

16. A plane traveling west flew 1000 miles in 2.5 hours. A plane traveling east flew 1350 miles in 3 hours. How fast was each plane traveling? On average, which plane had the greater speed?

17. Renate bought a 32-ounce jar of mayonnaise for $2.59. Dean bought a 48-ounce jar of mayonnaise for $3.59. How much did each person pay per ounce of mayonnaise? Round your answers to the nearest cent. Who paid less per ounce?

18. Keisha bought a 16-ounce bottle of ketchup for $1.19. Jules bought a 24-ounce bottle of ketchup for $1.99. How much did each person pay per ounce of mayonnaise? Round your answers to the nearest cent. Who paid less per ounce?

19. Mrs. Billings drove 96 miles in $1\frac{1}{2}$ hours. Mr. Lucas drove 175 miles in $2\frac{1}{2}$ hours. Find each driver's average speed. On average, who was driving faster?

20. Dena read 45 pages of a novel in $1\frac{1}{2}$ hours. Jamison read 88 pages of the same novel in $2\frac{3}{4}$ hours. On average, how many pages did each student read per hour? Who was reading at the faster rate?

21. A fabric store sells denim for $5.99 per yard. Find the price per foot. Round to the nearest cent.

22. A grocery store sells ground beef for $2.99 per pound. Find the price per ounce. Round to the nearest cent. (1 pound = 16 ounces)

23. A flooring store is advertising laminate flooring at $2.99 per square foot. Find the price per square yard. (1 square yard = 9 square feet)

24. A home improvement store sells carpet for as low as $1.79 per square foot. Find the corresponding price per square yard. (1 square yard = 9 square feet)

25. A tile store sells ceramic tile for $2.99 per square foot. Find the price per square inch. Round to the nearest cent. (1 square foot = 144 square inches)

26. A flooring store is selling laminate flooring for $33.99 per square yard. Find the price per square foot. Round to the nearest cent. (1 square yard = 9 square feet)

27. Vernon bought square tiles measuring 6 inches on each side to tile his bathroom. Each tile cost $1.19. Find the cost of the tile per square foot. (1 square foot = 144 square inches)

28. Halley bought square tiles measuring 10 inches on each side to tile her kitchen. Each tile cost $2.39. Find the cost per square foot. Round to the nearest cent. (1 square foot = 144 square inches)

Unit Rates and Dimensional Analysis *continued*

Change each rate to miles per hour. Round to the nearest whole number, if necessary.

29. 25 feet per second

30. 35 feet per second

31. 200 inches per second

32. 275 inches per second

33. 1500 feet per minute

34. 7500 feet per minute

35. 800 yards per minute

36. 1000 yards per minute

37. A meter on one pipe indicated that water was flowing through the pipe at a rate of 75 gallons per minute. A meter on a second pipe indicated that water was flowing through that pipe at a rate of 4350 gallons per hour. Express both rates in gallons per hour. Which pipe had water flowing through it at the faster rate?

38. Water was flowing through a pipe filling one swimming pool at a rate of 95 gallons per minute. Water was flowing through a pipe filling a second swimming pool at a rate of 6100 gallons per hour. Express both rates in gallons per hour. Which swimming pool is filling at the faster rate?

39. One store sells a particular chain for $0.19 per inch. Another store charges $2.29 per foot for the same chain. Express both rates in dollars per foot. Which store has the lower price?

40. A flooring store sells a particular carpet for $2.49 per square foot. A home improvement store sells the same carpet for $17.99 per square yard. Express both rates in dollars per square yard. Which store has the lower price?

CHAPTER 2 Deciding When to Use Cross Products

KEY CONCEPT

Rewrite Equations in order to Solve Using Cross Products

A proportion is a special type of equation where one ratio is equal to a second ratio. Proportions can be solved using cross products. Other equations containing ratios can be solved using cross products if you first rewrite them as proportions.

EXAMPLE 1 ## Determine whether an equation is written as a proportion

Determine whether each equation is written as a proportion.

a. $\dfrac{y}{9} - \dfrac{5}{12} = \dfrac{1}{6}$
b. $\dfrac{3}{b+4} = \dfrac{7}{b}$

Solution:

a. The equation $\dfrac{y}{9} - \dfrac{5}{12} = \dfrac{1}{6}$ is not a written as a proportion because the expression to the left of the equal sign is not in the form of a single ratio.

b. The equation $\dfrac{3}{b+4} = \dfrac{7}{b}$ is written as a proportion because the expressions on both sides of the equal sign are single ratios. ∎

Some equations can be rewritten as proportions as shown in the next example.

EXAMPLE 2 ## Rewrite an equation as a proportion

Rewrite each equation as a proportion.

a. $\dfrac{x+2}{3} - \dfrac{x+1}{4} = 0$
b. $\dfrac{8}{p} = \dfrac{7}{10} + \dfrac{1}{5}$
c. $\dfrac{m}{2} = 6$

Solution:

a. The equation $\dfrac{x+2}{3} - \dfrac{x+1}{4} = 0$ can be written as a proportion by adding $\dfrac{x+1}{4}$ to each side.

$$\dfrac{x+2}{3} - \dfrac{x+1}{4} = 0$$

$$\dfrac{x+2}{3} - \dfrac{x+1}{4} + \dfrac{x+1}{4} = 0 + \dfrac{x+1}{4}$$

$$\dfrac{x+2}{3} = \dfrac{x+1}{4}$$

Pre-AP Copymasters

Deciding When to Use Cross Products *continued*

b. The equation $\frac{8}{p} = \frac{7}{10} + \frac{1}{5}$ can be written as a proportion by expressing the sum of the fractions on the right side of the equal sign as a single fraction.

$$\frac{8}{p} = \frac{7}{10} + \frac{1}{5}$$

$$\frac{8}{p} = \frac{7}{10} + \frac{2}{10}$$

$$\frac{8}{p} = \frac{9}{10}$$

c. The equation $\frac{m}{2} = 6$ can be written as a proportion by expressing 6 as the ratio $\frac{6}{1}$.

$$\frac{m}{2} = \frac{6}{1} \quad \blacksquare$$

After an equation is rewritten as a proportion, we can use cross products to solve the equation.

EXAMPLE 3 ## Solve an equation using cross products

Solve the equation $\frac{x+2}{3} - \frac{x+1}{4} = 0$ using cross products.

Solution:

We first need to rewrite the equation as a proportion. This was done in Example 2. Then we use cross products to eliminate the fractions from the equation.

$$\frac{x+2}{3} = \frac{x+1}{4}$$

$$4(x+2) = 3(x+1)$$

$$4x + 8 = 3x + 3$$

$$x + 8 = 3$$

$$x = -5$$

The solution is -5. Check the solution by substituting -5 into the original equation. ■

Practice

Determine whether each equation is written as a proportion.

1. $\frac{x}{4} - \frac{3}{5} = 0$ **2.** $\frac{5}{y} - \frac{6}{11} = 0$ **3.** $\frac{s}{8} - \frac{1}{2} = \frac{s}{4}$ **4.** $\frac{1}{t} - \frac{3}{8} = \frac{5}{8}$

5. $\frac{x+9}{7} = \frac{x}{6}$ **6.** $\frac{1}{h-2} = \frac{2}{h}$ **7.** $\frac{4}{b+2} - \frac{1}{b} = 0$ **8.** $\frac{3+g}{2} - \frac{g}{3} = 0$

Deciding When to Use Cross Products *continued*

**Rewrite each equation as a proportion. Then solve the
equation using cross products.**

9. $\dfrac{x}{8} - \dfrac{3}{4} = 0$ **10.** $\dfrac{c}{14} + \dfrac{5}{7} = 0$ **11.** $\dfrac{3}{5} + \dfrac{d}{25} = 0$ **12.** $\dfrac{1}{6} - \dfrac{w}{24} = 0$

13. $\dfrac{10}{y} + \dfrac{5}{16} = 0$ **14.** $\dfrac{9}{v} - \dfrac{3}{7} = 0$ **15.** $\dfrac{6}{11} - \dfrac{12}{b} = 0$ **16.** $\dfrac{7}{13} + \dfrac{63}{g} = 0$

17. $\dfrac{z}{4} = 3 - \dfrac{1}{2}$ **18.** $\dfrac{m}{6} = 2 - \dfrac{1}{3}$ **19.** $\dfrac{1}{y} = \dfrac{1}{7} - \dfrac{1}{8}$ **20.** $\dfrac{1}{d} = \dfrac{1}{8} - \dfrac{1}{9}$

21. $\dfrac{x+1}{2} = 8$ **22.** $\dfrac{x+2}{5} = 3$ **23.** $\dfrac{10}{h+2} = 2$ **24.** $\dfrac{25}{n-9} = 5$

25. $\dfrac{y}{3} = y$ **26.** $\dfrac{m}{5} = m$ **27.** $\dfrac{k+2}{3} = k$ **28.** $\dfrac{\ell-3}{4} = \ell$

29. $\dfrac{z-1}{3} - \dfrac{z+1}{2} = 0$ **30.** $\dfrac{r+1}{5} - \dfrac{r-1}{4} = 0$

31. $\dfrac{m+2}{3} + \dfrac{m-5}{2} = 0$ **32.** $\dfrac{b-5}{2} + \dfrac{b+1}{5} = 0$

33. $\dfrac{p-5}{p-6} - \dfrac{1}{2} = 0$ **34.** $\dfrac{x+1}{x+2} + \dfrac{2}{3} = 0$

35. $\dfrac{1}{y-5} - \dfrac{1}{2y-4} = 0$ **36.** $\dfrac{1}{t-4} - \dfrac{1}{2t+5} = 0$

**Write an equation for each sentence. Then rewrite the
equation as a proportion, if necessary. Solve the
proportion using cross products.**

37. The sum of the quotient of x and 4 and the quotient of 2 and 3 is 0.

38. The sum of the quotient of y and 5 and the quotient of 3 and 4 is 0.

39. The difference between the quotient of a and 2 and the quotient of 4 and 5 is 0.

40. The difference between the quotient of b and 6 and the quotient of 1 and 7 is 0.

41. When the quantity $x + 5$ is divided by 8, the result equals $\dfrac{1}{2}$.

42. When the quantity $y - 1$ is divided by 10, the result equals $\dfrac{2}{5}$.

43. The quotient of 4 and the quantity $d + 2$ equals $-\dfrac{1}{3}$.

44. The quotient of 5 and the quantity $n + 1$ equals $-\dfrac{1}{4}$.

CHAPTER 2 Interpreting Percents

As you solve problems that involve percents, be sure that you understand what the percents in the problems mean.

In many situations, percents are used to describe a part of a whole.

EXAMPLE 1 Use a percent to describe a part of a whole

Of the 70 students who regularly attend drama club meetings, only 42 auditioned for parts in the school play. So, 42 out of 70 or 60% of the students who regularly attend drama club meetings auditioned for the school play. ■

Using percents to describe parts of a whole allows us to compare parts of two different wholes.

EXAMPLE 2 Use percents to compare parts of two different wholes

At Lake High School, 120 out of 480 students participated in a county-wide service project. At Morris High School, 150 out of 750 students participated in the same service project. The school with better participation will receive a trophy. If the trophy were awarded to the school with more participants, Morris High School would receive the trophy, but this wouldn't be fair because Morris has the advantage of having more students. By comparing the percentages of students who participated from each school, we eliminate Morris High School's advantage. At Lake High School, 25% of the students participated, and at Morris High School, 20% participated. Based on percentages, Lake High School will receive the trophy. ■

Tax and surcharge rates are often expressed in terms of percents. In these cases, the amount of tax or surcharge is proportional to another amount.

EXAMPLE 3 Find the amount of a surcharge

For some online auctions, there is a surcharge added to the winning bid. This surcharge is called the buyer's premium. Suppose that Mr. Johannes has a winning bid of $240 for an antique rug in an auction that has a 10% buyer's premium. Find the amount of the buyer's premium. Then find the total cost of the rug and the premium.

Solution:

The buyer's premium is proportional to the amount of the winning bid. We can use the formula $p = 0.10b$ to calculate the premium p for the winning bid b, where the percent has been expressed as a decimal. So, Mr. Johannes's premium is $p = 0.10(\$240) = \$24$.

To find the total cost, we can add the amount of the winning bid and the amount of the buyer's premium: $\$240 + \$24 = \$264$. ■

Some catalog and online vendors offer a flat rate for shipping, while others determine the amount of shipping based on the total price or weight of the products purchased.

EXAMPLE 4 Compare shipping prices

Troy wants to purchase a video game that is offered by two different online vendors for $39.95. Vendor A charges $7 for shipping and handling regardless of the size of the order. Vendor B charges 15% of the purchase price for shipping and handling. Find the amount that Vendor B would charge Troy for shipping and handling. Which vendor will charge him less?

CHAPTER 2	**Interpreting Percents** *continued*

Solution:

Vendor B will charge 15% of $39.95 for shipping and handling: 0.15($39.95) ≈ $5.99. Since $5.99 is less than $7, Vendor B will charge Troy less. ■

Percents are also used to describe changes in quantities, such as populations, prices of consumer products, and values of investments. In these situations, the amount that the quantity changes is proportional to its original value.

EXAMPLE 5 ## Estimate the value of a home

The Wests purchased a home one year ago for $295,000. Since then, home prices in their neighborhood have increased by about 14%. Estimate the value of the Wests' home.

Solution:

The value of the Wests' home is about 14% greater than the price they paid one year ago. This means that the value is now 114% of the price they paid: 114% of $295,000 is 1.14($295,000) = $336,300. ■

You should also be able to distinguish between a constant rate of growth and growth by a certain percentage.

EXAMPLE 6 ## Comparing population growth

Suppose that the population of a city was 100,000 a year ago and is now 103,000. What will its population be one year from now if it increases again by the same amount? What will its population be one year from now if it increases again by the same percentage? Which is greater?

Solution:

The population increased by 3000 in the past year. So, if the population increases by the same amount during the next year, the population one year from now will be 103,000 + 3000 = 106,000.

The population increased 3000 out of 100,000 or 3% over the past year. So, if the population increases by the same percentage during the next year, the population one year from now will be 103% of the current population or 1.03(103,000) = 106,090.

The population will be greater if it increases again by the same percentage. ■

Practice

1. Angela has two jobs. Last week she earned $30 babysitting for her nephew and $20 cleaning for her neighbor. What percentage of her total earnings for the week came from cleaning?

2. Quincy invited 25 people to his birthday party. Only 21 were able to attend. What percentage of the people was able to attend?

Interpreting Percents continued

3. Ms. Li earns $942 each week. If 28% of her earnings are withheld for taxes and social security, how much does she pay in taxes and social security each week?

4. A salesperson receives 35% of his total sales in commission. If the salesperson sells $12,500 in merchandise in one month, how much is his commission for the month?

5. At the end of last year, Mr. Rodriguez's financial portfolio was worth $450,000. His financial adviser earns a commission equal to 0.5% of the value of the portfolio. What was the financial adviser's commission for the year?

6. Sophie bought a necklace in an online auction. Because the seller was in a different state, she did not have to pay sales tax. However, she did have to pay shipping costs of $4.95 and a 10% buyer's premium on her winning bid of $29.50. What was her total?

7. At the beginning of the year, the population of a town is 42,156. If the population of the town grows by 3% during the year, what will its population be at the end of the year? Round to the nearest whole number.

8. Mr. Hassan took a job with a starting salary of $52,000. After one year, he will get a 5% raise. What will his salary be after the raise?

9. One online vendor charges a flat rate of $12 for the shipping and handling on any size order. A second vendor charges 6% of the merchandise total for shipping and handling. Find the value of the merchandise for which the shipping and handling costs are the same for both vendors.

10. One auction company charges a flat rate of $5 to sell an item. Another company charges 7% of the winning bid. For what winning bid would the charges for both companies be the same? Round to the nearest cent.

11. In a competition between two schools, the school whose team performs best on the obstacle course will receive ten new computers from a local businessman. Greene High School had ten participants in the event of whom six completed the course within the time limit. Hamilton High School had 15 participants of whom eight completed the course within the time limit.

    a. If the computers go to the school with more students finishing the course within the time limit, which school will win?

    b. If the computers go to the school with higher percentage of students finishing the course within the time limit, which school will win? Give the percentages as part of your answer.

12. Greg and Kayla live in two different states. The sales tax laws are different in the two states. Both want to buy a DVD from an online store that costs $18.95. The store charges $5.95 shipping and handling for a single DVD.

    a. Greg lives in a state where sales tax is charged on the total cost of the DVD and shipping and handling. If Greg's sales tax rate is 7%, what will be his total with shipping, handling and sales tax?

CHAPTER
2

Interpreting Percents *continued*

b. Kayla lives in a state where sales tax is charged only on the cost of the DVD and not on the shipping and handling. If Kayla's sales tax rate is 8%, what will be her total with shipping, handling and sales tax?

c. Who will pay more, Greg or Kayla?

13. Ms. Kumori bought several shares of a stock at $32.40 per share. One week later the stock was valued at $34.50 per share.

a. By how much did the value of a share increase during the week?

b. By what percentage did the value of a share increase? Round to the nearest tenth of a percent.

c. If the value of a share increases by the same amount during the next week how much will it be worth?

d. If the value of a share increases by the same percentage during the next week how much will it be worth? Round to the nearest cent.

e. Would Ms. Kumori prefer for the value to increase by the same amount or by the same percentage? Explain.

14. A candidate for a statewide office received 5482 votes in Marion County and 82,389 votes in Bay County. The candidate concludes that because he received more votes in Bay County than in Marion County, he is more popular in Bay County.

a. Explain the problem with the candidate's conclusion.

b. If the population of Marion County is 9492 and the population of Bay County is 344,678, what would you conclude about the candidate's popularity? Use percentages to support your reasoning.

15. Miss Cardoza bought a house for $217,000. One year later the house was valued at $289,000.

a. If the house's value increases by the same amount, what will it be worth after one more year?

b. If the house's value increases by the same percentage, what will it be worth after one more year? Round to the nearest hundred thousand.

16. Use the internet or some other reliable resource to find the percent increase in housing prices last year in a city near you. Then, assuming that housing prices will increase by the same percentage this year, estimate the value of a house on December 31 that was worth $500,000 on January 1.

17. The number of students at Garland High School participating in community service activities was 75 in 2004, 150 in 2005, and 200 in 2006. Why might the principal have been somewhat disappointed in the increase between 2005 and 2006?

Name _____ Date _____

Identifying the Domain of a Variable in a Formula

For most formulas modeling real-life situations, there are natural restrictions on the values that may be used for the variables in the formula. For a formula, the set of all values that may be meaningfully substituted for any variable in the formula is called the domain of that variable.

EXAMPLE 1 ## Identify the domain of a variable in a formula

Find the domain of each variable in the formula for the area of a rectangle, $A = \ell w$.

Solution:

The formula $A = \ell w$ models the area A of a rectangle, where ℓ represents the length of the rectangle and w represents its width. Because neither the length nor the width of a rectangle can be either negative or zero, the values of ℓ and w cannot be either negative or zero. It is also true that the value of A cannot be negative or zero. Therefore, each of the variables, A, ℓ, and w in the formula has the set of all positive real numbers as its domain. ■

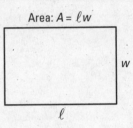

In real-life situations, given restrictions on the domain of certain variables in a formula will affect the domain of other variables in the formula.

EXAMPLE 2 ## Identify the domain of a variable in a formula

Suppose you have a rectangular yard that is 20 feet by 30 feet, and you want to create a rectangular garden within the yard as shown in the figure. Find the domain of each variable in the formula for the area of the garden, $A = \ell w$.

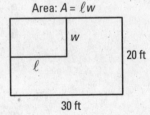

Solution:

As in Example 1, the values of ℓ and w cannot be either negative or zero. The length ℓ cannot be greater than 30 ft and the width w cannot be greater than 20 ft, since the garden must be within the yard. Therefore, the area of the garden A cannot be greater than (30 ft) • (20 ft) = 600 ft². The domain of ℓ is the set of positive real numbers less than or equal to 30, the domain of w is the set of positive real numbers less than or equal to 20, and the domain of A is the set of positive real numbers less than or equal to 600. ■

In the previous example, the domains of the variables were given as a range of real numbers. In some real-world situations, the domain of a variable can be further restricted to discrete values such as whole numbers or multiples of whole numbers.

CHAPTER 2 **Identifying the Domain of a Variable in a Formula** *continued*

EXAMPLE 3 **Identify the domain of a variable in a formula**

The formula $C = 8.50x$ models the cost C in dollars for x adults to see a movie. Find the domain of the variable x.

Solution:

In this situation, the variable x represents a number of people. This number cannot be negative. It also cannot be irrational or a rational number that is not a whole number: $\sqrt{3}$ people and 4.5 people are both meaningless. The domain of the variable x in the formula $C = 8.50x$ is the set of whole numbers. ∎

Before substituting a value for a variable in a formula, always ask whether the number is a meaningful value for the variable.

Practice

Find the domain of each variable in the formula.

1. Perimeter of a rectangle: $P = 2\ell + 2w$
2. Volume of a cube: $V = s^3$
3. Speed given distance and time: $s = \dfrac{d}{t}$
4. Density given mass and volume: $d = \dfrac{m}{v}$
5. Volume of a rectangular prism: $V = \ell wh$
6. Circumference of a circle: $c = \pi d$

Problem Solving

7. Suppose you have a square region that is 20 feet wide and 20 feet long and you wish to put a circular pool within that region. Find the domain of each variable in the formula for the area of the pool, $A = \pi r^2$.

8. Suppose you drive a car that gets 20 miles per gallon and the capacity of the tank is 14 gallons. The distance driven is given by the formula $d = 20g$. Find the domain of each variable in the formula assuming that the tank is not refilled.

9. The formula $R = 30x$ models the revenue R in dollars for selling x shirts. Find the domain of the variable x.

10. To use a gym for two weeks, you pay a sign-up fee of $30 and $5 for each day you use the gym. The formula $C = 30 + 5d$ models the cost C in dollars for going d days over the two week period. Find the domain of the variable d.

11. What are the possible values of the variable C in the formula $C = 8.50x$ from Example 3?

12. What are the possible values of the variable R in the formula $R = 30x$ from Exercise 9?

13. What are the possible values of the variable C in the formula $C = 30 + 5d$ from Exercise 10?

Solving Linear Equations with a Graphing Calculator

Your graphing calculator can be a powerful tool to help you solve equations and check your work that you have done by hand. As with any tool, you need to know how to use it properly if you want to use it effectively. There are several ways to solve an equation with a graphing calculator. At this point, we will look at one of them.

EXAMPLE **Solve a linear equation with a graphing calculator**

Solve the equation $5x + 1 = 3x - 1$ using a graphing calculator.

Solution:

Find the menu on your calculator where you can enter functions in order to graph them. On many calculators, this is accomplished by pressing a button similar to Y=. Then enter the left side of the equation, $5x + 1$, beside Y_1 and the right side of the equation beside Y_2.

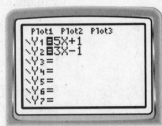

Then produce a graph of the two equations in a suitable viewing rectangle. Most calculators have a standard viewing rectangle that will be sufficient in this case. This viewing rectangle shows both the axes with units from -10 to 10. On some calculators, you can produce this graph by pressing ZOOM 6.

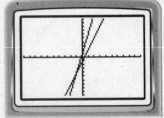

To find the solution, we identify the x-value of the point where the two lines intersect. Most calculators have a feature that will find the intersection point for you. Look for the CALC menu and select the intersect command under that menu.

The calculator may prompt you to select the graphs whose intersection you want to find as well as ask you for a guess. You may simply press ENTER at each of these prompts. The x-coordinate shown at the bottom of the screen is the solution of the equation.

Be sure to check the solution by substituting it back into the original equation. ∎

Practice

Solve the equations in Exercises 3–14 on page 157 of your textbook using your graphing calculator. Regardless of the letter used for the variable, you will enter it as x on your calculator. You should get the same answers as when you solved the equations by hand.

CHAPTER 3 | Scatter Plots

When data in the form of ordered pairs is graphed as points in a coordinate plane, the result is called a **scatter plot.** A scatter plot sometimes reveals a pattern in the relationship between two variables.

EXAMPLE 1 | Weight versus age for female babies

The table gives the age and weight for ten female babies, of various ages, born in the U.S. in 2005.

Age (months)	1	2	4	6	7	8	9	11	11	12
Weight (pounds)	8.6	12.5	13.1	17.9	16.5	17.2	18.4	18.3	22.8	23.9

a. Create a scatter plot of the data, with age on the horizontal axis and weight on the vertical axis.

b. Would you expect the relation between age and weight to be a function? *Discuss.* Review Lesson 1.7 as necessary.

c. What general trend is evident in the relation between age and weight?

d. What is a good estimate for the likely weight of a baby girl at the age of 10 months?

Solution:

a. The scatterplot is as shown.

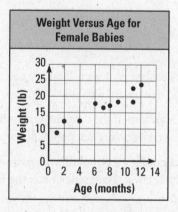

Weight Versus Age for Female Babies

b. Any one baby will have only a single recorded weight at each monthly checkup, so for an individual baby the age-weight relation can be considered a function. But in a population of babies, it is possible for the same age to correspond to several different weights, and then the relation is not a function. In the data given, for instance, the age of 11 months is associated with two different weights.

c. The trend is for babies to increase in weight as they get older.

d. A weight of about 20 pounds at 10 months would be well in line with the pattern of the data. ■

CHAPTER 3

Scatter Plots *continued*

Practice

1. **Reasoning** Identify pairs of real-world variables whose scatterplot would match each of the following descriptions. *Explain* your answers.

   a. One variable decreases as the other increases.

   b. There is no pattern to the relation between the variables.

2. **Writing** *Explain* why it would make no sense to try to construct a scatter plot relating different flavors of ice cream to the number of calories per scoop.

3. **World Geography** In the list of the world's most populous contries, China and India rank first and second. The table shows the next ten countries, as of mid-2004.

Country	Land area (millions of sq km)	Population (millions)
Russia	17.1	144
United States	9.6	293
Brazil	8.5	184
Mexico	2.0	105
Indonesia	1.9	238
Nigeria	0.9	137
Pakistan	0.8	159
Japan	0.4	127
Philippines	0.3	86
Bangladesh	0.1	141

   a. Construct a scatter plot with land area as the independent variable and population as the dependent variable.

   b. *Describe* the pattern of the data and comment on the relationship, for the countries shown, between land area and population size.

   c. How does a country's population *density* show up on the graph? (Hint: Of the countries on the list, Bangladesh has the highest density and Russia has the lowest.)

   d. **Challenge** Give two reasons why this scatter plot would not be a good tool for predicting the population of a country with a land area of 5 million square kilometers.

4. **Challenge** The plot from Example 1 is used to make two predictions: the weight of a baby girl aged 3 months, and the weight of a baby girl aged 14 months. Which prediction is likely to be more accurate? *Explain.* Give two separate reasons for your answer.

5. **Activity** Use an Internet search engine to locate real-world data in the form of a table relating two quantitative variables. Copy the table and paste it into a spreadsheet application. Use the application's chart utility to create a scatter plot. Describe the pattern of points and discuss the usefulness of the graph for making predictions.

Name _____ Date _____

CHAPTER 3 Distinguishing Between Discrete and Continuous Variables

The usual reason for a function $y = f(x)$ to be discrete rather than continuous is that one or both of the variables x and y are discrete variables. We are used to thinking of variables as ranging over the real numbers, but sometimes a variable can only take on discrete values, spaced out along the real number line.

The main use of discrete variables is for quantities of objects that must be present either as a whole or not at all. Whether this applies to a given type of object can depend on the context.

EXAMPLE 1 Distinguish between discrete and continuous variables

Would each of the named quantities be best represented by a continuous variable or a discrete one?

    a. gallons of milk in a family refrigerator   **b.** gallons of milk in a store refrigerator

Solution:

    a. Someone checking on how much milk a family has in its refrigerator will count a half-gallon container, or a partly-full gallon container, as a fraction of a gallon. This context calls for a continuous variable.

    b. Someone counting milk containers at a store (e.g., for inventory) will use whole numbers only. Gallon, half-gallon, and quart containers will be counted separately. This context calls for a discrete variable to represent gallons of milk. ■

Normally, discrete variables take on integer values. Sometimes, however, they can represent quantities that are not necessarily integer-valued.

EXAMPLE 2 Identify discrete values

What are the discrete possible values in each case?

    a. The price, in dollars, of an item on a store shelf.

    b. Number of people that show up for a meeting

    c. Number of right answers on a multiple-choice test

    d. Miles traveled by a car, as indicated by the odometer

Solution:

    a. Prices must be multiples of $0.01, so $0.01, $0.02, $0.03, . . .

    b. People are counted using the numbers 0, 1, 2, 3, . . .

    c. Correct answers are counted using the numbers 0, 1, 2, 3, . . .

    d. An odometer indicates miles in increments of 0.1 mile, so 0.0, 0.1, 0.2, 0.3, . . . ■

CHAPTER 3 · Distinguishing Between Discrete and Continuous Variables *continued*

In applied problems, we sometimes pretend that discrete variables are continuous, and then we round our results to a nearby discrete value.

EXAMPLE 3 ### Round to a discrete value

The population of a small town, t years after 2000, is given by $P(t) = 34e^{0.08t}$. What is the projected 2009 population? (Note: e is an irrational number with a value of approximately 2.72. Use the e^x key on your graphing calculator for this example.)

Solution:

The year 2009 corresponds to $t = 9$, and $P(9) = 34e^{0.08*9} \approx 69.85$. Rounded to the nearest whole number, the population in 2009 is projected to be 70 people. ■

Practice

State whether each of the following quantities is a discrete or a continuous variable.

1. Number of pages in a book

2. Amount of liquid in a glass

3. Gas prices (which typically end with "9/10")

4. Olympic finishing times in the men's 10k Olympic biathlon (which are measured to the nearest tenth-second).

5. Distance traveled by an airplane

6. Oven temperature in recipes (which are usually in increments of 25°F)

7. Number of apples on a tree

8. **Writing** Suppose we make it a practice to write the value of any variable as a decimal rounded to three decimal places. Does this mean all the variables we are working with are discrete variables? Why or why not?

CHAPTER 3

Intercepts of Horizontal and Vertical Lines

A slanting line in a graph will have both a y- and an x-intercept. What about vertical and horizontal lines?

A horizontal line has a y-intercept but no x-intercept–unless, that is, the line lies on top of the x-axis, in which case it has infinitely many x-intercepts! By the same token, a vertical line has exactly one x-intercept, and has no y-intercept unless it lies on the y-axis.

EXAMPLE 1 ## Find the intercepts of the graph of an equation

    a. $y = 5$ **b.** $x = 3$ **c.** $y = -2$

    d. $x = -\dfrac{3}{2}$ **e.** $y = 0$

Solution:

The graphs of the five lines are as shown.

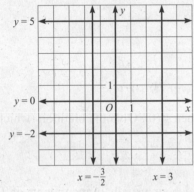

a. $y = 5$ has a y-intercept of 5 and no x-intercept.

b. $x = 3$ has an x-intercept of 3 and no y-intercept.

c. $y = -2$ has a y-intercept of -2 and no x-intercept.

d. $x = -\dfrac{3}{2}$ has an x-intercept of $-\dfrac{3}{2}$ and no y-intercept.

e. $y = 0$ has a y-intercept of 0 and infinitely many x-intercepts. ■

Practice

Find the x-intercept(s) and the y-intercept(s) of the graph of the equation.

    1. $y = 5$ **2.** $x = -4$ **3.** $y = -\dfrac{3}{4}$

    4. $x = 0$ **5.** $y = 9$ **6.** $y = 0$

Write the equation of the line that has the given intercepts.

    7. x-intercept: -2 **8.** x-intercept: none   **9.** x-intercept: 0
        y-intercept: none y-intercept: 7 y-intercepts: all
                                                    real numbers

CHAPTER 3 Integer Solutions of Linear Equations

Typically, the variables in a linear equation range over all real numbers. The graph of a linear equation in two variables is a continuous line.

EXAMPLE 1 Find solutions of linear equations

a. Graph the equation $4x + 6y = 16$.

b. List some ordered pair solutions, including solutions where x and/or y have non-integer values.

Solution:

a. We simplify the equation and rewrite it in the form
$y = -\frac{2}{3}x + \frac{8}{3}$ to find that the line has a slope
of $-\frac{2}{3}$ and a y-intercept of $\frac{8}{3}$.

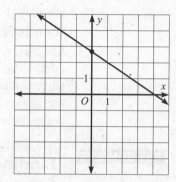

b. Substituting arbitrarily selected values of x into
$y = -\frac{2}{3}x + \frac{8}{3}$, we generate a list of ordered pairs.

y	x
-2	4
0	$\frac{8}{3}$
$\frac{1}{2}$	$\frac{7}{3}$
4	0
5	$-\frac{2}{3}$

We can confirm by inspection that the ordered pairs lie on the line in part a. ∎

Although it is common for x and y to range over the real numbers, there are many situations where the solutions to an equation can only involve integer values. For instance, an equation might relate numbers of male and female students, or it might relate two elements in a chemical formula. Integer-valued variables such as this are the most common type of *discrete* variables.

EXAMPLE 2 Find integer solutions of linear equations

Suppose that for the equation $4x + 6y = 16$, we require x and y to be integers. Identify two solutions from Example 1 and find at least one more solution.

Solution:

From the table in Example 1, $x = -2$, $y = 4$ and $x = 4$, $y = 0$ are both solutions. Since the solutions lie along a line with a slope of $-\frac{2}{3}$, it should be possible to find more solutions by starting with a known solution and counting up and over the appropriate number of units. Starting at $(-2, 4)$ and counting right 3 and down 2, we find the point

Integer Solutions of Linear Equations *continued*

(1, 2) on the line, which means that $x = 1$, $y = 2$ is a third integer solution. (We could equally well have counted left 3 and up 2 from point (4, 0).) Additional applications of the same process yield $x = -5$, $y = 6$ and $x = 7$, $y = -2$ as solutions. ∎

Equations with integer-only solutions are called *Diophantine equations*, after the mathematician Diophantus of Alexandria (200–284 AD). The constants in such equations are normally integers, as well. So in a linear Diophantine equation of the form $ax + by = c$, the constants a, b and c are integers, and integer values for x and y are sought.

We found the integer solutions in Example 2 by inspecting the graph. There are, however, ways to find the solutions algebraically. The standard method is surprisingly complicated; it involves something called the Euclidean algorithm. But there is also a simpler method, which uses carefully controlled trial and error. This method is based on the fact that any solutions will occur at fixed intervals along the graph of the continuous (non-discrete) version of the equation.

KEY CONCEPT

Finding Integer Solutions for an Equation of the Form $ax + by = c$

1. Find the greatest common factor (GCF) of a and b, and divide this number into $|b|$. Call the result d.

2. Pick any d consecutive integer values for x, and try them until you find one that produces an integer value for y. It helps to rewrite the equation in the form $y = -\frac{a}{b}x + \frac{c}{b}$.

3. If Step 2 produces no solutions, the equation has no integer solutions anywhere. If Step 2 produces a solution, then the equation has a series of solutions for which the x-values are spaced d units apart. (The spacing of the y-values will be the quotient of $|a|$ and the GCF of a and b.)

EXAMPLE 3

Find integer solutions of an equation of the for $ax + by = c$

Use controlled trial and error to find integer solutions for the linear equation $4x + 6y = 16$.

Solution:

1. The GCF of 4 and 6 is 2, and $|6| \div 2 = 3$.

2. Write the equation as $y = -\frac{2}{3}x + \frac{8}{3}$ and try any 3 consecutive integer values of x. We arbitrarily select $x = 0$ as a convenient starting value.

x	y	
0	$\frac{8}{3}$	y is not an integer
1	2	y is an integer - STOP
2		

CHAPTER 3 | **Integer Solutions of Linear Equations** *continued*

3. The ordered pair (1, 2) is a solution. Other solutions are found by changing the value of x up or down in increments of 3:

x	y
-5	6
-2	4
1	2
4	0
7	-2

Notice that the quotient of $a = 4$ and 2 (the GFC of 4 and 6) is 2, and the y-values occur at 2-unit intervals. The complete range of solutions can be represented as $x = 1 + 3n, y = 2 - 2n$, for $n = \ldots, -2, -1, 0, 1, 2, \ldots$ ∎

The trial and error method is not very efficient when one has to try many values. If $|a| < |b|$, it may be faster to divide the greatest common factor of a and b into $|a|$ and then try successive values of y.

Practice

Use controlled trial and error to find the integer solutions, if any, for each linear equation. Write them in terms of *n*, with *n* = ..., −2, −1, 0, 1, 2, ...

1. $5x + 2y = 1$
2. $4x - 3y = -7$
3. $2x + 7y = -10$

4. $4x - y = 7$
5. $-x + 3y = -9$
6. $x + 8y = 0$

7. $-6x + 9y = 11$
8. $-3x - 9y = 15$
9. $-12x + 4y = 6$

10. $-11x + 6y = 17$
11. $5x + 7y = -9$
12. $30x - 35y = 19$

13. Several ranchhands are in a corral, working with one or more horses. Counting both human and horse legs, there are 22 legs in the corral. How many cowboys and how many horses might there be? List all the possibilities.

14. One molecule of a certain chemical compound is known to have a mass of 160 atomic mass units (amu's). The molecule is believed to consist of carbon (12 amu per atom) and oxygen (16 amu per atom). Based on this information alone, what are the possible formulas for the compound, in the form $C_x O_y$, where x is the number of carbon atoms and y is the number of oxygen atoms?

15. **Explain** Suppose that the mass of the molecule in Exercise 14 were remeasured and found to be 162 atomic mass units. Explain why, with this mass, the compound would have to contain something else besides carbon and oxygen.

Name _____   Date _____

Interpreting the Slope and *y*-Intercept

When a linear equation is in slope-intercept form, $y = mx + b$, the graphical interpretation of m and b is that b indicates where the line crosses the *y*-axis, while m indicates the extent to which the line is tilted away from the horizontal.

However, we can also give an algebraic interpretation for m and b, based on the fact that the expression $mx + b$ contains two terms, one of which, b, is a *fixed term*, because its value doesn't change when x changes. The other term, mx, is a *variable term*, whose value varies with x in a way controlled by the value of m.

EXAMPLE 1 ## Interpret the slope and *y*-intercept

A large pot of water is boiling on a stove. As the water boils away, the amount left in the pot decreases. The number of gallons of water, y, remaining in the pot after x minutes, is given by $y = -\frac{3}{80}x + \frac{3}{4}$. Explain the meaning of the quantities $-\frac{3}{80}$ and $\frac{3}{4}$ in the equation.

Solution:

The quantity $\frac{3}{4}$ represents the value of y when $x = 0$. This is the initial quantity of water: the pot started out with $\frac{3}{4}$ gallons. When x increases by 1 minute, y decreases by $\frac{3}{80}$ gallons. In other words, $-\frac{3}{80}$ represents the change in the amount of water during one minute of boiling. The minus sign means that as time goes on, the amount of water decreases. ■

In Example 1, where x represented time, $b = \frac{3}{4}$ was the *initial value* and $m = -\frac{3}{80}$ was the *rate of change* over time, in gallons per minute.

The quantity mx represents the *total change* that has occurred at time x.

Of course, the variable x does not always represent time. It can instead, for instance, represent the output volume of a manufacturing process.

EXAMPLE 2 ## Interpret the slope and *y*-intercept

A factory produces fiber optic cable. The cost in dollars, y, of one day's worth of production is given by $y = 0.4x + 30,000$, where x is the number of meters of cable produced. Explain the meaning of the quantities 0.4 and 30,000.

Solution:

The quantity 30,000 represents the factory's *fixed cost* for one day of production. This would include the mortgage or rental cost of inhabiting the building and any other costs that do not depend on how many meters of cable are produced.

The quantity $0.4x$, on the other hand, represents the *variable cost*, which goes up or down depending on whether more or less cable is produced in a given day. The variable cost includes the cost of raw materials used during production. The quantity 0.4 can be interpreted as the cost of producing 1 meter of cable, given that the factory is already up and operating for the day. ■

| CHAPTER 3 | **Interpreting the Slope and *y*-Intercept** continued |

Practice

Writing For each formula in the following application contexts, explain the meaning of the constant term and of the coefficient in the variable term.

1. The population of a town, x years after 2003, is given by $P(x) = 15.6x + 1842$.

2. A student's score, y, on a test with 30 questions is calculated and recorded as $y = 40 + 2x$, where x is the number of questions answered correctly.

3. A plumber who retrofits old houses with new copper pipe charges $C(x) = 800 + 3.3x$ dollars for a house with x square feet of living area.

4. In a certain place, the air temperature (in degrees Celsius) over the course of the morning is a function of time according to the equation $T(t) = -10 + 0.15t$, where t is minutes after 6:00 A.M.

For each situation, give an appropriate linear equation in *y*-intercept form.

5. A water tank initially containing 150 liters of water has more water pumped in, at the rate of 7 liters per minute.

6. Each of four roommates contributes $450 per month toward the rent payment (which covers utilities) and also pays $\frac{1}{4}$ of the phone bill.

7. A car traveling at a constant speed of 55 miles per hour begins to accelerate, gaining 2 miles per hour in speed every second.

8. The cost of renting a car for one day is 48 dollars plus 15 cents per mile.

9. **Explain** What does it mean when a linear equation does not have a constant term—for instance, the equation $v(t) = 9.81t$, where v is the speed of a falling object in meters per second, and t is number of seconds after the object was released?

Pre-AP Copymasters

CHAPTER 3

Distinguishing Between Direct Variation and Other Linear Models

All direct variation is linear, but not all linear models represent direct variation. Direct variation is the special case of a linear model $y = mx + b$ where the y-intercept (the constant term b) equals 0.

EXAMPLE 1 ## Identify linear and direct variation relations

For each of the following, state whether the relation is linear, and if so, whether it represents direct variation.

a. $y = 3x - 6$ **b.** $y = 9x$ **c.** $y = \dfrac{5}{x}$

d. $x - 2y = 0$ **e.** $y + x = 4$

Solution:

a. $y = 3x - 6$ is a linear equation in slope-intercept form, so it is a linear model. However, the y-intercept is not 0, so this is not an instance of direct variation.

b. $y = 9x$ is a linear slope-intercept equation with $m = 9$ and $b = 0$. This is a linear relation that represents direct variation.

c. $y = \dfrac{5}{x}$ is not a linear equation. It cannot be written in either form
$ax + bx = c$ or $y = mx + b$.

d. $x - 2y = 0$ can be rewritten as $y = \dfrac{1}{2}x$. This is a linear slope-intercept equation with $m = \dfrac{1}{2}$ and $b = 0$. So this is a linear relation that represents direct variation.

e. $y + x = 4$ can be rewritten as $y = -x + 4$. This is a linear equation in slope-intercept form, but b equals 4, not 0. So this is not an instance of direct variation. ■

Graphically, a relation of direct variation appears as a straight line that passes through the origin.

EXAMPLE 2 ## Identify direct variation graphically

Use the graphs of the equations in parts d and e of Example 1 to show that one represents direct variation and the other does not.

Solution:

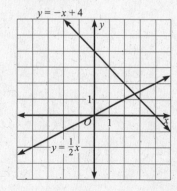

The graph of $x - 2y$, or $y = \dfrac{1}{2}x$, passes through the origin, so this is an instance of direct variation. By contrast, the graph of $y + x = 4$, or $y = -x + 4$, does not pass through the origin, so this is not direct variation. ■

Distinguishing Between Direct Variation and Other Linear Models *continued*

Practice

For each of the following, state whether the relation is linear, and if so, whether it represents direct variation.

1. $y - 3x = 7$ **2.** $y = 3x - 6$ **3.** $5x + y = 0$

4. $y = 4x^2$ **5.** $xy = 8$ **6.** $\dfrac{y}{x} = 10$

For each of the following, write an appropriate equation and state whether the linear relation represents direct variation.

7. A trip to the gas station costs $2.78 times the number of gallons pumped.

8. An automobile repair costs $178 for the part plus $65 per hour for labor.

9. The total number of pixels on a computer screen is determined by the area and the fact that the resolution is 9216 pixels per square inch.

10. Challenge An electric motor needs 1 ampere of current for every 120 watts of power produced, plus 0.5 amperes of current to run the control circuitry and instrument panel.

Representations of Lines

Lines can be determined given any of the following: a graph, an equation, a slope and one point, or two points. Given one form of a line, the other forms can be derived from it.

Two points, (1, 1) and (3, 5), are plotted on a graph to form the line shown.

From the points, the slope of the line can be found.

Slope $= m = \dfrac{y_2 - y_1}{x_2 - x_1} = \dfrac{5 - 1}{3 - 1} = \dfrac{4}{2} = 2$

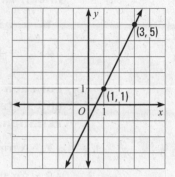

The slope with one of the given points can be used to find the equation of this line in point-slope form.

Point-slope form: $y - 1 = 2(x - 1)$

The point-slope form can be rewritten into slope-intercept form or general form.

Slope-intercept form: $y - 1 = 2x - 2 \rightarrow y = 2x - 1$

General form: $y - 1 = 2x - 2 \rightarrow 2x - y = 1$

Each of these forms represents the same line graphed through the two points (1, 1) and (3, 5).

EXAMPLE 1 ## Find the equation of a line from a graph

Find the point-slope form and slope-intercept form of the line shown in this graph.

Solution:

Two points located on this line are $(-3, 2)$ and $(1, -2)$.

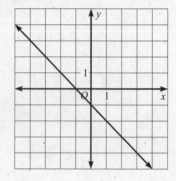

The slope of the line is $\dfrac{y_2 - y_1}{x_2 - x_1} = \dfrac{2 - (-2)}{-3 - 1} = \dfrac{4}{-4} = -1$.

The y-intercept is at -1.

One point-slope form of this line is $y - 2 = -1(x + 3)$.

The slope-intercept form of this line is $y = -x - 1$. ∎

Example 1 shows how equations of a line can be found given a graph or two points. Example 2 shows how the slope and one point can be found given the general form of a line.

EXAMPLE 2 ## Find the slope and a point on a line given its equation

Find the slope and a point on the line $3x + y = -4$.

Solution:

To find the slope, rewrite the equation in slope-intercept form as $y = -3x - 4$.

The slope is -3.

To find a point on the line, choose any x value and find the corresponding y value. When $x = -2$, $y = -3(-2) - 4 = 2$. A point on this line is $(-2, 2)$. ∎

Algebra 1
Pre-AP

CHAPTER 4

Representations of Lines *continued*

Since lines have an infinite number of points, the number of possible x and corresponding y values that can be found is infinite. As a result, the number of equations that can be written for one line in point-slope form is also infinite.

EXAMPLE 3 ## Write multiple equations for one line in point-slope form

Find more than one equation in point-slope form for the line containing points $(2, 1)$, $(3, 3)$, and $(4, 5)$.

Solution:

Slope $= m = \dfrac{y_2 - y_1}{x_2 - x_1} = \dfrac{3 - 1}{3 - 2} = \dfrac{2}{1} = 2$.

One equation in point-slope form is $y - 1 = 2(x - 2)$.

Other equations are $y - 3 = 2(x - 3)$ and $y - 5 = 2(x - 4)$.

All equations represent the line $y = 2x - 3$. Since there are infinitely many points on a line, each point can be used to write an infinite number of equations in point-slope form. ∎

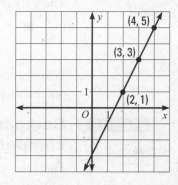

Practice

Write the point-slope form of the line containing the given slope and point.

1. $m = 3$, point $(0, 4)$ **2.** $m = \dfrac{1}{3}$, point $(3, 2)$ **3.** $m = \dfrac{4}{3}$, point $(-1, -1)$

4. $m = -5$, point $(6, 0)$ **5.** $m = -\dfrac{5}{2}$, point $(-4, 2)$ **6.** $m = -1$, point $(4, -4)$

Write the slope-intercept form of the line containing the given two points.

7. $(1, 4)$ and $(2, 5)$ **8.** $(0, -3)$ and $(4, 3)$ **9.** $(5, 0)$ and $(0, 3)$

10. $(-3, 1)$ and $(2, -3)$ **11.** $(3, -4)$ and $(-1, 2)$ **12.** $(-1, -2)$ and $(-3, -3)$

Write the slope-intercept form of the line graphed below.

13. 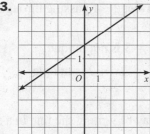   **14.** 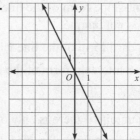   **15.**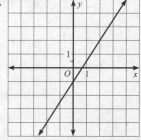

Problem Solving

16. Mark bought a \$50 tennis racket and paid \$20 an hour for tennis lessons. Find Mark's total cost for the tennis racket and 1, 2, 3, and 4 hours of tennis lessons. Use this information to write four equations in point-slope form to model Mark's total cost for tennis racket and lessons.

CHAPTER 4 ## Unique Representations

Numbers can be expressed in several ways. The fraction $\frac{6}{3}$, the mixed number $1\frac{5}{5}$, the expression $-7 + 9$, and $\sqrt{4}$ all describe the number 2.

EXAMPLE 1 ### Show that rational numbers are not uniquely represented

Show that $\frac{2}{3}$ is not uniquely represented as a rational number.

Solution:

The fractions $\frac{4}{6}, \frac{6}{9}, \frac{10}{15}$, and $\frac{20}{30}$ are just some of the other rational numbers equivalent to $\frac{2}{3}$. ∎

While rational numbers have an infinite number of equivalent fractions, all rational numbers can be written in lowest terms as one unique fraction.

EXAMPLE 2 ### Compare the uniqueness of prime and composite factorizations

Find unique factorizations for the numbers 11 and 28.

Solution:

11 is prime, so its factorization 1×11 is unique.

28 is composite. It can be factored in many ways, such as 1×28, 2×14, and 4×7. There is only one way to break a composite number into prime factors. The prime factorization of 28, $2 \times 2 \times 7$, is unique. ∎

Examples 1 and 2 show there are many ways of describing numbers and their factorizations. Example 3 explores the concept of uniqueness as it pertains to equations of lines.

EXAMPLE 3 ### Determine representations of lines that are unique

Show each of the following:

a. The point-slope form of the line with slope -1 passing through points $(3, 1)$ and $(-2, 6)$ is not unique.

b. The standard form of the line $x + 4y = 3$ is not unique.

c. The slope-intercept form of the line $y = 3x - 2$ is unique.

Solution:

Equations are unique if there is only one way of writing the line in a specific form.

a. Two point-slope forms for this line are $y - 1 = -1(x - 3)$ and $y - 6 = -1(x + 2)$. Since more than one equation in point-slope form describes the line, this representation is not unique.

b. Two additional standard forms for the line $x + 4y = 3$ are $2x + 8y = 6$ and $-x - 4y = -3$. Since more than one equation in standard form describes the line, this representation is not unique.

Unique Representations *continued*

c. All lines have exactly one slope and no more than one y-intercept. If the slope or y-intercept in $y = 3x - 2$ were different, the equation would represent a different line. Suppose the slope and y-intercept were both doubled, changing $y = 3x - 2$ to $y = 6x - 4$. These equations are not the same since both lines intersect the y-axis at different points and have different slopes. There is only one unique way of writing an equation in slope-intercept form. ■

Practice

Write two other representations for the given number.

1. $\dfrac{10}{35}$ **2.** $\dfrac{9}{16}$ **3.** $-\dfrac{8}{12}$ **4.** $-\dfrac{24}{18}$

5. factors of 24 **6.** factors of 36 **7.** factors of 150 **8.** factors of 76

Write the unique representation as a fraction in lowest terms.

9. $\dfrac{6}{15}$ **10.** $\dfrac{35}{14}$ **11.** $\dfrac{8}{18}$ **12.** $-\dfrac{56}{100}$

Write the unique prime factorization.

13. 45 **14.** 60 **15.** 200 **16.** 99

Problem Solving

17. Ticket prices to the school play are $6 for students and $10 for adults. The school hopes to raise $1500 from the ticket sales. Write three equations in standard form that model this situation.

18. Jenny bought 3 shirts for the same price from a catalog company that charges a flat fee of $5 for shipping. The total amount she paid was $41. Meghan bought 2 of the same shirts from the same catalog and paid a total of $29. Determine the price for each shirt. Then write three equations in point-slope form that model this situation.

19. Josh makes and sells model trains for $12 each. His cost for materials was $60. Write an equation in slope-intercept form that models the amount of profit Josh makes after each sale, until he uses up his materials.

20. A freight elevator lifts barrels and boxes. Each barrel weighs 40 pounds and each box weighs 25 pounds. The most weight the elevator can lift at once is 1000 pounds. Write three equations in standard form that represent the possible combinations for the most number of boxes and barrels the freight elevator can lift.

21. William has cheese and crackers for a 300-calorie snack. Each slice of cheese has 50 calories and each cracker has 30 calories. Write three equations in standard form that show the possible number of crackers and slices of cheese that William can have for his snack.

22. Write an equation in slope-intercept form that shows all possible combinations for the number of dimes and quarters totaling $10.

Name _____ Date _____

KEY CONCEPT

Discrete Functions

In Chapter 1, you made data plots given a finite set of domain values corresponding to a distinct set of range values. These non-continuous graphs were **discrete functions.**

A **sequence** is a discrete function whose domain is the set of positive integers. Example 1 examines the graph of a sequence.

EXAMPLE 1 ### Graph sequences

Graph the function defined by this sequence.

x	1	2	3	4	5	...
$2x + 1$	3	5	7	9	11	...

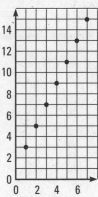

Solution:

This graph represents a discrete function since its points are not connected by a straight line or curve and each member of the domain corresponds to exactly one member of the range. ∎

Linear functions differ from discrete functions since the domain of linear functions is the set of real numbers and not positive integers. Example 2 examines the difference between the graphs of both function types.

EXAMPLE 2 ### Compare graphs of sequences and linear functions

Compare the sequence defined by $3x - 5$ and the function $y = 3x - 5$ by graphing each.

Solution:

The table of values shows the first 5 terms in the sequence.

x	1	2	3	4	5	...
$3x - 5$	−2	1	4	7	10	...

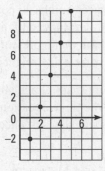

The graph of the sequence at the left shows non-connected points and only positive integer values for the domain.

The graph of the linear function at the right shows a continuous set of points connected by a straight line and all real numbers for the domain. ∎

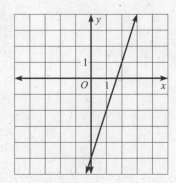

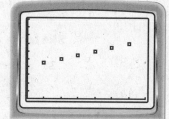

CHAPTER 4 **Sequences as Discrete Functions** *continued*

EXAMPLE 3 **Graph sequences using a graphing calculator**

Use a graphing calculator to graph the first six terms of the sequence defined by $\frac{1}{2}x + 4$.

Solution:

Enter $1-6$ into L_1. Then enter $\frac{1}{2} L_1 + 4$ into L_2.

Set Stat Plots, Plot1 to On, and Type to be a scatter plot. Be sure the Window is set for the appropriate domain and range shown in each list. Then graph. ■

Graphs of sequences and scatter plots appear to be similar since they both depict discrete data with positive domain values. Scatter plots differ, though, in several ways. While the domain of sequences is restricted to the set of positive integers, scatter plots can have domains that include any real number. Also, scatter plots may or may not be functions since some domain values could correspond to more than one range value.

EXAMPLE 4 **Compare graphs of sequences and scatter plots**

Make a plot of the data in each table. Then explain whether each plot represents a function.

a.

1	2	3	4	5	6
0	2	4	6	8	10

b.

2	4	3	4	1	2
1	2	3	4	5	6

Solution:

a. This plot represents a function. Each member of the domain corresponds to exactly one member of the range.

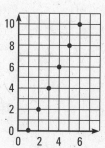

b. This plot does not represent a function. Some members of the domain correspond to more than one member of the range. ■

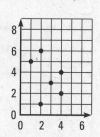

CHAPTER 4 | Sequences as Discrete Functions _continued_

Practice

1. **Writing** Describe the differences between a sequence and a linear function.

2. **Writing** Describe the differences between the graph of a sequence and a scatter plot.

Sketch a graph of each sequence and linear function.

3. sequence defined by $x - 3$;
   linear function $y = x - 3$

4. sequence defined by $-x + 5$;
   linear function $y = -x + 5$

Use a graphing calculator to plot the first eight terms in each sequence.

5. $4x + 2$
6. $-2x + 6$
7. $\frac{1}{3}x$
8. $\frac{x + 3}{2}$

Sketch a graph of the data. Then explain whether or not the graph represents a function.

9.

2	5	8	11	14	17
3	5	8	3	5	8

10.

5	7	4	7	3	2
0	2	4	6	8	10

11.

6	5	4	3	2	1
1	2	3	4	5	6

12.

1	2	3	4	5	6
4	4	4	4	4	4

Problem Solving

13. A sequence starts with 8 and subtracts 2 to get each following term. Sketch a graph of the first six terms of this sequence.

14. Alyssa kept track of the money she earned each day she worked last week.

Hours Worked	5	2.5	6	3	5
$ Earned	40	24	48	30	35

Plot this data on a graph. Then explain whether or not the graph represents a function.

15. Marcus read 5 pages of a book the first day of vacation. Each following day, he read 5 more pages than the previous day. Explain whether or not the graph of $y = 5x$ can be used to show the number of pages Marcus read each day of vacation.

Activity

16. Find the shoe sizes and heights, in inches, of fifteen people. Plot the data showing the relationship between shoe size and height on a graph using a graphing calculator. Then explain whether or not the data represents a function.

CHAPTER 5 **The Meanings of *And* and *Or* in Logic**

The words *and* and *or* are used frequently in everyday language. They are also significant in a branch of mathematics called logic. The meanings of each word in everyday language and in mathematics are compared here.

KEY CONCEPT

The Meaning of *And*

For a statement containing **and** to be true, *both* parts of the statement must be true. If one part is not true, the entire statement is false.

EXAMPLE 1 **Determine the truth value of statements containing *and***

Determine whether each statement is true or false.

  a. The day before Thursday is Wednesday and there are twelve months in one year.

  b. $12 \div 3 = 4$ and $6 - (-1) = 5$

  c. $8 \cdot 7 = 56$ and $4 - 15 < -9$

Solution:

  a. The day before Thursday *is* Wednesday. There *are* twelve months in one year. The statement is true since both parts are true.

  b. Since $12 \div 3 = 4$ is true but $6 - (-1) = 5$ is false, the entire statement is false.

  c. Since $8 \cdot 7 = 56$ is true and $4 - 15 < -9$ is true, the entire statement is true. ■

KEY CONCEPT

The Meanings of *Or*

There are two types of *or* statements with varied meanings in everyday language and mathematics.

One *or* is the **inclusive or**.

For statements containing the *inclusive or* to be true, *one or the other or both* parts must be true. If neither part is true, the entire statement is false. This meaning of *or* is typically associated with mathematical statements.

The other *or* is the **exclusive or**.

For statements containing the *exclusive or* to be true, *one or the other* parts must be true, *but not both*. If both parts are true, the entire statement is false. This meaning of *or* is typically associated with statements in everyday language.

The Meanings of *And* and *Or* in Logic *continued*

EXAMPLE 2 ## Determine the parts that make *or* statements true

In the statements below, determine what must be true for the entire statement to be true.

a. After school, Michael walks home or rides the bus.

b. $x + 6 = 2$ or $y - 7 = 4$

Solution:

a. Michael walks home after school, or Michael rides the bus after school. But, both cannot be true. The or in this statement is the *exclusive or*.

b. In order for the statement to be true: $x = -4$, $y = 11$, or both $x = -4$ and $y = 11$. The *or* in this statement is the *inclusive or*.

Note that context is important in determining the type of *or* in everyday language. For example, in the statement "Michael walks to school or Michael rides the bus home from school," the *or* does not have to be *exclusive or*. It is possible for both parts to be true in order for the statement entire statement to be true.

In mathematics a statement such as "$x + 6 = 2$ or $x - 7 = 4$" is true if $x = -4$, $x = 11$, or both $x = -4$ and $x = 11$. You might notice that even though the condition $x = -4$ and $x = 11$ is not possible, the mathematical usage of *or* implies that the entire statement would be true if it was possible.

Practice
Determine whether the statement is true or false.

1. A mile is longer than a kilometer and a quart is more than a pint.

2. A rectangle has four congruent sides or a parallelogram has two pairs of congruent angles.

3. All men are taller than women or have larger shoe sizes than women.

4. A red traffic light means stop or a green traffic light means go.

5. Some triangles are scalene and all squares are rectangles.

6. $24 - 8 = 16$ or $7 + 3 = 21$

7. $4 \cdot 5 = 20$ and $-4 \cdot -5 = -20$

8. $36 < 6 \cdot 6$ or $17 - 9 \geq 36 \div 4$

Determine what must be true for the entire statement to be true.

9. All students in the math class are girls or all students in the math class are boys.

10. Ashley went to bed at 9:00 P.M. or she read a book at 9:00 P.M.

11. Adam mowed the lawn on Saturday and he cleaned the garage on Sunday.

12. $3q - 8 = 1$ or $q + 7 = -6$

13. $-7 \leq 2a + 7$ and $2a + 7 \leq 3$

14. $m + \frac{1}{3} < \frac{8}{9}$ or $-3 - n > -5$

Compound Inequalities with No Solution or All Real Numbers as Solutions

CHAPTER 5

Some compound inequalities have no solution. Other compound inequalities have the set of all real numbers as solutions.

KEY CONCEPT

Compound Inequalities with No Solution

When no values for a variable make a compound inequality true, there is no solution. We describe the solution set as the empty set $\varnothing$. When the solution set is $\varnothing$, the solution cannot be graphed.

Compound inequalities with no solutions usually come from solving compound inequalities with *and*.

EXAMPLE 1 ## Identify a compound inequality with no solution

Solve the inequality $8 \le x - 3 < 4$. Graph the solution, if possible.

Solution:

$$8 \le x - 3 \qquad and \qquad x - 3 < 4$$
$$8 + 3 \le x - 3 + 3 \quad and \quad x - 3 + 3 < 4 + 3$$
$$11 \le x \qquad and \qquad x < 7$$

It is not possible for x to be greater than or equal to 11 *and* also be less than 7. The solution set is $\varnothing$ and cannot be graphed. ■

Notice that the compound inequality in Example 1 is false for all x values because it uses the conjunction *and*.

KEY CONCEPT

Compound Inequalities with All Real Numbers as Solutions

When all values for a variable make a compound inequality true, the solution set is the set of all real numbers. The graph of this solution set is the entire number line.

Compound inequalities with all real numbers as the solution usually come from solving compound inequalities with *or*.

EXAMPLE 2 ## Identify a compound inequality with all real numbers as solutions

Solve the inequality $-7 < 2p - 5$ *or* $p + 1 > 3p - 4$. Graph the solution, if possible.

Solution:

$$-7 < 2p - 5 \qquad or \qquad p + 1 > 3p - 4$$
$$-2 < 2p \qquad or \qquad 1 > 2p - 4$$
$$5 > 2p$$
$$-1 < p \qquad or \qquad \frac{5}{2} > p$$

Compound Inequalities with No Solution or All Real Numbers as Solutions *continued*

The solution set is all real numbers greater than -1 *or* less than $\frac{5}{2}$.

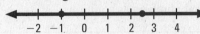

The graph of this solution shows both sets of numbers overlapping and continuing on infinitely in both directions. This shows that the set of all real numbers make this compound inequality true. ■

Notice that the inequality in Example 2 is true for all values of p because it uses the conjunction *or*.

Practice

Solve each inequality. Graph each solution, if possible.

1. $-5 < k + 6 < 0$
2. $15 \le 6w - 9 \le 6$
3. $4 < -2m \le 10$
4. $12 < 3x + 6 \text{ or } -3x \ge -9$
5. $3 < 2g + 1 < g$
6. $1 > 4 - d \text{ or } -1(d - 6) \ge -1$
7. $5 + a < 1 \text{ or } -5 > 3 - 2a$
8. $4 \ge -q - 4 \text{ or } 2 - 3q > 1$
9. $2(3 - b) \le b \text{ or } 2b \le 9 - b$
10. $18 < 4z + 2 < -14$
11. $-1 > -7 - h > 3$
12. $j \le 3j + 2 \text{ or } -2(-j - 1) \le -6$

13. Five more than y is greater than 2 *or* three less than twice y is less than or equal to 1.

14. The difference of 3 and v is greater than or equal to 4 *and* less than or equal to 3.

15. Four times the sum of 2 and n is less than -8 *and* 6 is less than twice n.

16. Seven less than 5 times c is less than 3 *or* 10 more than c is greater than -4 times c.

Problem Solving

17. The amount of money, including tips, that Gina earned working h hours last week is given by the compound inequality $300 \ge 10h + 60 \ge 400$. Discuss the number of hours that Gina could have worked.

18. Three identical blocks on one balance scale weigh less than 12 pounds *and* 8 of the same identical blocks on another scale weigh more than 40 pounds. Explain whether or not this is possible. If it is, what is the possible weight of each block? If it is not possible, explain why not.

19. The highest test score Scott can receive is 100. The sum of his first four test scores is at least 360. Find the range of scores Scott must get on his fifth test to have an average greater than 70.

20. If the length of Theresa's rectangular garden is 30 feet, she wants the perimeter to be at least 80 feet. *Or*, if the length is 20 feet, she wants the perimeter to be at most 90 feet. Describe the possible widths that Theresa's garden can be.

21. Carina's profit, in dollars, selling j pieces of jewelry in a month is shown by the inequality $100 \ge 50 + 2j > 200$. Discuss the likelihood of Carina earning this profit.

CHAPTER 5 · Graphing Calculators and Logic

A graphing calculator can be used to test whether or not a mathematical statement containing equalities, inequalities, and logical connectors is true.

The TEST menu on a graphing calculator contains the functions $=$, $\neq$, $>$, $\geq$, $<$, and $\leq$. Example 1 shows how to test and interpret the results of these functions.

EXAMPLE 1 Test equalities and inequalities

Use a graphing calculator to determine whether each statement is true or false.

a. $\dfrac{6}{8} = \dfrac{8}{12}$

b. $-5 \cdot (3 + 1) < -16 \div (6 - 2)$

Solution:

a. Enter this sequence into the calculator: $6 \div 8$ 2nd TEST $=$ $8 \div 12$ ENTER

The output shows 0. This means the statement is false.

b. Enter this sequence into the calculator:

$-5 \cdot (3 + 1)$ 2nd TEST $<$ $-16 \div (6 - 2)$ ENTER

The output shows 1. This means the statement is true. ∎

Logical connectors for *and*, the inclusive or (*or*), and the exclusive or (*xor*) are featured in the LOGIC menu within the TEST menu.

EXAMPLE 2 Test logic statements

Use a graphing calculator to determine whether each statement is true or false.

a. $-8 \div -4 \neq -2$ *and* $5 + 8 < 15 - 3$ **b.** $5 + (-9) \geq 0$ *or* $-3 \cdot -3 > -3 \cdot 3$

c. $6 > -2 - (-5)$ *xor* $3 \cdot 2 = 30 \div 5$

Solution:

a. $-8 \div -4$ 2nd TEST $\neq$ -2 2nd TEST LOGIC *and*

$5 + 8$ 2nd TEST $<$ $15 - 3$ ENTER

The output shows 0. This means the statement is false. Although the first part of this statement is true, the second part is not. With *and* statements, both parts need to be true. Otherwise, the entire statement is false.

b. $5 + (-9)$ 2nd TEST ≥ 0 2nd TEST LOGIC *or*

$-3 \cdot -3$ 2nd TEST $> -3 \cdot 3$ ENTER

The output shows 1. The statement is true. Only one part of an *or* statement needs to be true for the entire statement to be true.

c. 6 2nd TEST $> -2 - (-5)$ 2nd TEST LOGIC *xor*

$3 \cdot 2$ 2nd TEST $= 30 \div 5$ ENTER

The output shows 0. The statement is false. With *exclusive or* statements, only one part, *not* both parts, must be true for the entire statement to be true. Here both parts are true, so the entire statement is false. ∎

CHAPTER 5

Graphing Calculators and Logic *continued*

You can also use the TABLE feature of a graphing calculator to test different values of a variable in an algebraic statement.

EXAMPLE 3 ## Test logic connectors on algebraic statements

Use a graphing calculator to determine whether $-x + 1 < 0$ *and* $x \geq -2$ is true or false for $x = -3, -2, -1, 0, 1, 2, 3$.

Solution:

In the Y= screen, enter the algebraic statement for Y_1 as shown below on the left. Then set the table to evaluate $x = -3, -2, -1, 0, 1, 2, 3$ and press 2nd TABLE to get the get the screen shown below on the right.

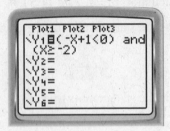 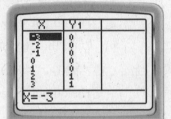

This shows that the statement is true for $x = 2, 3$, but false for $x = -3, -2, -1, 0, 1$. ∎

Practice

Use a graphing calculator to determine whether each statement is true or false.

1. $1.5 \cdot 6 \neq 9$ 2. $13 - (-4) < 8$ 3. $64 \div 6 \geq 50 \div 4$ 4. $8 = 4 + 2 \cdot 2$

Use a graphing calculator to determine whether each logic statement is true or false.

5. $6 - 2 < -5$ *or* $4 \div 2 \neq -3 - (-5)$ 6. $11 > -2 + 14$ *xor* $-4 \cdot -6 \leq -24$

7. $5 \div 2 \cdot 4 = 10$ *and*
   $3 - (-4 \cdot -1) = -1$

8. $1 - 3 \cdot 4 \geq -7 - 8$ *and*
   $20 \div 4 < 0.5 \div 0.1$

9. $1 - 8 \leq -2 \div 2$ *xor*
   $3 + 2 \neq 10 \div 5$

10. $5 + 3 \leq -12 \div -4$ *or*
    $8 \cdot 2 = 7 - (1 - 10)$

Use a graphing calculator to determine whether each algebraic statement is true or false for the given values.

11. $7 - x < -2$ *and* $5 \geq 10x$ for $x = -3, -2, -1, 0, 1, 2, 3$

12. $4x + 2 = -10$ *or* $3x > -6$ for $x = -3, -2, -1, 0, 1, 2, 3$

13. $9 < 3x + 12$ *or* $-2x \neq 4$ for $x = -3, -2, -1, 0, 1, 2, 3$

14. $x + 1 \leq 0$ *xor* $21 \geq 8x - 5$ for $x = -1, 0, 1, 2, 3, 4, 5$

15. $3 \div 5 < 2x$ *and* $3 - x = 2x$ for $x = -1, 0, 1, 2, 3, 4, 5$

16. $x - (-3) \neq 5$ *xor* $x \div 2 < -1$ for $x = -3, -2, -1, 0, 1, 2, 3$

CHAPTER 5 — A Closer Look at Absolute Value

Piecewise functions define more than one rule or expression over separate intervals. The absolute value function can be seen as an example of a piecewise-defined function.

KEY CONCEPT

Definition of Absolute Value as a Piecewise-Defined Function

The definition of absolute value can be written as a piecewise-defined function.

$$y = |x| = \begin{cases} x, & \text{when } x \geq 0 \\ -x, & \text{when } x < 0 \end{cases}$$

You can use this definition to evaluate the absolute value of given values of x.

EXAMPLE 1 ## Find the absolute value of x

Find $y = |x|$ for each value of x.

a. $x = 5$ 　　　　　　　　　　　**b.** $x = -7$

Solution:

a. Since $5 \geq 0$, $y = |5| = 5$. 　　　**b.** Since $-7 \leq 0$, $y = -(-7) = 7$. ■

The absolute value of other expressions can be derived from the above definition.

EXAMPLE 2 ## Find the absolute value of $-x$

Find $y = |-x|$ for each value of x.

a. $x = 6$ 　　　　　　　　　　　**b.** $x = -15$

Solution:

First, write $y = |-x|$ as a piecewise-defined function by substituting $-x$ for x in the above definition.

$$y = |-x| = \begin{cases} -x, & \text{when } -x \geq 0 \\ -(-x), & \text{when } -x < 0 \end{cases}$$

This can be rewritten as

$$y = |-x| = \begin{cases} -x, & \text{when } x \leq 0 \\ x, & \text{when } x > 0 \end{cases}$$

a. Since $6 > 0$, $y = |-6| = 6$. 　　**b.** Since $-15 \leq 0$,
　　　　　　　　　　　　　　　　　　　$y = |-(-15)| = -(-15) = 15$. ■

Piecewise-defined functions can be written for any absolute value function, as shown in Example 3.

EXAMPLE 3 ## Write absolute value functions as piecewise-defined functions

Write a piecewise-defined function for $y = |x + 5|$.

A Closer Look at Absolute Value *continued*

Solution:

If $x < -5$, then $x + 5$ is negative and $|x + 5| = -(x + 5)$. If $x \geq -5$, then $x + 5$ is positive and $|x + 5| = (x + 5)$.

$$|x + 5| = \begin{cases} x + 5, \text{ when } x \geq -5 \\ -(x + 5), \text{ when } x < -5 \end{cases} \blacksquare$$

Practice

Find each absolute value when $x = -10$.

1. $|x - 8|$ 2. $|-5x|$ 3. $|-(x + 1)|$

4. $|-x - 9|$ 5. $-|16 - 3x|$

Write each absolute value function as a piecewise-defined function.

6. $y = |-x|$ 7. $y = -|x|$ 8. $y = -|-x|$ 9. $y = |4x|$

10. $y = |2 - x|$ 11. $y = |2x + 3|$ 12. $y = |-5x|$ 13. $y = -|7 + x|$

14. $y = |-(x - 6)|$ 15. $y = -|3 - 6x|$

Problem Solving

16. A quality control analyst uses the function $y = |x - 0.75|$ to measure the error when weighing packages of seeds. Write a piecewise-defined function for this error measure.

17. Shannon's car averages 25 miles per gallon. She uses the function $y = |x - 25|$ to describe the amount this mileage varies. Write a piecewise-defined function showing the amount of variation for the car's mileage per gallon.

18. During the first basketball game of the season, the captain of the team scored 12 points. The function $y = |x - 12|$ describes the variation in points scored by other members of the basketball team. Write a piecewise-defined function showing the amount of variation for the points scored by the other team members.

19. A toy company projected earnings of 5.3 hundred thousand dollars during each quarter of the year. Write a piecewise-defined function showing the amount each quarter's actual earnings varied from the projected profits.

20. Eric's gym teacher expects students to finish a race in about 45 seconds. Write a piecewise-defined function showing the amount each student's finish time varies from the gym teacher's expected finish time.

21. On a geography quiz, the average class score is an 86. Write a piecewise-defined function showing the amount each student's score varies from the average score.

22. **Challenge** Write a piecewise-defined function for $y = |x - 1| + |x + 3|$.

CHAPTER 5 · Solving Absolute Value Equations by Graphing

Absolute value equations in the form $|ax + b| = c$, where a, b, and c are constants, can be solved by graphing corresponding functions in the form $y = |ax + b| - c$ and finding the zeros. The x-values of the points where the graphs intersect the x-axis are the solutions.

KEY CONCEPT

Number of Possible Solutions to an Absolute Value Equation

An absolute value equation can have zero, one, or two solutions.

Examples of each type are shown in Example 1.

EXAMPLE 1 ## Determine the number of solutions to an absolute value equation by graphing

Determine the number of solutions to each absolute value equation by graphing.

a. $|x + 1| = 2$ **b.** $\frac{1}{2}|x - 2| = 0$ **c.** $2|x - 1| = -1$

Solution:

a. Graph $y = |x + 1| - 2$. There are two zeros; one at $x = 1$ and the other at $x = -3$.

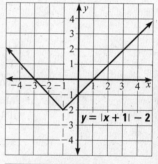

b. Graph $y = \frac{1}{2}|x - 2|$. There is one zero at $x = 2$.

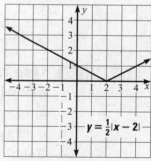

c. Graph $y = 2|x - 1| + 1$. There are 0 solutions. ∎

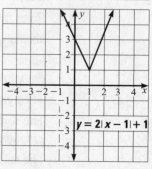

Solving Absolute Value Equations by Graphing *continued*

Notice the values of the constant c in each equation. In Example 1a, $c = 2$. When $c > 0$, there are 2 solutions. In Example 1b, $c = 0$. When $c = 0$, there is 1 solution. In Example 1c, $c = -1$. When $c < 0$, there are 0 solutions.

EXAMPLE 2 Find solutions to $|ax + b| = c$ by graphing $y = |ax + b|$ and $y = c$

a. Show how the graphs of $y = |3x + 2|$ and $y = 1$ can be used to find the solutions of $|3x + 2| = 1$.

b. Explain what the graphs of $y = -|x - 5|$ and $y = 2$ tell about the solutions of $y = -|x - 5| - 2$.

Solution:

a.

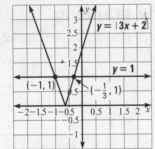

b.

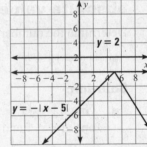

The x-coordinates of the points where these two graphs intersect are the solutions. The solutions to $|3x + 2| = 1$ are $x = -1$ and $x = -\frac{1}{3}$.

The graphs of $y = -|x - 5|$ and $y = 2$ do not intersect. Therefore, there are no solutions to the equation $y = -|x - 5| - 2$. ■

The solutions to absolute value equations can be found using a graphing calculator, as shown in Example 3.

EXAMPLE 3 Use a graphing calculator to solve absolute value equations

Solve the absolute value equation $0 = |2x + 5| - 4$ by using a graphing calculator.

Solution:

Enter the absolute value function into $\boxed{Y=}$ using the absolute value function (abs) found in the $\boxed{MATH}$ menu under NUM. Be sure the $\boxed{WINDOW}$ is set for an appropriate domain and range.

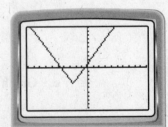

Then graph. The graph of the absolute value function $y = |2x + 5| - 4$ is shown.

The solutions can be found using the zero command from the $\boxed{2nd}$ CALC menu on the graphing calculator.

The solutions are at $x = -0.5$ and $x = -4.5$. ■

Name _____ Date _____

Solving Absolute Value Equations by Graphing *continued*

Practice

Determine the number of zeroes in each graph.

1.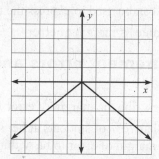

2.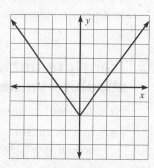

Determine the number of solutions to each absolute value equation.

3. $|x - 4| = 0$

4. $|4 - 3x| = 7$

5. $-|-(2 + x)| = 1$

6. $-|x - 3| = -6$

Solve each absolute value equation using a graphing calculator.

7. $0 = |x + 3|$

8. $0 = |-x - 2|$

9. $0 = -|2x|$

10. $0 = |2x - 3| + 1$

11. $0 = |x + 6| - 2$

12. $|4x + 3| = 3$

13. $|7 - x| = 0$

14. $-|2 - x| = 3$

15. $|-0.5x| = -0.5$

Problem Solving

16. Justin graphed $y = |2x - 4|$ and $y = 1$ on the same coordinate grid. Randy graphed the function $y = |2x - 4| - 1$ on another grid. How do the solutions of Justin's graphed functions compare to the zeros of Randy's graphed function?

17. Alesha graphed $y = -|x + 6|$ and $y = 1$ on the same coordinate grid. Explain how Alesha can use these graphs to find the solution to the equation $-|x + 6| = 1$. Then find the solution to the equation $-|x + 6| = 1$.

18. Draw a graph of an absolute value equation that has no solution. Explain why it has no solution.

19. Write an absolute value equation with exactly one solution. Then find its solution.

20. Mattie wrote an equation in the form $y = |ax + b| - c$ that had no solution. What possible values for a, b, and c could Mattie have used?

21. Dave wrote an equation in the form $y = |ax + b| - c$ that had two solutions. What possible values for a, b, and c could Dave have used?

22. Taylor wrote an equation in the form $y = |ax + b| - c$ that had exactly one solution. What possible values for a, b, and c could Taylor have used?

CHAPTER 5 Margins of Error

Many measurements are not exact. Errors due to the measuring tool used or to rounding are called **margins of error**. Absolute value inequalities can be used to express the range of possible values.

If x represents the values acceptable within the margin of error of a given value, then the following absolute value inequality can be used to express the range of values:

$$|x - \text{given value}| \leq \text{margin of error}$$

EXAMPLE 1 Translate between measurement errors and absolute value inequalities

Write an absolute value inequality or describe the margin of error for the situation.

a. In a recent study, Camille found that 70% of students at her school play an after school sport. She determined the margin of error to be within 6%.

b. To the nearest foot, the length of Damien's desk is 5 feet.

c. At the supermarket, a watermelon's weight in pounds is given by $|x - 14| \leq 3$.

Solution:

a. Since the range of values can be 6% more or 6% less than 70%, the absolute value inequality is $|x - 70| \leq 6$.

b. Measurements to the nearest foot are at most 0.5 feet shorter or longer, so the absolute value inequality is $|x - 5| < 0.5$. Note that in this case, the inequality does not include the boundary values.

c. The weight of an average watermelon at the supermarket is within 3 pounds of 14 pounds, or between 11 pounds and 17 pounds. The margin of error is 3 pounds. ∎

EXAMPLE 2 Determine margins of error

A gear on a machine part has a tolerance within 0.06 centimeters of 2.4 centimeters.

a. Write an absolute value inequality describing the margin of error for the tolerance of this gear.

b. Determine the tolerance range, in centimeters, for this gear.

Solution:

a. $|x - 2.4| \leq 0.06$

b. First rewrite the absolute value inequality as a compound inequality:

$$-0.06 \leq x - 2.4 \leq 0.06$$

Therefore, $2.34 \leq x \leq 2.46$ or the tolerance range is between 2.34 cm and 2.46 cm. ∎

The range of values within a margin of error can be graphed on a number line, as shown in Example 3.

Margins of Error *continued*

EXAMPLE 3 ## Express margins of error on a number line

The number of bagels made each day at a bakery is within 24 of 360. Using the margin of error, find the total number of bagels that can be made each day. Then graph this range on a number line.

Solution:

The margin of error is 24. The absolute value inequality describing the range of values is $|x - 360| \le 24$ Rewrite the absolute value inequality as a compound inequality:

$$-24 \le x - 360 \le 24$$

Therefore, $336 \le x \le 384$, so the range of bagels is between 336 and 384.

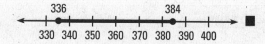

Practice

Write the absolute value inequality describing the margin of error.

1. The length of a computer monitor, to the nearest inch, is 14 inches.

2. In a survey, the number of people favoring the development of a new shopping mall was within 4 percentage points of 28%.

3. In a game, points are awarded if a player's marker lands within 5 feet of a line 40 feet away.

Describe the margin of error shown by the absolute value inequality.

4. The starting salary in dollars of employees at a retail shop is given by $|x - 24{,}500| \le 1500$.

5. The average tensile strength of a spring, in pounds, is given by $|x - 35| < 2.5$.

6. The precision of a measurement, in centimeters, is given by $|x - 9.6| < 0.05$.

7. The number of minutes it takes Malcolm to run a mile is given by $|x - 7.75| \le 0.25$.

Problem Solving

8. When mixing substances in the chemistry lab, Audrey's measurements can be off by no more than 10%. Describe the range of measures Audrey can make for 80 milliliters of a substance.

9. To the nearest 10 millimeters, the length of a square's side is 50 millimeters. Find the possible range in area A of this square. Graph this range on a number line.

10. In an experiment, Logan found that the equation $d = 60 - 0.75p$ describes the distance d, in feet, traveled by an object weighing p pounds when projected off a platform. The margin of error is within 8 feet. What is the expected distance an object weighing 20 pounds would travel? Graph this distance range on a number line.

CHAPTER 5 Problem Solving with Linear Equations in Two Variables

We have learned that linear inequalities result when the $=$ sign in a linear equation is replaced with one of the inequality symbols $<$, $>$, $\leq$, or $\geq$. Here, we explore various problem situations involving each equality and inequality symbol and learn to recognize key words and phrases that help determine which symbols model these situations.

KEY CONCEPT

Meanings of Equality and Inequality Symbols

The table below shows each equality and inequality symbol, their meanings, and some key phrases that are indicators of each symbol.

Symbol	Meaning	Key Phrases
$=$	equals	is, exactly, the same as
$<$	less than	less than, fewer, below, smaller
$>$	greater than	greater than, more, over, above, larger, exceeds
$\leq$	less than or equal to	less than or equal to, at most, no more than
$\geq$	greater than or equal to	greater than or equal to, at least, no less than

Situations using inequality symbols can often appear similar. You should to be able to distinguish the differences among various situations and know when to use each type of inequality. Example 1 investigates this further.

EXAMPLE 1 ## Identify equality and inequality symbols modeling situations

Identify the equality or inequality symbol most appropriate for the situation.

  a. Sierra studied no more than 6 hours for her exam.

  b. The number of points Maria scored in this game exceeded her prior record.

  c. Today's high temperature is seven degrees more than yesterday's high temperature.

  d. The highest grade Timothy can receive is a 90%.

Solution:

  a. Since the sentence uses the phrase, *no more than*, the appropriate symbol is $\leq$.

  b. Since the sentence use the word *exceeded*, the appropriate symbol is $>$

  c. Since the sentence uses the word *is*, the appropriate symbol is $=$

  d. In this case, the highest grade has to be at most 90%. Therefore, the appropriate symbol is $\leq$. ■

Problem Solving with Linear Equations in Two Variables *continued*

Notice that the situation in part c uses the = sign and not the > symbol, even though the phrase *more than* is used. Here the phrase *more than* implies addition and not the inequality >. The situation described in part d does not use any of the key words or phrases shown in the table. However, the meaning of the word *highest* is synonymous with the phrase *at most* or *no more than*. For that reason, the inequality ≤ is most appropriate.

Determining which equality and inequality symbol to use involves more than just recognizing key phrases. It requires the ability to understand the situation being modeled as a whole and to use reasoning skills.

EXAMPLE 2 ## Write equations and inequalities to model situations

Write an equation or inequality that best describes the situation. Then explain why the equality or inequality symbol used best models the situation.

- **a.** Dry cleaning costs $3 for each shirt and $2 for each pair of pants. This month, Jesse budgeted no more than $24 for dry cleaning.

- **b.** The freshman class is selling tickets to a sporting event. Student tickets cost $5 each. Adult tickets cost $8 each. The goal is to sell at least $1500 worth of tickets.

- **c.** A crate of m magazines weighs p pounds. Each magazine weighs 0.75 pounds and the crate weighs 1.25 pounds.

Solution:

- **a.** Let the variable s represent the number of shirts and p the number of pants. The cost for dry cleaning shirts is $3s$ and the cost for dry cleaning pants is $2p$. The inequality that best describes the situation is:

$$3s + 2p \leq 24$$

The inequality symbol ≤ is used this situation because the phrase *no more than $24* implies that amounts less than $24 or exactly $24 can be spent.

- **b.** Let the variable s represent the number of student tickets sold and a the number of adult tickets sold. The amount from selling student tickets is $5s$ and the amount from selling adult tickets is $8a$. The inequality that best describes the situation is:

$$5s + 8a \geq 1500$$

The inequality symbol ≥ is used in this situation because the phrase *at least $1500* implies that amounts equal to $1500 or greater than $1500 are needed to meet the goal.

- **c.** The situation can be best modeled by the equation:

$$0.75m + 1.25 = p$$

The equality symbol = is used in this situation because a linear relationship exists between the number of magazines and the total weight of the crate with magazines. No comparison is being made to suggest the total weight is less than or greater than a certain amount. ∎

| CHAPTER 5 | # Problem Solving with Linear Equations in Two Variables *continued* |

EXAMPLE 3   ## Compare problems modeled by inequalities and equations

Carlos has at most $20 to spend on a bouquet of flowers. Carnations cost $1 each and roses $2 each.

a.   Describe the inequality that shows the number of carnations and roses Carlos can buy.

b.   Carlos spends exactly $20 on the bouquet. Write an equation describing the number of carnations and roses he buys.

Solution:

a.   Let c be the number of carnations that Carlos buys and r the number of roses. The amount he spends on carnations is $1c$ or c, and the amount he spends on roses is $2r$. Since Carlos has *at most* $20 to spend, he can spend exactly $20 or any amount less than $20. The inequality describing this is $c + 2r \leq 20$.

b.   Since Carlos spends *exactly* $20, the $\leq$ symbol in the inequality above is replaced with an $=$ symbol. The equation is $c + 2r = 20$.   ■

The two models in Example 3 are similar. The only difference that distinguishes *at most* $20 from *exactly* $20 is the inequality and equality symbols. Example 4 explores the similarities and differences between the graphs of these two models.

EXAMPLE 4   ## Compare graphs of inequalities and equations

Compare the graphs of $c + 2r = 20$ and $c + 2r \leq 20$ from Example 3. Identify at least six flower combinations that Carlos can get that satisfy each model.

Solution:

The graph of the equation $c + 2r = 20$ is a straight line containing all points on that line. The graph of the inequality $c + 2r \leq 20$ shows the same straight line but contains all points on that line *and* all points beneath that line as indicated by the shaded region.

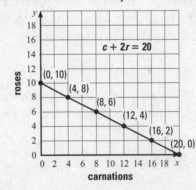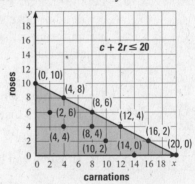

Some flower combinations in the form (carnations, roses) satisfying $c + 2r = 20$ include (0, 10), (4, 8), (8, 6), (12, 4), (16, 2) and (20, 0).

Some flower combinations in the form (carnations, roses) satisfying $c + 2r \leq 20$ include all points on the graph of $c + 2r = 20$ as well as (2, 6), (4, 4), (8, 4), (10, 2), and (14, 0).

Problem Solving with Linear Equations in Two Variables *continued*

Practice

Identify the equality or inequality symbol modeling each situation.

1. Dehlia babysat fewer hours last month compared to this month.

2. Victoria's monthly phone bill shows a charge of $0.15 for each minute she talks plus a service fee of $12.95.

3. The maximum weight capacity a bridge can hold is 12 tons.

4. Liam has a risk of getting sunburned if his time outdoors exceeds 45 minutes.

5. Monica plans to save at least 40% of her earnings.

6. Jasmine earns $10 an hour tutoring and $8 an hour working at the library. She wants to earn a minimum of $400 this month.

Describe all points satisfying each equation or inequality.

7. $y = 4x - 3$ 8. $y \geq 4x - 3$ 9. $y < 4x - 3$

10. $2x - 3y > -3$ 11. $2x - 3y \leq -3$ 12. $2x - 3y = -3$

Graph each equation or inequality on separate coordinate grids and compare their solutions.

13. $y < 0.5x + 2$
    $y > 0.5x + 2$

14. $y = -2x - 1$
    $y \leq -2x - 1$

15. $4x + 3y > 6$
    $4x + 3y = 6$

16. $-5x - 2y = 4$
    $-5x - 2y < 4$

Problem Solving

17. One side of a balanced scale has 3 square weights and 4 triangular weights. The other side of the scale has 4 square weights and 1 triangular weight. What equation or inequality can be used to model this situation?

18. The cost to park in a parking garage is $2.50 for the first hour and $1.50 each additional hour. Janelle plans to spend at most $10 to park for the day. Write an equation or inequality that shows the number of hours h Janelle can park in the garage and still meet her budget.

19. In a trivia game, Lyle earns 3 points for each question he answers correctly in the main round and 5 points for each question he answers correctly in the bonus round. Lyle earned at least 30 points in the game he played. Write and graph an equation or inequality showing the number of questions Lyle could have answered correctly in both rounds. Use the graph of the equation or inequality to explain whether or not Lyle could have answered 6 questions correctly in the main round and 2 questions correctly in the bonus round.

CHAPTER 6

Graph Systems of Two Equations and Three Equations

We already know that the graph of the solutions to a linear equation can be a vertical line, a horizontal line, or a line that lies at an angle to both the vertical and the horizontal axis. In this chapter we explore the solutions of *systems of linear equations*.

Among other things, we want to know what the solution graph for a system of equations looks like. To answer this question, we first need to consider what happens when we graph several equations in the same coordinate plane. We begin with scenarios involving just two equations in two variables.

EXAMPLE 1 ## Graph two equations in the same plane

For each of each of the following pairs of equations, graph the two equations together in one coordinate plane.

a. $x + 2y = 8$
     $y = x - 2$

b. $y = -2x + 6$
     $y = -2x - 3$

c. $2y - x = 4$
     $-6y + 3x = -12$

Solution:

a.

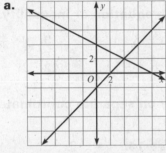

b.

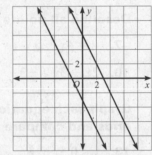

c.

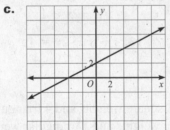

The three graphs in Example 1 cover all the basic possibilities. Two linear equations may represent the same line (part c). But if the lines are distinct, they will either intersect (part a) or they will not (part b).

Now we can consider how the graphs of the equations in a system relate to the graph of the solution to the system as a whole.

KEY CONCEPT

Graphing the Solutions of a System of Equations

The graph of the solution or solutions of a system of equations consists of all points that lie on the line for every individual equation in the system.

<table>
<tr><td>CHAPTER
6</td><td colspan="2"># Graph Systems of Two Equations
and Three Equations continued</td></tr>
</table>

This principle comes from the definition of the solution of a system of equations: an ordered pair (x, y) is a solution of the system if it is a solution for every one of the individual equations.

EXAMPLE 2 ## Graph the solution of a two-equation linear system

Refer to Example 1, and graph the solution in each of the three cases.

Solution:

a.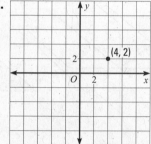

The point that lies on both lines is the point of intersection, (4, 2). That point is the graph of the solution of the sytem.

b.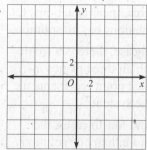

No point lies on both lines, so the system has no solution. The graph of the solution is the empty graph.

c.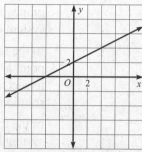

The two equations represent the same line. Every (x, y) pair on that line is a solution for both equations, and therefore is a solution for the system. ∎

Part a in Examples 1 and 2 is the "typical" system. Systems like those in parts b and c are examined in more detail in Section 7.5.

What we have learned can be extended to systems of more than two equations. The solution of a single one-variable equation of the form $ax = b$ is a point (0 dimensions) on the number line (1 dimension). The solution of a single two-variable equation of the form $ax + by = c$ is a line (1 dimension) in the coordinate plane (2 dimensions). Similarly, the solution of a single three-variable equation of the form $ax + by + cz = d$ is a plane (2 dimensions) in the coordinate xyz-space (3 dimensions).

A similar pattern also applies to systems of equations as well. Just as the solution of a system of two linear equations in two variables is the intersection of two lines, the solution of a system of three linear equations in three variables is the intersection of three planes. As the number of dimensions grows, however, there are two problems. First, it gets harder to visualize and graph the solutions. And second, there are more and more ways for the solution graphs of the individual equations to intersect. With two equations in two variables, there are three possibilities. For three equations in three variables, there are four different possibilities for the intersection of the three solution planes: no intersection, a point, a line, or a plane.

CHAPTER 6

Graph Systems of Two Equations and Three Equations *continued*

Here are some illustrations of how each type of intersection may come about. Each illustration represents three planes in three-dimensional *xyz*-space. The axes are omitted for clarity.

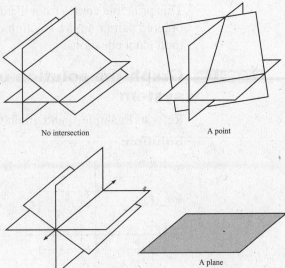

No intersection   A point

In the first case, each pair of planes has an intersection, but there is no point at which all three planes intersect. If these three planes are solution graphs for three linear equations, the system of equations has no solution.

In the second case, there is a single point at which all three planes intersect, and that point represents the solution of the system.

A line   A plane

In the third and fourth cases, the system has more than one solution.

In the third case, all solutions lie along a line running through the three-dimensional *xyz*-space, the line where all three planes intersect. And in the fourth case, all three equations have the same solution plane, and every point on that plane is a solution to the system.

Practice

Graph the solution of each system of equations. State whether the solution is a point, a line, or the empty graph.

1. $2x + y = 0$
$y = x + 3$

2. $x + y = 2$
$-3x - 3y = -6$

3. $3x + 2y = 2$
$4y = x - 10$

4. $-x + 4y = 8$
$4y = x - 12$

5. $3x + 8y = -20$
$16y + 40 = -6x$

6. $x + 2y = -5$
$3y = 2x + 3$

Each of the following two figures depicts graphs of three linear equations in three variables. State whether the graph of the solution to the system of three equations is empty or is a point, a line, or a plane.

7.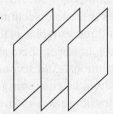

8.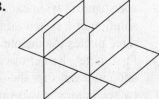

9. With three planes, it is possible for two planes to coincide but the third plane to be distinct. What two possibilities does this lead to for the intersection of all three planes? Draw both situations. If each plane represents the graph of a linear equation, what does each of the two outcomes imply about the solution of the system?

CHAPTER 6

Exploring Systems of Three Linear Equations

Solving a system of three linear equations in three variables is hard to do graphically, even with a graphing calculator. However, graphing calculators provide another means of solving linear systems by using matrices. This method can be used with systems of two equations in two unknowns, three equations in three unknowns, four equations in four unknowns, and so on.

Recall from the Extension on pages 94 and 95 of the textbook, that an $n \times m$ matrix is a rectangular block of numbers that has n rows and m columns. The numbers n and m are called the **dimensions** of the matrix.

To solve a linear system of equations, you will use a graphing calculator to multiply the **inverse** of a matrix and another matrix. The inverse of an $n \times n$ matrix A is an $n \times n$ matrix, denoted A^{-1}, such that when the two matrices are multiplied under matrix multiplication, the resulting matrix is an $n \times n$ matrix with 1's along the diagonal from the upper left to lower right and 0's everywhere else. This matrix is called an **identity matrix.** We will not go into the details of matrix multiplication here, but we will use a graphing calculator to perform this operation.

EXAMPLE 1 ## Solve a linear system using matrices

On a graphing calculator, use matrices to solve the system $\begin{cases} 5x + 2y = 6 \\ x - 3y = -5 \end{cases}$.

Solution:

Make sure the equations are in standard form, with variables on the left side and constants on the right, and zero coefficients included as needed. On the calculator, set matrix A as a 2×2 matrix and enter the coefficients of the system—one row for each equation, one column for each variable. (Consult the manual for your particular calculator as necessary.)

Now set matrix B as a 2×1 matrix and enter the constants from the right side of each equation, making sure to keep them in correct order.

Finally, go to the main screen and multiply the inverse of matrix A by matrix B, using the x^{-1} key on your calculator to indicate the matrix inverse operation.

The resulting matrix gives the solution values. Note that these values, with $x \approx 0.47$ and $y \approx 1.8$, match the solution found by graphing in the Graphing Calculator Activity on page 434 of the textbook. ■

Pre-AP Copymasters

Exploring Systems of Three Linear Equations *continued*

This method works for larger systems, such as three equations in three variables, as long as the number of variables equals the number of equations and the system has a single, well-defined solution.

KEY CONCEPT

Solving a Linear System Using Matrices

In general, to solve a linear system with n equations and n variables, multiply the inverse of the $n \times n$ matrix of coefficients by the $n \times 1$ matrix of constants. The result is the matrix of solution values.

EXAMPLE 2
Solve a linear system using matrices

On a graphing calculator, use matrices to solve the following system:
$$2x + 3y + z = 6$$
$$-x + 2y + 3z = 4$$
$$3x - z = 2$$

Solution:

Using a graphing calculator, enter $A = \begin{bmatrix} 2 & 3 & 1 \\ -1 & 2 & 3 \\ 3 & 0 & -1 \end{bmatrix}$ and $B = \begin{bmatrix} 6 \\ 4 \\ 2 \end{bmatrix}$ Then compute $A^{-1}B$,

which results in the matrix $\begin{bmatrix} 1 \\ 1 \\ 1 \end{bmatrix}$. Therefore, the solution is $x = 1$, $y = 1$, $z = 1$. ■

Sometimes the calculator will display an error message like "SINGULAR MAT". When this message occurs, it means that the system has either infinitely many solutions or no solution at all. A message like "INVALID DIM" or "DIM MISMATCH" means that one or both matrices have been entered with incorrect dimensions.

Practice

Use the matrix method to verify the solutions obtained by the graphing method for each of the Practice Exercises in the Graphing Calculator Activity on page 434 of the textbook. Then solve the linear systems.

1. $5x + y = -4$
   $x - y = -2$

2. $y = x + 4$
   $y = -3x - 2$

3. $-0.45x - y = 1.35$
   $-1.8x + y = -1.8$

4. $-0.4x + 0.8y = -16$
   $1.2x + 0.4y = 1$

Use the matrix method to solve the linear systems.

5. $2x + y - 3z = -11$
   $-x + 8y - z = 15$
   $-4x - 5y - z = -5$

6. $-x - y + z = 3.2$
   $y - 4z = -15.2$
   $-2x + 5y + 2z = -2$

7. $w + 3x + 2y + z = 5$
   $2w + x - y + z = 1$
   $3w - 5x - y + 2z = -3$
   $-w + x - 4y + z = 7$

8. Name two advantages and one disadvantage of the matrix method, compared to the graphical method.

The Symmetric, Reflexive, and Transitive Properties of Equality

CHAPTER 6

When we manipulate equations, we often use the familiar properties of arithmetic operations, such as the commutative and associative properties of addition. However, we also make use of three properties of the equality relation, properties so much taken for granted they often do not even get mentioned.

KEY CONCEPT

Three Properties of Equality

Reflexive Property	For any a, $a = a$.
Symmetric Property	For any a and b, if $a = b$ then $b = a$.
Transitive Property	For any a, b and c, if $a = b$ and $b = c$ then $a = c$.

The reflexive property says that any number is equal to itself. The symmetric property says that equality is a two-way street: whenever one number is the same as another number, the second number is also the same as the first. And the transitive property says that equality is always direct: if a and c are connected by the chain of equalities $a = b$, $b = c$, then they are also directly connected by the equality $a = c$.

These properties are used to justify simple but necessary steps in various solution procedures.

EXAMPLE ## Identify the properties of equality

For each of the three procedures, identify the property of equality used in the final step, and state why it was used.

a. $4 = 2x$
  $2 = x$ **Divide both sides by 2.**
  $x = 2$ **?**

b. $C(x) = 3(x - 5)$
  $3(x - 5) = 3x - 15$ **Distributive property**
  So $C(x) = 3x - 15$ **?**

c. Check $x = -1$, $y = 6$ as a solution for $2x + 3y = 16$.
   $2x + 3y = 16$
  $2(-1) + 3(6) = 16$ **Substitute.**
       $16 = 16$ **Simplify.**
  The solution checks.   **?**

Solution:

a. The symmetric property is being used to write the final equation with the variable on the left.

b. The transitive property is being used to relate the final expression $3x - 15$ back to the function name $C(x)$.

c. The reflexive property is being used to conclude that $16 = 16$ is a true statement, and that therefore, $x = -1$, $y = 6$ is a solution for $2x + 3y = 16$. ∎

Pre-AP Copymasters

CHAPTER 6

The Symmetric, Reflexive, and Transitive Properties of Equality *continued*

Part (c) of Example 1 actually assumes a fourth property of equality, which is quite important and is used frequently.

KEY CONCEPT

The Substitution Property of Equality
For any a and b, if $a = b$, then b can be substituted for a in any equation.

This is the property that allows us to substitute values in for variables in equations, or to replace one variable expression with another, equivalent variable expression.

Practice
Use the given property or properties to write an equation not already given.

1. $-6y$
   reflexive property

2. $7x = 12$
   symmetric property

3. $3x - 11 = 9, 9 = 2y$
   transitive property

4. $8y = 2x + 9$
   symmetric property

5. $19 + x = 3x, 5 = 19 + x$
   transitive property

6. $3x = 2y, (3x)^2 = 8$
   substitution property

7. $11a = 5,\ 11a + 9b = y, y = 2z$
   substitution property, transitive property

8. **Proof** Use two properties of equality to show that if $x = y$ and $x = z$, then $y = z$.

9. **Proof** Show that if $a = b$, $b = c$, and $c = d$, then $a = d$.

Challenge
Do the reflexive, symmetric, and transitive properties apply to the inequality relations >, <, ≥, and ≤ for real numbers? Explain your answers to each question.

10. Is the "greater than" relation
    a. reflexive? (Is $a > a$ is true for any a?)
    b. symmetric? (When $a > b$, must it also be true that $b > a$?)
    c. transitive? (When $a > b$ and $b > c$, is it also true that $a > c$?)

11. Is the "less than" relation
    a. reflexive?   b. symmetric?   c. transitive?

12. Is the "greater than or equal to" relation
    a. reflexive?   b. symmetric?   c. transitive?

13. Is the "less than or equal to" relation
    a. reflexive?   b. symmetric?   c. transitive?

14. Consider the "is 1 more than" relation, as in "x is 1 more than y." Is this relation transitive? Why or why not?

CHAPTER 6 Adding Equals to Equals

The reflexive, symmetric, and transitive properties of equality are not the only properties of equality that are used to find solutions to equations. Here is another property that is used frequently.

KEY CONCEPT

The Addition Property of Equality

If $a = b$, then $a + c = b + c$.

This is the property that allows us to add the same thing to both sides of an equation.

EXAMPLE 1 Solve equations using the addition property of equality

Solve each of the following equations.

  a. $x - 7 = 12$ **b.** $-3 = x + 9$

Solution:

  a. $x - 7 = 12$
       $x - 7 + 7 = 12 + 7$ **Add 7 to both sides.**
             $x = 19$ **Simplify.**

  b. $-3 = x + 9$
       $-3 + (-9) = x + 9 + (-9)$ **Add −9 to both sides.**
             $-12 = x$ **Simplify.**
             $x = -12$ **Symmetric property of equality** ∎

Part (b) illustrates how the addition property of equality can be used to justify *subtracting* the same quantity (in this case, 9) from both sides of an equation, because subtracting a number is the same as adding its opposite.

The addition property of equality can be combined with the substitution property of equality to get the following result of adding equals to equals.

If $a = b$ and $c = d$, then $a + c = b + d$.

This can be shown as follows.

       $a = b$ Given
   $a + c = b + c$ Addition property of equality
   $a + c = b + d$ Substitution property of equality

This result is the basis for the elimination method of solving linear systems introduced in Lesson 7.3.

EXAMPLE 2 Add equals to equals and use the elimination method

Explain how adding equals to equals makes it possible to solve the following linear system by the elimination method.

Algebra 1
Pre-AP **111**

Adding Equals to Equals *continued*

$$5x + 3y = 13$$
$$-2x - 3y = 11$$

Solution:

Since $5x + 3y = 13$ and $-2x - 3y = 11$, we know by adding equals to equals that $(5x + 3y) + (-2x - 3y) = 13 + 11$. By adding and simplifying,

$$5x + 3y = 13$$
$$\underline{-2x - 3y = 11}$$
$$3x \quad\quad = 24$$

It follows that $x = 8$. Substituting back into either equation and solving for y yields $y = -9$. ■

The other version of the elimination method, where equations are subtracted instead of added, is justified by a combination of adding equals to equals and another property, the multiplication property of equality (see Exercise 4).

Practice

1. Tickets to a school fair are $3 per adult and $1 per student. A total of 1395 people attend, and the ticket sales amount to $2867.

   a. Write a linear system that could be solved to find the number of adults and the number of students who attend the fair.

   b. Suppose the system is solved by subtracting the equation that describes ticket sales from the equation that describes attendance numbers. Does the resulting equation have an interesting interpretation? Why or why not?

   c. Solve the system to find the number of adults and the number of students who attended the fair.

2. **Writing** Suppose someone decided to solve the given linear system by adding the equations instead of subtracting.

   $$8x + 7y = 22$$
   $$-5x + 7y = 9$$

   Would this method be successful? Why or why not?

3. **Writing** Suppose someone decided to solve the linear system by switching the two sides of the second equation and then adding the result to the first equation.

   $$-3x + 4y = -2$$
   $$7x + 4y = -10$$

   Would this method be successful? Why or why not?

4. **Challenge** According to the Multiplication Property of Equality, if $a = b$ and $c = d$, then $ac = bd$. Explain how the Multiplication Property can be used, together with the Addition Property, to justify the subtraction version of the Elimination Method for solving linear systems. (Hint: Remember that subtracting a number is the same as adding its opposite.)

CHAPTER 6 Describing Polygons with Systems of Inequalities

With two linear inequalities, we can define a wedge-shaped region in the coordinate plane. With three or more linear inequalities, we can define a finite, polygon-shaped region—three inequalities for a triangle, four for a quadrilateral, and so on. Since in most applications we will want to include the border of the region, the inequalities will normally be non-strict. That is, we will usually (but not always) use ≤ and ≥ rather than < and >.

EXAMPLE 1 Graph systems of inequalities

Graph each system of inequalities.

a. $x + y \leq 3$
$y \leq x + 3$
$y \geq \frac{1}{2}x$

b. $x \geq -2$
$x \leq 3$
$y \leq 4$
$y \geq \frac{2}{3}x - 2$
$y \geq -2x - 4$

Solution:

a.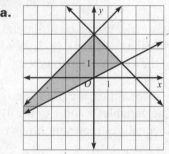

b.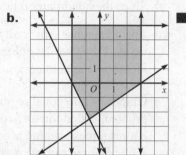

Sometimes, we will need to write the system of inequalities using other information, such as the vertices of the polygon. In that case, we take two vertices at a time and use the procedure for finding the equation of a line through two points. We then convert each equation into the appropriate inequality.

EXAMPLE 2 Describe a region with a system of inequalities

Write a system of inequalities to describe the quadrilateral region with corners at $(-5, -4)$, $(-2, 2)$, $(3, 2)$, and $(3, -2)$.

Solution:

We begin by graphing the region.

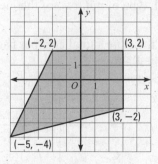

Describing Polygons with Systems of Inequalities *continued*

Taking two adjacent vertices at a time, we find the equations for the lines through them. The slope of the line through $(-5, -4)$ and $(-2, 2)$ is $\dfrac{2 - (-4)}{-2 - (-5)} = \dfrac{6}{3} = 2$, and the line through the two points is given in point-slope form as $y - 2 = 2(x + 2)$ or in slope-intercept form as $y = 2x + 6$. The slope of the line through $(-2, 2)$ and $(3, 2)$ is $\dfrac{2 - 2}{3 - (-2)} = \dfrac{0}{5} = 0$, and the line through the two points is $y = 2$.

Using the pairs of points $(3, 2)$, $(3, -2)$ and $(-5, -4)$, $(3, -2)$, we find the two remaining equations: $x = 3$ and $y = \dfrac{1}{4}x - \dfrac{11}{4}$.

Now we write the corresponding inequalities by substituting $\geq$ or $\leq$ for $=$ in each equation, depending on which side of the line represents the interior of the polygon.

Since the quadrilateral lies *below* the line $y = 2x + 6$, we write $y \leq 2x + 6$.

Since the quadrilateral lies *below* the line $y = 2$, we write $y \leq 2$.

Since the quadrilateral lies *to the left of* the line $x = 3$, we write $x \leq 3$.

Since the quadrilateral lies *above* the line $y = \dfrac{1}{4}x - \dfrac{11}{4}$, we write $y \geq \dfrac{1}{4}x - \dfrac{11}{4}$.

The points that satisfy all four inequalities make up the quadrilateral region. In other words, the quadrilateral region with vertices at $(-5, -4)$, $(-2, 2)$, $(3, 2)$, and $(3, -2)$, including the boundaries, is the graph of the system of inequalities. ■

Graphs of polygonal regions, defined by inequalities, are used in a type of application problem called **linear programming**. The variables x and y typically represent different resources in some process, and the inequalities represent limits on how much of each resource can be used.

EXAMPLE 3 ## Graph a system of inequalities

A specialty store plans to sell large bags of nuts containing some mix of peanuts and cashews. The store buys its nuts wholesale at $0.50 per pound for peanuts and $2 per pound for cashews. Each bag should contain at least 0.5 pound of each type of nut, but one bag's worth of nuts should not cost the store more than $4. Using x for pounds of peanuts and y for pounds of cashews, write a system of inequalities that defines the possible amounts of peanuts and cashews that go into each bag of mixed nuts. Graph the system.

Solution:

Since there must be at least 0.5 pound of each type of nut, two of the inequalities are $x \geq 0.5$ and $y \geq 0.5$.

The third inequality comes from the limit on the store's total cost per bag: $0.5x + 2y \leq 4$, or in slope-intercept form, $y \leq -0.25x + 2$.

We graph the system of three inequalities.

$x \geq 0.5$

$y \geq 0.5$

$y \leq -0.25x + 2$ ■

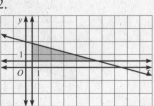

CHAPTER 6 Describing Polygons with Systems of Inequalities *continued*

If Example 3 were a typical linear programming problem, a possible question might be "Which mix of nuts will produce the maximum profit per bag?" The answer would depend on how much customers were willing to pay for a given mix of nuts.

Suppose that customers only cared about the amount of nuts, and were willing to pay the same per pound regardless of the cashews-to-peanuts ratio. Profit would be maximized by putting in the minimum amount of cashews and then filling the bag up to the limit with peanuts. The lower right corner of the solution graph shows that a bag would contain 0.5 pound of cashews and 6 pounds of peanuts.

Practice

Graph each system of inequalities.

1. $x \le 0$
   $y \ge -3$
   $2x - y \ge -3$

2. $x + y \le 0$
   $y \ge -2$
   $4x - y \ge -10$

3. $x + 2y < 2$
   $3x - 2y \ge 6$
   $5x + 2y \ge -6$

4. $x \ge -2$
   $y \ge -3$
   $y \le 1$
   $3x + y \le 6$

5. $x \le 3$
   $y \le 4x + 2$
   $2x - 3y \ge -3$
   $x + 3y \ge -6$

6. $y \le -3x + 8$
   $4y + x \le 10$
   $y \ge -5x - 7$
   $4y - x > -7$

Use inequalities to describe each graph. Write your inequalities in slope-intercept form.

7.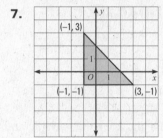

8.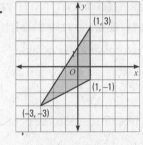

9.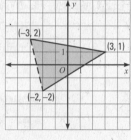

10.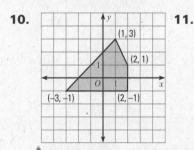

11.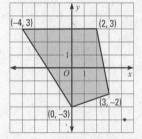

12.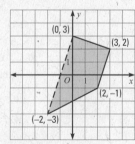

13. In Example 3, suppose that all customers really care about (and are willing to pay for) is cashews. Which mix of nuts would maximize the profit per bag?

14. **Writing** When a solid boundary meets a dashed boundary, is the corner point part of the solution of the system? Why or why not?

Pre-AP Copymasters

Adding and Subtracting Exponential Expressions

CHAPTER 7

Adding and subtracting exponential expressions differs from multiplying them. To add or subtract, like terms are combined. In other words, exponential expressions with the same base and exponent can be added or subtracted. The coefficients of the like terms are added or subtracted while the variable and power of the variable remain the same.

EXAMPLE 1 Add exponential expressions

Simplify the expression, if possible.

a. $y^2 + 2y^2$ **b.** $5x^3 + 6x + 4x^3 + 3x^2$ **c.** $2k + 5$

Solution:

a. y^2 and $2y^2$ are like terms. Add the coefficients. Keep the variable and power the same.

$$y^2 + 2y^2 = 3y^2$$

b. Add the like terms $5x^3$ and $4x^3$.

$$5x^3 + 6x + 4x^3 + 3x^2 = 5x^3 + 4x^3 + 6x + 3x^2$$
$$= 9x^3 + 6x + 3x^2$$

c. There are no like terms in $2k + 5$. This is in simplest form. ■

Example 2 shows how adding differs from multiplying exponential expressions.

EXAMPLE 2 Compare addition and multiplication of exponential expressions

Simplify the expression, if possible.

a. $3m^2 + 2m^2$ **b.** $3m^2 \cdot 2m^2$ **c.** $z^3 + z^2$ **d.** $z^3 \cdot z^2$

Solution:

a. To add like terms, add the coefficients and keep the variable and the power the same.

$$3m^2 + 2m^2 = 5m^2$$

b. To multiply powers with the same base, multiply the coefficients and add the exponents.

$$3m^2 \cdot 2m^2 = (3 \cdot 2)m^{2+2}$$
$$= 6m^4$$

c. There are no like terms in $z^3 + z^2$. This is in simplest form.

d. $z^3 \cdot z^2 = z^{3+2} = z^5$ ■

CHAPTER 7 Adding and Subtracting Exponential Expressions *continued*

Example 3 shows how to subtract exponential expressions.

EXAMPLE 3 **Subtract exponential expressions**

Simplify the expression, if possible.

a. $6c^3 - c^3$
b. $2t^4 + 2s^2 - s^2 - 3t^4$
c. $(q^3 - 2q) - (q^2 + 2q)$

Solution:

a. Subtract the coefficients and keep the variables the same.

$$6c^3 - c^3 = 5c^3$$

b. Subtract like terms only. Here, there are two sets of like terms. $2t^4$ and $3t^4$ are like terms, and $2s^2$ and s^2 are like terms.

$$2t^4 + 2s^2 - s^2 - 3t^4 = 2t^4 - 3t^4 + 2s^2 - s^2$$
$$= -t^4 + s^2$$

c. Subtract each term in the second set of parentheses by first distributing. Then subtract like terms.

$$(q^3 - 2q) - (q^2 + 2q) = q^3 - 2q - q^2 - 2q$$
$$= q^3 - q^2 - 2q - 2q$$
$$= q^3 - q^2 - 4q \ \blacksquare$$

Practice

Simplify the expression, if possible.

1. $12a^3 + 4a^3$
2. $5h^2 + 3h$
3. $6g^2 \cdot 3g^2$
4. $8j^3 - j^3$

5. $2p^2 \cdot p^2$
6. $4x + 2x^3 + 2x$
7. $3u^2 - 4u^2$
8. $6y^3 + (-4y^3)$

9. $(2w + 5y^2) + (7w + 3y^2)$
10. $(3b^2 + 5a) - (b^2 + 5a)$

11. $(2v - w^2) - (2w^2 - v)$
12. $12q^2 + 8q + 4q^2$

13. $3n^2 \cdot 4n^2 \cdot 2n$
14. $y^3 - 3y^2 + 3z^2 - y^3 + z^2$

15. $(a^2 - 2b^3 + 2) - (2a^2 - b^3 - 2)$
16. $5x^4 - (2x^3 - 4x^5 + 3x^2)$

Problem Solving

17. A square has a side length of $5x^2$ units. Find the perimeter of the square. Then find the area of the square.

18. The length of a rectangle is $2x + 3$ inches. The width of the rectangle is $4x - 5$ inches. What is the perimeter, in inches, of this rectangle?

19. The perimeter of a triangle is equal to $2x^2 - 4x + 1$ centimeters. One side of the triangle is $6x - 5$ centimeters long. Another side is $x^2 - 2x + 3$ centimeters long. Find the length of the remaining side of the triangle.

20. The perimeter of a rectangular garden is equal to $10x + 2$ yards. The width of the garden is $3x + 4$ yards. What is the length of the garden in yards?

CHAPTER 7 Simplifying Exponential Expressions

Exponential expressions can be combined through addition, subtraction, multiplication, division, and raising to powers. Examples 1 through 3 show different ways of combining these operations when simplifying exponential expressions.

EXAMPLE 1 ## Simplify exponential expressions with addition and multiplication

Simplify the expression.

$$(2x^2)^3 + (4x^2)(3x^4) = 2^3 \cdot (x^2)^3 + (4 \cdot 3)(x^2 \cdot x^4)$$
$$= 8 \cdot x^6 + 12 \cdot x^6$$
$$= 20x^6 \ \blacksquare$$

EXAMPLE 2 ## Simplify exponential expressions with addition and division

Simplify the expression.

$$\left(\frac{x}{2y^2}\right)^4 + \left(\frac{3x^2}{2y^4}\right)^2 = \frac{(x)^4}{(2y^2)^4} + \frac{(3x^2)^2}{(2y^4)^2}$$
$$= \frac{x^4}{2^4(y^2)^4} + \frac{3^2(x^2)^2}{2^2(y^4)^2}$$
$$= \frac{x^4}{16y^8} + \frac{9x^4}{4y^8}$$
$$= \frac{x^4}{16y^8} + \frac{36x^4}{16y^8}$$
$$= \frac{37x^4}{16y^8} \ \blacksquare$$

EXAMPLE 3 ## Simplify exponential expressions with subtraction, multiplication, and division

Simplify the expression.

$$\left(\frac{2m}{n^2}\right)^3 - \left(\frac{m}{n^2}\right)^5 \left(\frac{2n^2}{m}\right)^2 = \frac{2^3 m^3}{(n^2)^3} - \frac{m^5}{(n^2)^5} \cdot \frac{2^2(n^2)^2}{m^2}$$
$$= \frac{8m^3}{n^6} - \frac{m^5}{n^{10}} \cdot \frac{4n^4}{m^2}$$
$$= \frac{8m^3}{n^6} - \frac{4m^3}{n^6}$$
$$= \frac{4m^3}{n^6} \ \blacksquare$$

Simplifying Exponential Expressions *continued*

Practice

Simplify the expression.

1. $3(c^3)^2 + c^2(2c)^4$ **2.** $4(s^3)^2 - 3s^4(2s)^2$ **3.** $(6vw)^2 - 12(vw)^2$

4. $(4xy^2)^2 + (xy)(3x^3y)$ **5.** $(4ab^2)^3(a^2b^4) - (2ab^2)^5$ **6.** $(2u^4v^8)^3 + 2(u^3v^6)^4$

7. $3\left(\dfrac{h^3}{k^6}\right)^2 + 7\left(\dfrac{h^2}{k^4}\right)^3$ **8.** $\left(\dfrac{2x^3}{y}\right)^4 - \left(\dfrac{3x^6}{2y^2}\right)^2$ **9.** $\left(\dfrac{3np}{p^2}\right)^3 + \left(\dfrac{n}{p}\right)^3$

10. $4\left(\dfrac{y^6}{z^2}\right) - \left(\dfrac{-3y^3}{z}\right)^2$ **11.** $\left(\dfrac{-q^3r^2}{2qr^4}\right)^3 - \left(\dfrac{q^4r}{qr^4}\right)^2$

12. $\left(\dfrac{3r^5s^3}{4t^4}\right)^2 + \left(\dfrac{3r^4s^2}{2t^4}\right)^3\left(\dfrac{st^2}{2rs}\right)^2$ **13.** $3\left(\dfrac{2a^4bc^5}{a^2b^2c^3}\right)^2\left(\dfrac{a}{b}\right)^4 - 2\left(\dfrac{a^4c^2}{b^3}\right)^2$

14. $\left(\dfrac{-j^3}{k}\right)^4 + \left(\dfrac{j^7k}{k^5}\right) - \left(\dfrac{2j^6}{k^2}\right)^2$ **15.** $\left(\dfrac{2x^4z^2}{y^3}\right)^3 - 4\left(\dfrac{x^2z}{y}\right)^6 - \left(\dfrac{2x^6z^3}{y^3}\right)^2$

Problem Solving

16. A sidewalk with exterior dimensions 5*xy* units by 3*xy* units surrounds a rectangular pool at the town park. The pool is 2*xy* units wide and *xy* units long. Write an expression to find the area of the sidewalk. Then find the area.

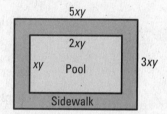

17. A rectangular piece of land is $6x^4$ feet long and $4y^2$ feet wide. A square piece of the land is used for a flower display. The display is $3x^2y$ feet long on each side. Write an expression for the area of land not covered by the flower display. Then find the area.

Name _____ Date _____

Exploring Non-Integer Exponents with a Graphing Calculator

Some of the ways to evaluate non-integer exponents with a graphing calculator are explored here.

EXAMPLE 1 ## Evaluate exponents that are multiples of $\frac{1}{2}$ with a graphing calculator

Evaluate the expression with a graphing calculator.

a. $196^{1/2}$ **b.** $4^{5/2}$

Solution:

a. Use the $\sqrt{}$ command to evaluate $196^{1/2}$.

Enter these keystrokes: [2nd] $\sqrt{}$ 196 [ENTER]

Display reads: 14

b. Another way to evaluate *any* fractional exponent is to use the [▲] command.

Enter these keystrokes: 4 [▲] [(] 5 [÷] 2 [)] [ENTER]

Display reads: 32

Notice what happens when parenthesis are *not* used to evaluate $4^{5/2}$.

Enter the keystrokes: 4 [▲] 5 [÷] 2 [ENTER]

Display reads: 512

This is not correct. By *not* using parentheses, the calculator evaluates $4^5 \div 2$.

Parentheses are used to tell the calculator to raise 4 to the $\frac{5}{2}$ power. ∎

EXAMPLE 2 ## Evaluate exponents that are multiples of $\frac{1}{3}$ with a graphing calculator

Evaluate the expression with a graphing calculator.

a. $64^{1/3}$ **b.** $125^{4/3}$ **c.** $27^{-1/3}$

Solution:

a. $64^{1/3}$ is the same as $\sqrt[3]{64}$. Use the $\sqrt[3]{}($ command found in the [MATH] menu.

Use these keystrokes: [MATH] $\sqrt[3]{}($ 64 [ENTER]

Display reads: 4

b. $125^{4/3}$ is the same as $\left(\sqrt[3]{125}\right)^4$.

Use these keystrokes: [MATH] $\sqrt[3]{}($ 125 [)] [▲] 4 [ENTER]

Display reads: 625

c. Use these keystrokes: 27 [▲] [(] −1 [÷] 3 [)] [ENTER]

Displays reads: .33333333333 ∎

| CHAPTER 7 | **Exploring Non-Integer Exponents with a Graphing Calculator** *continued* |

EXAMPLE 3 **Evaluate other non-integer exponents with a graphing calculator**

Evaluate the expression with a graphing calculator.

a. $81^{1/4}$ **b.** $32^{3/5}$

Solution:

a. $81^{1/4}$ is the same as $\sqrt[4]{81}$. Use the $\sqrt[x]{\ }$ command found in the MATH menu.

Use these keystrokes: 4 MATH $\sqrt[x]{\ }$ 81 ENTER

Display reads: 3

b. $32^{3/5}$ is the same as $\left(\sqrt[5]{32}\right)^3$.

Use these keystrokes: 5 MATH $\sqrt[x]{\ }$ 32 ▲ 3 ENTER

Display reads: 8 ■

When using the $\sqrt[x]{\ }$ function, notice the root is entered *before* the $\sqrt[x]{\ }$ function key.

EXAMPLE 4 **Evaluate expressions containing multiple fractional exponents with a graphing calculator**

Evaluate $8^{-5/3} \cdot \dfrac{64^{3/2}}{512^{-1/3}}$ with a graphing calculator.

Solution:

Use these keystrokes: 8 ▲ (((−) 5 ÷ 3) ✕ 64 ▲ (3 ÷ 2) ÷ 512 ▲ ((−) 1 ÷ 3) ENTER

Display reads: 128 ■

Practice

Evaluate the expression using a graphing calculator.

1. $9^{5/2}$ **2.** $1024^{2/5}$ **3.** $(243^{-9/10})^{2/3}$

4. $(27^{4/3})(81^{-1/4})$ **5.** $\dfrac{16^{3/4}}{(512^{-1/3})^{4/3}}$ **6.** $\dfrac{256^{5/8}}{8^{-5/3}} \cdot 64^{-2/3}$

Find two sets of keystrokes that can be used to evaluate the expression with a graphing calculator. Then evaluate the expression.

7. $25^{5/2}$ **8.** $343^{-1/3}$ **9.** $64^{5/6}$

10. $(8^{2/3})(16)^{3/4}$ **11.** $\dfrac{36^{1/2}}{(8^{2/3})^{1/2}}$ **12.** $125^{2/3} \cdot \dfrac{225^{-1/2}}{9^{3/2}}$

Pre-AP Copymasters

CHAPTER 7

Average Rates of Change

KEY CONCEPT

Average Rate of Change

A function's *average rate of change* is the amount the function increases or decreases over an interval. For a linear function, slope is a measure of the average rate of change.

EXAMPLE 1 ## Average rate of change in a linear function

Find and compare the average rates of change in each interval for the linear function $y = 4x$.

    a. $0 \le x \le 1$ **b.** $1 \le x \le 2$ **c.** $0 \le x \le 2$

Solution:

	Interval	Endpoints	Average Rate of Change
a.	$0 \le x \le 1$	$(0, 0)$ and $(1, 4)$	$\dfrac{4 - 0}{1 - 0} = 4$
b.	$1 \le x \le 2$	$(1, 4)$ and $(2, 8)$	$\dfrac{8 - 4}{2 - 1} = 4$
c.	$0 \le x \le 2$	$(0, 0)$ and $(2, 8)$	$\dfrac{8 - 0}{2 - 0} = 4$

The average rates of change are the same in each interval. Since the function is linear, the average rate of change is constant. ■

EXAMPLE 2 ## Average rate of change in an exponential function

Find and compare the average rates of change in each interval for the exponential function $y = 4^x$.

    a. $0 \le x \le 1$ **b.** $1 \le x \le 2$ **c.** $0 \le x \le 2$

Solution:

	Interval	Endpoints	Average Rate of Change
a.	$0 \le x \le 1$	$(0, 1)$ and $(1, 4)$	$\dfrac{4 - 1}{1 - 0} = 3$
b.	$1 \le x \le 2$	$(1, 4)$ and $(2, 16)$	$\dfrac{16 - 4}{2 - 1} = 12$
c.	$0 \le x \le 2$	$(0, 1)$ and $(2, 16)$	$\dfrac{16 - 1}{2 - 0} = \dfrac{15}{2} = 7.5$

The average rates of change are all different. The average rate of change is not constant. ■

Since the slope of a linear function is constant, its average rate of change is the same over all intervals. For an exponential function, its average rate of change is not constant and depends on the interval.

Average Rates of Change *continued*

EXAMPLE 3 ## Average rates of change in other non-linear functions

Describe each function's average rate of change by finding the average rate of change over two intervals.

   a. quadratic function: $y = x^2 - 3$ **b.** cubic function: $y = 2x^3 + 1$

Solution:

a.

Interval	Endpoints	Average Rate of Change
$0 \leq x \leq 1$	$(0, -3)$ and $(1, -2)$	$\dfrac{-2 - (-3)}{1 - 0} = 1$
$1 \leq x \leq 2$	$(1, -2)$ and $(2, 1)$	$\dfrac{1 - (-2)}{2 - 1} = 3$

The two average rates of change are different, so the average rate of change varies in a quadratic function.

b.

Interval	Endpoints	Average Rate of Change
$1 \leq x \leq 2$	$(1, 3)$ and $(2, 17)$	$\dfrac{17 - 3}{2 - 1} = 14$
$2 \leq x \leq 3$	$(2, 17)$ and $(3, 55)$	$\dfrac{55 - 17}{3 - 2} = 38$

The two average rates of change are different, so the average rate of change varies in a cubic function. ∎

Practice

Describe the average rate of change of the function. Explain your reasoning.

  1. $y = -2^x + 2$ **2.** $y = \dfrac{x + 1}{2}$ **3.** $y = x^2 + x - 6$ **4.** $y = \sqrt{x}$

Problem Solving

  5. Write a function that has a constant rate of change. Explain how you know it has a constant rate of change.

  6. Write a function that does not have a constant rate of change. Explain how you know the rate of change is not constant.

  7. Find the average rate of change of the function $y = x^3$ over the intervals $-1 \leq x \leq 0$, $0 \leq x \leq 1$, and $-1 \leq x \leq 1$. Explain whether or not it can be concluded that the average rate of change is constant for this function.

  8. The function below has a constant rate of change.

x	2	4	6	8	. . .
y	-7	n	-1	2	. . .

What is the value of n?

  9. A coin in Amber's collection increases in value 20% each year. Last year, the coin was worth $2.00. What is the value of the coin this year? What is the expected value of the coin 5 years from now?

CHAPTER 7

Exponential Functions: Continuous or Noncontinuous

Many of the functions you have seen so far are continuous. A *continuous* function is defined over all real numbers. Its graph is a smooth curve with no holes, breaks, jumps, or sharp turns. If a function is not defined over all real numbers, or its graph has holes, breaks, jumps, or sharp turns, then it is a *noncontinuous* function.

EXAMPLE 1 ## Identify continuous and noncontinuous functions

Graph the functions and explain whether they are continous or noncontinuous.

a. $y = \dfrac{1}{x^2}$

b. $y = \begin{cases} 2x, \text{ when } x > 2 \\ x^2, \text{ when } x < 2 \end{cases}$

c. $y = 2^x$

Solution:

a.

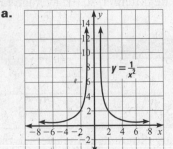

The function $y = \dfrac{1}{x^2}$ is noncontinuous since there is a break in the graph at $x = 0$. This is because the function is undefined at $x = 0$.

b.

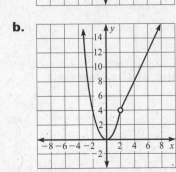

The function $y = \begin{cases} 2x, \text{ when } x > 2 \\ x^2, \text{ when } x < 2 \end{cases}$ is noncontinuous since there is a hole in the graph at $x = 2$. This is because the function is not defined at $x = 2$.

c.

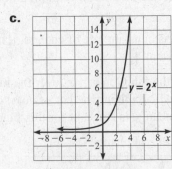

The function $y = 2^x$ is continuous since there are no breaks or holes anywhere in the graph. This is because the function is defined for all real numbers. ∎

In Example 1, part c shows a continuous exponential function, $y = 2^x$. Other exponential functions and their graphs are explored in Example 2 to determine whether they are continuous or noncontinuous.

CHAPTER
7

Exponential Functions: Continuous or Noncontinuous continued

EXAMPLE 2 **Graph exponential functions**

Graph the exponential functions and determine whether they are continuous or noncontinuous.

  a. $y = -3^x$ **b.** $y = 4^{(x-2)}$ **c.** $y = 2 \cdot \left(\frac{1}{4}\right)^x$

Solution:

a.
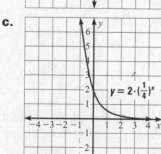
The graph of this exponential function is continuous.

b.
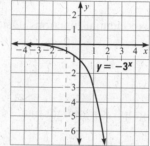
The graph of this exponential function is continuous.

c.
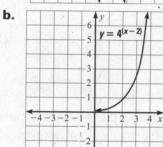
The graph of this exponential function is continuous. ■

Notice that each graph in Example 2 is continuous since each exponential function is defined for all real numbers. An exponential function will always be continuous unless there are values for which the function is undefined.

Examples 3 and 4 explore irrational exponents to determine if an exponential function could have any undefined values.

EXAMPLE 3 **Irrational exponents**

Use a graphing calculator to give an approximate value of the expression. Determine if the result is a real number.

  a. 2^π **b.** $3^{\sqrt{2}}$ **c.** $2^{\sqrt{3}}$ **d.** $\pi^{\sqrt{2}}$

Solution:

  a. $2^\pi \approx 8.825$ **b.** $3^{\sqrt{2}} \approx 4.7288$ **c.** $2^{\sqrt{3}} \approx 3.322$ **d.** $\pi^{\sqrt{2}} \approx 5.0475$

Each result is an irrational number. Therefore, each result is a real number. ■

CHAPTER
7

Exponential Functions: Continuous or Noncontinuous *continued*

Consider the exponential function $y = 2^x$ from Example 1, part c. We saw that the graph of this function is continuous since there are no breaks or holes in its graph. So, $y = 2^x$ is defined for any real number. Suppose the value of the exponent is an irrational number such as π or $\sqrt{3}$. We know that $y = 2^\pi$ and $y = 2^{\sqrt{3}}$ must be defined.

EXAMPLE 4 ## Exponential functions with irrational exponents

Use a graphing calculator to graph the exponential functions. Determine whether the graphs are continuous or noncontinuous.

a. $y = 2^\pi$ **b.** $y = \pi^{(\sqrt{2})x}$

Solution:

a. 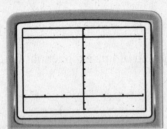   This graph is a straight line, so it is continuous.

b. 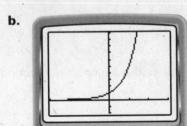   The graph of this exponential function with an irrational number in the exponent is continuous. ∎

Exponential functions are defined for all rational and irrational numbers, so they are defined for all real numbers. As a result, their graphs are continuous.

Practice

1. **Writing** Explain the difference between graphs of a continuous and a noncontinuous function.

2. **Writing** Explain whether or not all exponential functions are continuous.

Sketch a graph of the function. Determine whether the graph is continuous or noncontinuous.

3. $y = \begin{cases} \sqrt{x}, & \text{when } x > 0 \\ -2x, & \text{when } x < 0 \end{cases}$ 4. $y = \begin{cases} \frac{1}{2}x^2, & \text{when } x \leq 2 \\ x, & \text{when } x > 2 \end{cases}$

5. $y = \frac{2}{x}$ 6. $y = -|x|$ 7. $y = x^4$

8. $y = 4^x$ 9. $y = 2 \cdot 3^x$ 10. $y = -2^{(\pi x)}$

CHAPTER 7

Exponential Functions: Continuous or Noncontinuous *continued*

Problem Solving

11. Michaela bought a new car for $25,000. The value of the car depreciates 15% each year. After t years, the value of the car, v, is given by the function $v = 25,000(0.85)^t$. Find the value of the car to the nearest dollar after 1, 2, and 3 years. Then graph this function and determine whether it is continuous or noncontinuous.

12. Mr. Gordon increases the price of each bicycle in his bicycle shop by 5% each year. A bicycle that costs $200 this year will cost $200(1.05)^y$ y years from now. Explain whether this function is continuous or noncontinuous.

13. The population of a city is expected to increase by 0.8% each year. The current population is approximately 16 million. After t years, the population of this city, in millions, is expected to be $p = 16(1.008)^t$. Use a graphing calculator to graph this function. Explain whether it is continuous or noncontinuous.

14. Alex bought a computer for school last year. The value of the computer n years from now is modeled by the function $v = 750 \cdot 0.875^{(n + 1)}$. Use a graphing calculator to graph this function. Explain whether the graph of this function is continuous or noncontinuous. Determine whether or not the value of Alex's computer ever equals $0.

15. An environmentalist studying a certain endangered species counts 120 of these animals in their habitat. The population, p, of this species is decreasing according to the model $p = 120(0.96)^y$, where y is the number of years from now. About how many of these animals are expected to remain in their habitat 10 years from now? Graph this function.

16. The monthly sales of cell phones have increased at one retail shop according to the model $s = 250(1.35)^m$, where m is the number of months from now. Explain whether this function is continuous or noncontinuous.

17. The half-life of a substance is the amount of time it takes half of the substance to decay or decompose. A chemist determined the half-life of a radioactive substance to be 18 hours. The function $a = 500 \cdot \left(\frac{1}{2}\right)^{h/18}$ models the amount left, a, of 500 milligrams of this substance h hours from now. Use a graphing calculator to graph this function. Determine whether the graph of this function is continuous or noncontinuous.

CHAPTER 7

Model Limitations

Many exponential models are valid for predicting the rate of growth or decay over a short period of time. However, these models are often limited when it comes to making predictions farther into the future or when making conclusions about occurrences too far in the past.

EXAMPLE ## Limitations of a population model

During the 1990s, the population of a certain city increased from 80,000 to 180,000. The chart below lists the population of the city by year.

Year	1990	1991	1992	1993	1994	1995	1996	1997	1998	1999
Population (thousands)	80	88	95	110	129	131	140	152	167	180

This data is approximated by the exponential growth model $P = 80(2.5)^{0.1t}$, where t is the number of years since 1990.

a. The actual population of this city in the year 2005 is approximately 301,000. Explain whether or not this model is a good predictor of this population.

b. Use the growth model to predict the population of this city in the year 100 years after 1990. Explain whether you believe this prediction could be accurate.

c. Use the growth model to calculate the population of this city in the year 1989 and then in 1980. What conclusions can be made about this population model based on these results?

Solution:

a. In 2005, $t = 15$. $P = 80(2.5)^{0.1(15)} \approx 316$ thousand. The actual population and the model's population differ by about 15,000. So, the model gives a fairly close approximation and is a good predictor of the actual population in the year 2005.

b. $t = 100$. $P = 80(2.5)^{0.1(100)} \approx 763,000$ thousand or 763 million. This prediction is not very realistic. It is highly unlikely for one city to be able to have this many people.

c. In 1989, $t = -1$ and in 1980, $t = -10$. In 1989, $P = 80(2.5)^{0.1(-1)} \approx 73$ thousand. A population of approximately 73,000 in 1989 seems reasonable. In 1980, $P = 80(2.5)^{0.1(-10)} = 32$ thousand. While it is possible that this city had a population of 32,000 back in 1980, it seems too small for a city. It can be concluded that for years close to 1990, the model seems to give a more reasonable population than for years farther in the past. ■

The population model in the example made good predictions for years close to and between 1990 and 1999. However, the model seemed less accurate for years farther out into the past or future. Many exponential models are valid for only a brief period of time close to when observed data is gathered to make the model.

Practice

1. **Writing** An exponential model is used to predict the amount of defoliation on trees caused by a gypsy moth t years from now. Name at least two possible limitations of this model.

CHAPTER
7

Model Limitations continued

2. **Writing** Mrs. Wyman tracked the height of her infant daughter for 36 months, as shown in this growth chart.

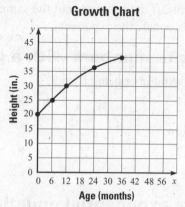

Growth Chart

Would this chart be a good predictor of height at 48 months? Would it be a good predictor of height at 480 months? Explain.

3. **Writing** In 1995, the model $P = 1000(1.025)^t$ was developed to predict the student population, P, at Lexington High School t years after 1995. The population at the high school in 2005 is approximately 1800. Is the model from 1995 a good predictor of the student population in 2005? Explain.

Problem Solving

4. Beginning in 2000, new subscriptions to a magazine could be ordered through the internet. The percent of new subscriptions being processed through the internet each year has increased according to the model $S = 9(1.2)^t$, where t is the number of years since 2000. What percent of new subscriptions were processed through the internet in 2000? Use the model to predict the percent of new subscriptions that are expected in the years 2010 and 2025. What do these percents tell about the validity of this model?

5. Daniel bought a used car for $12,000 in 2002. The value of the car after it depreciates is shown in the chart below.

Year	2002	2003	2004	2005	2006
Value ($)	12,000	8500	6000	4500	2800

The value of the car can be approximated by the function $V = 12,000(0.7)^t$, where t is the number of years since 2002. What is the expected value of the car in 2010? If the car was new in 1997, explain whether or not this model can be used to approximate the value of the car when it was new.

6. At an accessory shop, the price of sunglasses is related to the number of sunglasses, s, the shop has available for sale each month. The price, in dollars, can be modeled according to the function $P = 100 - 0.5(2)^{0.03s}$. Last month, the shop had 100 sunglasses available for sale. Use the model to find the price of the sunglasses last month. This month, the shop has 300 sunglasses available for sale. Use the model to find the price of the sunglasses this month. What does this tell you about the validity of this model?

Solving Exponential Equations

CHAPTER 7

In exponential equations, if the bases are the same, then the corresponding exponents are equivalent. To solve exponential equations when the bases are the same, equate the exponents. If the bases are not the same, try rewriting them so that they are the same and then equate the exponents.

EXAMPLE 1 ## Rewrite numbers with a given base

Write the number using base 3.

  a. 27   **b.** 81   **c.** $\frac{1}{9}$

Solution:

  a. $27 = 3 \cdot 3 \cdot 3 = 3^3$ **b.** $81 = 3 \cdot 3 \cdot 3 \cdot 3 = 3^4$ **c.** $\frac{1}{9} = \frac{1}{3 \cdot 3} = \frac{1}{3^2} = 3^{-2}$ ∎

EXAMPLE 2 ## Solve exponential equations by inspection

Solve the equation.

  a. $2^x = 8$ **b.** $9^x = 81$ **c.** $\frac{1}{25} = 5x$

Solution:

  a. $8 = 2^3$ so $2^x = 2^3$ and $x = 3$.

  b. $81 = 9^2$ so $9^x = 9^2$ and $x = 2$.

  c. $\frac{1}{25} = 5^{-2}$ so $5^x = 5^{-2}$ and $x = -2$. ∎

EXAMPLE 3 ## Solve exponential equations by equating the exponents

Solve the equation.

  a. $4^{2x} = 64$ **b.** $5^{3x-1} = 25^x$ **c.** $2^{3-2x} = \frac{1}{16}$

Solution:

  a. $64 = 4^3$, so $4^{2x} = 4^3$. Since the bases are the same, the exponents can be set equal to each other.

  $2x = 3$, so $x = \frac{3}{2}$.

  b. $25 = 5^2$, so $5^{3x-1} = 5^{2x}$; $3x - 1 = 2x$, so $x = 1$.

  c. $\frac{1}{16} = 2^{-4}$, so $2^{3-2x} = 2^{-4}$; $3 - 2x = -4$, so $7 = 2x$ and $x = \frac{7}{2}$. ∎

Solving Exponential Equations *continued*

Sometimes both base numbers may need to be rewritten in order to solve an exponential equation.

EXAMPLE 4 ## Solve exponential equations by rewriting the bases

Solve the equation.

a. $9^{2x-5} = 27^{3x}$ **b.** $4^{3x+5} = 8^{4x+2}$

Solution:

a. $9 = 3^2$ and $27 = 3^3$, so $3^{2(2x-5)} = 3^{3(3x)}$;
The bases are the same, so equate the exponents.

$$2(2x-5) = 3(3x)$$
$$4x - 10 = 9x$$
$$-10 = 5x$$
$$x = -2$$

b. $4 = 2^2$ and $8 = 2^3$, so $2^{2(3x+5)} = 2^{3(4x+2)}$.
The bases are the same, so equate the exponents.

$$2(3x+5) = 3(4x+2)$$
$$6x + 10 = 12x + 6$$
$$4 = 6x$$
$$x = \frac{2}{3} \blacksquare$$

Practice

Rewrite the number with a positive exponent using the smallest base possible.

1. 32   **2.** 625   **3.** 64   **4.** 243

Rewrite the number with a negative exponent using the smallest base possible.

5. $\frac{1}{36}$ **6.** $\frac{1}{1000}$ **7.** $\frac{1}{4}$ **8.** $\frac{1}{256}$

Solve the equation.

9. $2^x = 128$ **10.** $10^x = 100,000$ **11.** $4^x = 32$

12. $6^x = \frac{1}{216}$ **13.** $3^x = 27^{2x+1}$ **14.** $9^x = 3$

15. $16^{3x} = 4^{2x+1}$ **16.** $81^x = \frac{1}{27}$ **17.** $25^{3x-1} = 125^{x+2}$

18. $5^{2x} = 625^{3x+5}$ **19.** $\left(\frac{1}{2}\right)^{x+2} = 8$ **20.** $\left(\frac{1}{8}\right)^{2-x} = \frac{1}{16}$

21. $1000^{(2-x)} = 100^{(4-3x)}$ **22.** $\left(\frac{8}{27}\right)^{2x} = \frac{2}{3}$ **23.** $\left(\frac{125}{8}\right)^{x-3} = \left(\frac{25}{4}\right)^{2x+1}$

Pre-AP Copymasters

A Multiplication Strategy

You learned to multiply polynomials horizontally, vertically, using a table, and using the FOIL pattern. With each method, each term of the first polynomial is multiplied by each term of the second polynomial. As the number of terms in each polynomial increases, the need for organizing this multiplication becomes more important. You can use the methods learned for multiplying polynomials as tools to help with this organization.

EXAMPLE 1 ## Organize polynomial products

Find the product $(2x - 1)(3x^3 + 4x^2 - 5x - 2)$ horizontally and using a table.

Solution:

Horizontally:

$$(2x - 1)(3x^3 + 4x^2 - 5x - 2) = 2x(3x^3 + 4x^2 - 5x - 2) - 1(3x^3 + 4x^2 - 5x - 2)$$
$$= 2x(3x^3) + 2x(4x^2) + 2x(-5x) + 2x(-2) - 1(3x^3) - 1(4x^2) - 1(-5x) - 1(-2)$$
$$= 6x^4 + 8x^3 - 10x^2 - 4x - 3x^3 - 4x^2 + 5x + 2$$
$$= 6x^4 + 5x^3 - 14x^2 + x + 2$$

Using a table:

	$3x^3$	$4x^2$	$-5x$	-2
$2x$	$6x^4$	$8x^3$	$-10x^2$	$-4x$
-1	$-3x^3$	$-4x^2$	$5x$	2

$6x^4 + 8x^3 - 10x^2 - 4x - 3x^3 - 4x^2 + 5x + 2 = 6x^4 + 5x^3 - 14x^2 + x + 2$ ■

Regardless of which method is chosen, the same product results. Organization is key in helping to achieve the correct product.

In both methods used in Example 1, the two terms in the first polynomial were multiplied by the four terms in the second polynomial. The total number of multiplications that took place was 2×4 or 8. This can be verified by counting the multiplications in the horizontal method or seen visually by the 2×4 table in which the 8 spaces are filled.

When multiplying binomials by binomials, the FOIL method provides a convenient method for keeping the multiplication well organized.

KEY CONCEPT

Multiplications of Polynomials

Multiplying a polynomial with m terms by a polynomial with n terms will involve mn total multiplications.

EXAMPLE 2 ## Find the number of multiplications

Find the total number of multiplications involved.

   a. $(n^2 + 3)(4n + 1)$

   b. $(2d^5 - 6d^4 + d^2 + 4)(d^2 - 5d - 5)$

   c. $6k^2(3k^4 + 5k^2 - 2k^2 - 7k - 8)$

CHAPTER 8   # A Multiplication Strategy *continued*

Solution:

a. 2 terms in the first polynomial × 2 terms in the second polynomial = 4 total multiplications

b. 4 terms in the first polynomial × 3 terms in the second polynomial = 12 total multiplications

c. 1 term in the first polynomial × 5 terms in the second polynomial = 5 total multiplications ■

The number of terms in a polynomial product is not the same as the number of multiplications.

KEY CONCEPT

Multiplications of Polynomials

The number of terms in a polynomial product with mn multiplications will be less than or equal to mn. This is because in many polynomial products, like terms are combined. Only when there are no like terms to combine will there be a total of mn terms in the product.

Practice

Find the number of multiplications involved.

1. $w^2(3w^2 + 5w + 1)$

2. $(2q^5 - 7q^4)(2q^2 - 15q + 8)$

3. $(a^4 + 3a^3 + 6a^2 - 4)(3a^2 - 5a)$

4. $(2d^2 + 4g^2 - g)(d^2 + d - g)$

Find the number of terms in the simplified product.

5. $(2k^5 - 3k^3 + k)(k^2 - 4)$

6. $(r^3 + r^2 + 2r + 2)(r^2 - 2r - 2)$

7. $(x^2 - 2y^2)(x + 3y^2)$

8. $(2s^4 - 6s^2 + t^2)(s^2 + 6t + 1)$

Find the product.

9. $(u^4 - u^3 - u^2)(2u^2 - 3u + 2)$

10. $(2b^5 - 5b^4 + b^2 + 4b)(-5b^3 - 1)$

11. $(4p^5 + p^3 + n^4 + 4n^2)(p^3 + 3n^2 + 3)$ **12.** $(v^2 - 7z^2 + v - 2)(7v^2 + z^2 + 2v - z)$

Problem Solving

13. Four congruent squares are cut from each corner of a 30 centimeter by 50 centimeter piece of cardboard. The sides of the cardboard are then folded up to form a box. The length of each cut square is $2x$ centimeters. What are the dimensions of the box? Find an expression for the volume of the box in cubic centimeters.

14. Two years ago, Paul's rectangular garden was $x + 3$ feet long and $2x - 1$ feet wide. Last year, he lengthened each dimension by $4y - 5$ feet. This year, he lengthened the dimensions by another $z + 6$ feet. What are the new dimensions of Paul's garden? Find an expression for the area, in square feet, of the garden this year.

CHAPTER 8 **More Special Products**

Finding the cube of a binomial can be done in more than one way. One of the ways is to multiply the binomial by itself three times.

$$(a + b)^3 = (a + b)(a + b)(a + b)$$

Start by multiplying the first two binomials together.

$$(a + b)(a + b) = a^2 + 2ab + b^2$$

Multiply this result by the third binomial.

$$(a^2 + 2ab + b^2)(a + b) = a^3 + 3a^2b + 3ab^2 + b^3$$

Another way to find the product is to use the cube of a binomial pattern.

KEY CONCEPT

> ## Cube of a Binomial Pattern
>
> Algebra
>
> $(a + b)^3 = a^3 + 3a^2b + 3ab^2 + b^3$
>
> $(a - b)^3 = a^3 - 3a^2b + 3ab^2 - b^3$
>
> Example
>
> $(x + 4)^3 = x^3 + 12x^2 + 48x + 64$
>
> $(3x - 2)^3 = 27x^3 - 54x^2 + 36x - 8$

Recall that $(a + b)^2 \neq a^2 + b^2$ and $(a - b)^2 \neq a^2 - b^2$. That is because $(a + b)^2 = (a + b)(a + b)$ and $(a - b)^2 = (a - b)(a - b)$.

Notice, too, that $(a + b)^3 \neq a^3 + b^3$ and $(a - b)^3 \neq a^3 - b^3$ since $(a + b)^3 = (a + b)(a + b)(a + b)$ and $(a - b)^3 = (a - b)(a - b)(a - b)$. Each binomial is multiplied together to find the product.

EXAMPLE 1 **Use the cube of a binomial pattern**

Find the product.

  a. $(2x + 5)^3$

  b. $(4x - 1)^3$

Solution:

  a. $(2x + 5)^3 = (2x)^3 + 3(2x)^2(5) + 3(2x)(5)^2 + 5^3$
  $$= 8x^3 + 60x^2 + 150x + 125$$

  b. $(4x - 1)^3 = (4x)^3 - 3(4x)^2(1) + 3(4x)(1)^2 - 1^3$
  $$= 64x^3 + 48x^2 + 12x - 1 \blacksquare$$

Trinomials can be squared in a similar way. Grouping trinomials such as $(a + b + c)^2 = [(a + b) + c]^2$ allows for the square of a binomial pattern to be used, as shown in Example 2.

EXAMPLE 2 **Square trinomials by grouping**

Find the product.

  a. $(x^2 + 4x + 3)^2$

  b. $(6x - 2y - z)^2$

More Special Products continued

Solution

a. $(x^2 + 4x + 3)^2 = [(x^2 + 4x) + 3]^2$
$$= (x^2 + 4x)^2 + 2(x^2 + 4x)(3) + 3^2$$
$$= (x^2)^2 + 2(x^2)(4x) + (4x)^2 + 6x^2 + 24x + 9$$
$$= x^4 + 8x^3 + 16x^2 + 6x^2 + 24x + 9$$
$$= x^4 + 8x^3 + 22x^2 + 24x + 9$$

b. $(6x - 2y - z)^2 = [(6x - 2y) - z]^2$
$$= (6x - 2y)^2 - 2(6x - 2y)(z) + z^2$$
$$= (6x)^2 - 2(6x)(2y) + (2y)^2 - 12xz + 4yz + z^2$$
$$= 36x^2 - 24xy + 4y^2 - 12xz + 4yz + z^2 \blacksquare$$

Practice

1. **Writing** Explain why $(x + 3)^2 \neq x^2 + 9$.

2. **Writing** Explain why $(3x - 2y)^3 \neq 9x^3 - 4y^3$.

3. **Writing** Explain whether or not the product of $(x + y + z)^2$ is $x^2 + y^2 + z^2$. Justify your reasoning.

Find the cube of the binomial.

4. $(m + 2)^3$ 5. $(t - 7)^3$ 6. $(5k + 6)^3$

7. $(2q - 1)^3$ 8. $(c + d)^3$ 9. $(f - g)^3$

10. $(w + 2z)^3$ 11. $(4r - 3s)^3$ 12. $(-7v - 2w)^3$

Find the square of the trinomial.

13. $(x^2 + 6x + 4)^2$ 14. $(h^2 - 2h + 7)^2$ 15. $(3j^2 - j + 4)^2$

16. $(x - 3y - 2)^2$ 17. $(4y + 3w - 2z)^2$ 18. $(5m - 3r - 2q)^2$

Problem Solving

19. A moving box is shaped like a cube. Each side of the moving box is $4x - 3$ inches long. Write a polynomial that gives the volume of the moving box in cubic inches.

20. A square area of the gymnasium floor has been marked off for a sports tournament. The length of each side in feet is given by $2x^2 + 5x - 3$. Write a polynomial that gives the area, in square feet, of the floor marked off for the sports tournament.

Prime Trinomials of the Form $x^2 + bx + c$

CHAPTER 8

In Lesson 9.5, you factored trinomials of the form $x^2 + bx + c$. Sometimes trinomials of this type will not be factorable. Non-factorable trinomials are called **prime trinomials**.

KEY CONCEPT

Prime Trinomials

A trinomial of the form $x^2 + bx + c$ is prime if there are no integer factors of c whose sum equals b.

EXAMPLE

Identify prime trinomials of the form $x^2 + bx + c$

Factor the trinomial $x^2 + 3x - 6$, if possible.

Solution:

Find two factors of -6 whose sum is 3 by checking all possibilities.

Factors of -6	Sum of Factors
$1, -6$	$1 + (-6) = -5$
$-1, 6$	$-1 + 6 = 5$
$2, -3$	$2 + (-3) = -1$
$-2, 3$	$-2 + 3 = 1$

Since no two factors of -6 sum to 3, the trinomial is prime. ■

Note it can be concluded that a trinomial of the form $x^2 + bx + c$ is prime only after all possible factor combinations of c have been tried and none sum to b.

Practice

Show that the trinomial is prime.

1. $b^2 + 3b + 4$ **2.** $d^2 + 8d + 9$ **3.** $x^2 - 6x + 4$

4. $p^2 + 7p - 12$ **5.** $r^2 + 15r - 28$ **6.** $q^2 - 12q + 16$

7. $t^2 - 8t - 15$ **8.** $m^2 - 10m - 20$ **9.** $k^2 + 28k + 45$

Factor the trinomial, if possible. Otherwise write *prime*.

10. $y^2 + 15y + 24$ **11.** $s^2 + 11s - 40$ **12.** $w^2 - 18w + 36$

13. $z^2 - 12z + 27$ **14.** $u^2 + 26u - 25$ **15.** $g^2 - 11g - 42$

16. $q^2 + 20q - 100$ **17.** $h^2 - 15h - 76$ **18.** $x^2 - 30x + 64$

Name _____ Date _____

CHAPTER 8

Prime Trinomials of the Form $ax^2 + bx + c$

Recall that when factoring trinomials of the form $ax^2 + bx + c$, factors of both a and c must be combined to have a sum equaling b.

KEY CONCEPT

Prime Trinomials

A trinomial of the form $ax^2 + bx + c$ is prime if there is no integer factor combination of a and c whose sum equals b.

EXAMPLE

Identify prime trinomials of the form $ax^2 + bx + c$

Factor the trinomial $3x^2 + 5x - 4$, if possible.

Solution:

Combine factors of a and c to find a sum equaling b.

Factors of 3	Factors of −4	Possible factorization	Middle term when multiplied
1, 3	1, −4	$(x + 1)(3x - 4)$	$-4x + 3x = -x$
1, 3	−1, 4	$(x - 1)(3x + 4)$	$4x - 3x = x$
1, 3	4, −1	$(x + 4)(3x - 1)$	$-x + 12x = 11x$
1, 3	−4, 1	$(x - 4)(3x + 1)$	$x - 12x = -11x$
1, 3	2, −2	$(x + 2)(3x - 2)$	$-2x + 6x = 4x$
1, 3	−2, 2	$(x - 2)(3x + 2)$	$2x - 6x = -4x$

Since no combination of the factors of $3x^2$ and -4 sum to a middle term of $5x$, the trinomial is prime. ■

Note it can be concluded that a trinomial is prime only after all possible combinations of the factors of ax^2 and c have been tried and none sum to bx.

Practice

Show that the trinomial is prime.

1. $2x^2 + 14x + 7$ 2. $3g^2 + 15g + 6$ 3. $5y^2 - 11y + 9$

4. $4s^2 - 6s - 1$ 5. $-3p^2 + 8p - 8$ 6. $-2q^2 - 9q + 10$

Factor the trinomial, if possible. Otherwise write *prime*.

7. $3n^2 + n + 1$ 8. $7d^2 + 14d + 2$ 9. $4v^2 + 13v + 5$

10. $-k^2 - 6k + 6$ 11. $8m^2 + 19m - 3$ 12. $-4w^2 - 7w + 15$

13. $5z^2 - z - 7$ 14. $-2h^2 + 21h - 12$ 15. $6j^2 - 7j - 3$

Pre-AP Copymasters

Features of the Graph of $y = x^2$

CHAPTER 9

The **equation** $y = x^2$ is called the **parent quadratic function**. Understanding some of the properties of the graph of this equation, called a **parabola**, is essential to understanding quadratic functions and their many applications.

x	-2	-1	0	1	2
y	4	1	0	1	4

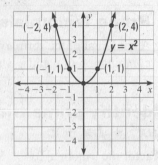

EXAMPLE 1 Demonstrate symmetry

Show that the graph of $y = x^2$ is symmetric with respect to the y-axis.

Solution:

If the graph $y = x^2$ contains the point (a, b), then it also contains the point $(-a, b)$. This is true because $b = a^2 = (-a)^2$. The points (a, b) and $(-a, b)$ are reflections of each other in the y-axis.

So, the graph of $y = x^2$ is symmetric with respect to the y-axis. ■

EXAMPLE 2 Demonstrate increasing and decreasing

Determine when the graph of $y = x^2$ is decreasing and when it is increasing.

Solution:

Looking at the graph of $y = x^2$, you can see that the graph is decreasing (downhill from left to right) when $x < 0$, and is increasing (uphill from left to right) when $x > 0$. ■

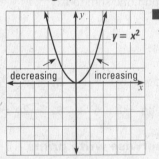

Practice

1. Find the geometric definition of a parabola in a book or on the Internet. Relate the definition to the parent quadratic function.

2. Use a reference book or the Internet to find some real life examples of parabolas.

CHAPTER 9

Average Rates of Change of Quadratic Functions

Geometrically, the **average rate of change** of a function is equal to the slope of the line through two specified points on the graph of the function.

KEY CONCEPT

Average Rate of Change

Suppose (x_1, y_1) and (x_2, y_2) are two points on a graph of a function, and that $x_1 < x_2$.

The average rate of change from x_1 to x_2 is equal to $\dfrac{y_2 - y_1}{x_2 - x_1}$.

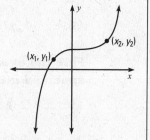

EXAMPLE 1

Find the rate of change of a quadratic function

Given the quadratic function with equation $y = x^2 + 4$, find the average rate of change from $x = 1$ to $x = 3$.

Solution:

When $x = 1$, $y = 5$ and when $x = 3$, $y = 13$.

Average rate of change from $x = 1$ to $x = 3$ is equal to $\dfrac{13 - 5}{3 - 1} = \dfrac{8}{2} = 4$. ■

EXAMPLE 2

Compare slope of a line and average rate of change

The slope of the line with equation $y = 2x - 1$ is 2. Find the average rate of change from $x = a$ to $x = b$. Show that the average rate of change is equal to the slope of the line.

Solution:

The average rate of change is $\dfrac{(2b - 1) - (2a - 1)}{b - a} = \dfrac{2b - 2a}{b - a} = \dfrac{2(b - a)}{(b - a)} = 2$

The slope of the line is equal to the average rate of change. ■

EXAMPLE 3

Find the interval given the average rate of change

Given the quadratic function with equation $y = x^2 + 2x$, find the value a for which the average rate of change from $x = 0$ to $x = a$ is equal to 4.

Solution:

When $x = 0$, $y = 0$ and when $x = a$, $y = a^2 + 2a$.

Average rate of change from $x = 0$ to $x = a$ is equal to $\dfrac{a^2 + 2a - 0}{a - 0} = \dfrac{a^2 + 2a}{a} = a + 2$.
Therefore, $a + 2 = 4$ or $a = 2$. ■

CHAPTER 9 — Average Rates of Change of Quadratic Functions *continued*

Practice

Find the average rate of change from $x = -1$ to $x = 2$ for the function.

1. $y = x^2$ **2.** $y = 3^x$ **3.** $y = -\frac{1}{2}x - 4$ **4.** $y = x^2 - 2x + 3$

5. $y = \left(\frac{1}{2}\right)^x - 1$ **6.** $y = 2x^2 - 1$ **7.** $y = -10x$ **8.** $y = (5 - x)^2$

Find the average rate of change of $y = 2x^2 + x$ over the specified interval.

9. $x = 2$ to $x = 4$ **10.** $x = -2$ to $x = -4$

11. $x = 0.25$ to $x = 1.25$ **12.** $x = -\frac{1}{2}$ to $x = 0$

If $a > 0$, find the value of a for which the average rate of change from $x = 0$ to $x = a$ is equal to 2.

13. $y = 4x^2$ **14.** $y = \frac{1}{2}x^2$

15. $y = x^2 + x + \frac{1}{2}$ **16.** $y = (x - 6)^2$

If $a < 0$, find the value of a for which the average rate of change from $x = a$ to $x = 0$ is equal to $-\frac{1}{2}$.

17. $y = 2x^2$ **18.** $y = x^2 + x$ **19.** $y = (x + 1)^2$ **20.** $y = x^2 - 1$

Find the average rate of change of the graph of the function from $x = -3$ to $x = -1$.

21.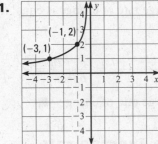

22.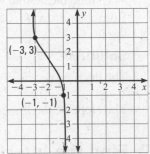

CHAPTER 9 Area Under a Graph

The area between a graph and the x-axis can be found or estimated using some familiar area formulas from geometry. This is referred to as "area under a graph".

The formulas for the area of a triangle $\left(A = \frac{1}{2}bh\right)$, a rectangle $(a = bh)$, and a trapezoid $\left(A = \frac{1}{2}h(b_1 + b_2)\right)$ are essential in finding or estimating the area under a graph.

EXAMPLE 1 Find the area under a graph: horizontal line

Find the area under the graph of $y = 2$ from $x = -3$ to $x = 5$.

Solution:

The figure below shows that the region is rectangular.

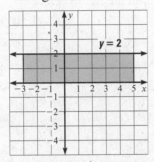

The height of the rectangle is $h = 2$ and the base of the rectangle is $b = 5 - (-3) = 8$.

So, the area under the graph is $A = bh = 8 \cdot 2 = 16$. ∎

EXAMPLE 2 Find the area under a graph: non-horizontal line

Find the area under the graph of $y = 4 - x$ from $x = -1$ to $x = 3$.

Solution:

The figure below shows that the region is in the shape of a trapezoid.

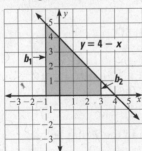

The bases, b_1 and b_2, are the vertical sides of the trapezoid and have lengths 5 and 1 respectively. The height $h = 3 - (-1) = 4$.

So, the area under the graph is $A = \frac{1}{2}h(b_1 + b_2) = \frac{1}{2} \cdot 4(5 + 1) = 12$. ∎

CHAPTER 9 | Area Under a Graph *continued*

When the graph is curved (e.g. not linear), rectangles provide an estimate of the area. The method of **inscribed rectangles** provides a good estimate of area, but will always be less than the actual area. **Circumscribed rectangles** also provide a good estimate, but will always be more than the actual area. The estimate for an area becomes increasingly accurate as more rectangles are used.

EXAMPLE 3

Use inscribed rectangles to estimate area

Find an estimate of the area under the graph of $y = 4 - x^2$ from $x = -2$ to $x = 2$ using inscribed rectangles with base length $b = 0.5$.

Solution:

There are a total of 6 such rectangles as shown in the figure below.

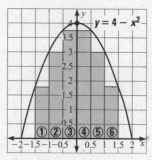

Now, we compute the area of each of the 6 rectangles as shown in the table below.

Rectangle	1	2	3	4	5	6
base b	0.5	0.5	0.5	0.5	0.5	0.5
height h	1.75	3	3.75	3.75	3	1.75
area A	0.875	1.5	1.875	1.875	1.5	0.875

Adding up the numbers in the bottom row of the table, we get an estimate of 8.5 for the area under the curve. Because we are using inscribed rectangles, this estimate is less than the actual area. ∎

EXAMPLE 4

Use circumscribed rectangles to estimate area

Find an estimate of the area under the graph of $y = 4 - x^2$ from $x = -2$ to $x = 2$ using circumscribed rectangles with base length $b = 0.5$.

Solution:

There are a total of 8 such rectangles as shown in the figure below.

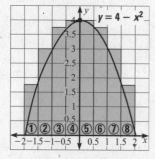

Area Under a Graph *continued*

Now, we compute the area of each of the 8 rectangles as shown in the table below.

Rectangle	1	2	3	4	5	6	7	8
base *b*	0.5	0.5	0.5	0.5	0.5	0.5	0.5	0.5
height *h*	1.75	3	3.75	4	4	3.75	3	1.75
area *A*	0.875	1.5	1.875	2	2	1.875	1.5	0.875

Adding up the numbers in the bottom row of the table, we get an estimate of 12.5 for the area under the curve. Because we are using circumscribed rectangles, this estimate is more than the actual area. ■

EXAMPLE 5   Use a graphing utility to find the area

Use a graphing utility to find the area under a curve over a certain interval.

Solution:

The **CALC** menu in most graphing calculators will have the option $\int f(x)dx$ which allows you to find the area under the curve.

We can now find a more accurate of the estimate of the area under $y = 4 - x^2$ from $x = -2$ to $x = 2$. Use -2 as our lower limit and 2 as our upper limit.

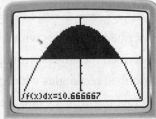

So, the area under the curve (rounded to the nearest hundredth) is approximately equal to 10.67. Notice that $8.5 < 10.67 < 12.5$. ■

Practice

Draw a graph of each situation. Then use the area formulas for triangles, rectangles, and trapezoids to solve.

1. Find the area under the graph of $y = 2x - 1$ from $x = 1$ to $x = 3$.

2. Find the area under the graph of $y - 10 = 0$ from $x = 0.25$ to $x = 1.25$.

3. Find the area under the graph of $y = -\frac{1}{2}x$ from $x = -20$ to $x = 0$.

4. Find the area under the graph of $y = x + 4$ from $x = 15$ to $x = 35$.

Area Under a Graph *continued*

Estimate the area under the graph of the function. Round decimal answers to the nearest hundredth.

5. $y = x^2 + 4$ from $x = -2$ to $x = 2$

   a. Use inscribed rectangles with base length 0.5.

   b. Use circumscribed rectangles with base length 0.5.

   c. Use a graphing utility.

6. $y = 2^x$ from $x = 0$ to $x = 1.5$

   a. Use inscribed rectangles with base length 0.5.

   b. Use circumscribed rectangles with base length 0.5.

   c. Use a graphing utility.

7. $y = 3 - x^2$ from $x = 0$ to $x = 1.5$

   a. Use inscribed rectangles with base length 0.5.

   b. Use inscribed rectangles with base length 0.4.

   c. Use inscribed rectangles with base length 0.2.

   d. Use a graphing utility. Compare with your answers to a – c.

8. $y = x^2 - 4x + 5$ from $x = 0$ to $x = 2$

   a. Use inscribed rectangles with base length 0.5.

   b. Use inscribed rectangles with base length 0.4.

   c. Use inscribed rectangles with base length 0.2.

   d. Use a graphing utility. Compare with your answers to a – c.

CHAPTER 9 Solving Quadratic Inequalitites by Graphing

Graphing can be a convenient way to solve a quadratic inequality. When a graph or part of a graph lies above the x-axis, then the y-values are positive, or greater than zero (>0). When a graph or part of a graph lies below the x-axis, then the y-values are negative, or less than zero (<0).

EXAMPLE 1 Use a graph of a quadratic function

Find where the value of the quadratic function $y = x^2 - 6x + 5$ is greater than 0 and where it is less than 0.

Solution:

Below is the graph of the quadratic function $y = x^2 - 6x + 5$.

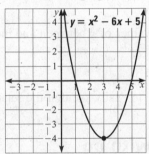

The graph lies above the x-axis for values of x less than 1 or greater than 5. Therefore, since $y > 0$ for these values of x, the solution of the inequality $x^2 - 6x + 5 > 0$ is $x < 1$ or $x > 5$.

The graph lies below the x-axis for values of x between 1 and 5. Therefore, since $y < 0$ for these values of x, the solution of the inequality $x^2 - 6x + 5 < 0$ is $1 < x < 5$. ∎

EXAMPLE 2 Graph to solve a quadratic inequality

Solve $-2x^2 + 8x \geq 0$ by graphing.

Solution:

The quadratic inequality $-2x^2 + 8x \geq 0$ can be solved by first drawing the graph of $y = -2x^2 + 8x$.

First, observe that $a = -2$. Because $a < 0$, the parabola opens down.

The line of symmetry and the x-coordinate of the vertex is $-\frac{b}{2a}$, or 2. The y-coordinate of the vertex is $y = -2(2)^2 + 8(2) = 8$. So, the vertex is (2, 8).

The table of values reveals two additional points on the graph.

x	1	4
y	6	0

Solving Quadratic Inequalitites by Graphing *continued*

Use all of this information to draw the graph.

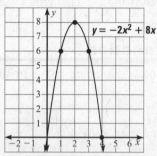

The graph is greater than or equal to zero for values of x between and including 0 and 4.

The solution set of the inequality is $0 < x < 4$. ■

The graph of a quadratic function can be used to easily see that the related quadratic inequality has no solution.

EXAMPLE 3 ## Solve a quadratic inequality with no solution

Solve $x^2 + 1 < 0$ by graphing.

Solution:

Graph $y = x^2 + 1$.

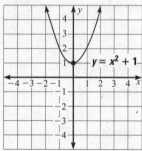

No part of the graph lies below the x-axis.

So, the inequality $x^2 + 1 < 0$ has no solution. ■

CHAPTER 9

Solving Quadratic Inequalitites by Graphing *continued*

Similarly, the graph of a quadratic function can be used to easily see that the related quadratic inequality has the set of all real numbers as its solution.

EXAMPLE 4 **Quadratic inequality with all real numbers as the solution**

Solve $-x^2 + 2x - 2 < 0$ by graphing.

Solution:

Graph $y = -x^2 + 2x - 2$. Because $a = -1$, the graph points down, and the vertex is $(1, -1)$. No portion of the graph lies above the x-axis.

The graphs shows that the solution of the quadratic inequality $-x^2 + 2x - 2 < 0$ is the set of all real numbers. So, the solution is the set of all real numbers. ■

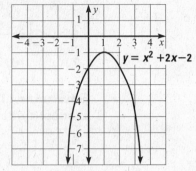

EXAMPLE 5 **Solve a quadratic inequality using a graphing calculator**

The quadratic inequality $-0.2x^2 - 1.2x + 1.2 < 0$ can be solved by graphing $y = -0.2x^2 - 1.2x + 1.2$ using a graphing calculator.

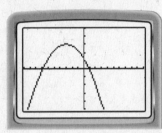

Then use the CALC menu to find zeros using a graphing calculator. The x-intercepts are 0.87 and -6.87.

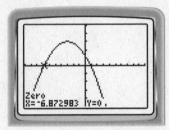
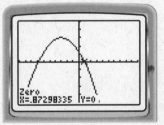

The graph lies below the x-axis for values of x less than -6.87 or greater than 0.87.

Therefore, the solution set of the inequality $-0.2x^2 - 1.2x + 1.2 < 0$ is approximately $x < -6.87$ or $x > 0.87$. ■

Pre–AP Copymasters

Solving Quadratic Inequalitites by Graphing *continued*

Practice

Solve the quadratic inequality by graphing.

1. $2x^2 - 4x > 0$

2. $-x^2 + 4x - 3 \geq 0$

3. $9 - x^2 < 0$

4. $0 \leq x^2 + x$

5. $0 < \frac{1}{4}x^2 - 6x$

6. $0 > 3x^2 + 1$

7. $x^2 + 10x \geq 0$

8. $\frac{1}{2}x^2 + x - 4 \leq 0$

Determine all values of *k* for which each quadratic inequality has no solution.

9. $x^2 + k \leq 0$

10. $kx^2 < 0$

Use a graphing calculator to solve the quadratic inequality. Round your answer to the nearest hundredth.

11. $0 > 4.6x^2 - 3.7x$

12. $0.34x^2 - 2.8 > 0$

13. $\frac{2}{3}x^2 + 3.7x - 4.9 \geq 0$

14. $\frac{1}{0.67}(4x + x^2) < 0$

Systems of Equations with at Least One Nonlinear Equation

CHAPTER 9

The solution to a system of equations can be found using algebraic methods or by graphing.

KEY CONCEPT

Solving a System of One Quadratic Equation and One Linear Equation

There are three cases to consider for a system of one quadratic equation and one linear equation.

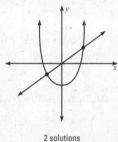

2 solutions

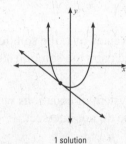

1 solution

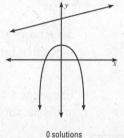

0 solutions

A system of one quadratic equation and one linear equation gives a graph of one parabola and one line.

The first case is a system with two solutions. In other words, the graphs of the parabola and line intersect in two places. You can solve a system by graphing using a graphing calculator.

EXAMPLE 1 ## Solve by graphing: two solutions

Solve the system by graphing: $x + 2y = 6$
$$y = x^2 - 3x + 4$$

Solution:

Write each equation as a function of x. Use a graphing calculator to graph the following system.

$$y_1 = -\frac{1}{2}x + 3$$

$$y_2 = x^2 - 3x + 4$$

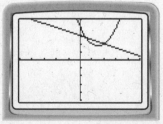

You can see that there are two intersection points. Since there are two intersection points, there are two solutions. Use the intersection option in the CALC menu of the graphing calculator to find the coordinates of the points of intersection.

The solutions of the system are (0.5, 2.75), (2, 2). ■

CHAPTER 9 Systems of Equations with at Least One Nonlinear Equation *continued*

Next, solve a system algebraically.

EXAMPLE 2 **Solving algebraically: two solutions**

Solve the system: $y = x^2 + 1$
$\qquad\qquad\qquad y = 5$

Solution:

Obtain the following equation by substitution: $x^2 + 1 = 5$

Solve for x: $x^2 = 4$
$\qquad\qquad x = \pm 2$

Because $y = 5$ for all values of x, the solutions are $(-2, 5)$, $(2, 5)$. You should always check that both ordered pairs are solutions to both equations. ∎

The second case is a system of equations with no solution. In other words, the graphs of the parabola and line do not intersect.

EXAMPLE 3 **Solve by graphing: no solution**

Solve the system: $y = 2x^2 + 1$
$\qquad\qquad\qquad 3y = x$

Solution:

Write each equation as a function of x. Use a graphing calculator to graph the following system

$y_1 = 2x^2 + 1$

$y_2 = \dfrac{1}{3}x$

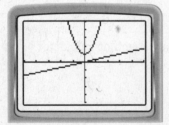

There are no intersection points, so the system has no solution. ∎

CHAPTER 9

Systems of Equations with at Least One Nonlinear Equation *continued*

EXAMPLE 4 ## Solve algebraically: no solution

Solve the system: $5x - x^2 = y$
$5x - y = -1$

Solution:

Substitute equation 1 into equation 2: $5x - (5x - x^2) = -1$

Solve for x: $x^2 = -1$

Since there is no number that can be squared to equal -1, there are no real number solutions to this equation. The system has no solution. ■

The third case is a system of equations with one solution. In other words, the graphs of the parabola and line intersect at only one point.

EXAMPLE 5 ## Solve by graphing: one solution

Solve the system: $y = x^2 + 2$
$y - 2x = 1$

Solution:

Write each equation as a function of x. Use a graphing calculator to graph the following system.

$y_1 = x^2 + 2$
$y_2 = 2x + 1$

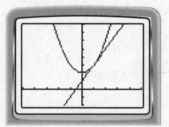

There is one intersection point. Use the intersection option in the CALC menu of a graphing calculator to find the coordinates of the point of intersection.

The solution to the system is $(1, 3)$. ■

CHAPTER 9 — Systems of Equations with at Least One Nonlinear Equation *continued*

EXAMPLE 6 — Solve algebraically: one solution

Solve the system in Example 5 algebraically: $y = x^2 + 2$
$$y - 2x = 1$$

Solution:

Solve by substituting the first equation into the second.

$$y - 2x = 1$$
$$(x^2 + 2) - 2x = 1$$
$$x^2 - 2x + 1 = 0$$
$$(x - 1)^2 = 0$$
$$x - 1 = 0$$
$$x = 1$$

Substitute $x = 1$ into the first equation, $y = 1^2 + 2 = 3$.

Therefore, the solution set is $(1, 3)$. ∎

In the examples so far, you have looked at a system of a quadratic equation and a linear equation. This concept can be extended to systems of other equations such as circles and lines, circles and parabolas, two parabolas, and two circles.

EXAMPLE 7 — Solve a system involving two parabolas: two solutions

Solve the system: $y = 4.5x^2 + 2.5x - 2.9$
$$y = -0.5x^2$$

Solution:

Use a graphing calculator to view the intersection points.

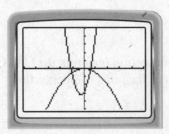

Use the intersection option in the CALC menu of the graphing calculator to approximate the intersection points.

Rounding to the nearest hundredth of a decimal place, the solutions to the system are $(0.55, -0.15)$, $(-1.05, -0.55)$. ∎

Systems of Equations with at Least One Nonlinear Equation *continued*

CHAPTER 9

EXAMPLE 8 **Solve a system involving two parabolas: no solution**

Solve the system: $y + x^2 = 0$
$ y = 2x^2 + 3$

Solution:

Write each equation as a function of x. Use a graphing calculator to graph the following system.

$y_1 = -x^2$
$y_2 = 2x^2 + 3$

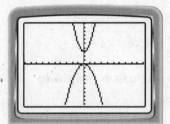

There are no intersection points, so the system has no solution. ■

Recall that an equation for a circle is given in the form $x^2 + y^2 = r^2$ where the center of the circle is at $(0, 0)$ and the radius is r. Systems with a line and a circle or a parabola and a circle can be solved graphically or algebraically.

If you solve graphically using a graphing calculator, the equation of a circle $x^2 + y^2 = r^2$, will be entered as $y_1 = \sqrt{r^2 - x^2}$ and $y_2 = -\sqrt{r^2 - x^2}$.

EXAMPLE 9 **Solve a system involving a circle and a parabola: three solutions**

Solve the system: $x^2 + y^2 = 25$
$ y = 5 - x^2$

Solution:

The first equation represents a circle with center $(0, 0)$ and radius 5. The second equation represents a parabola with vertex $(0, 5)$ that points down. Graph the following on a graphing calculator.

$y_1 = \sqrt{25 - x^2}$

$y_2 = -\sqrt{25 - x^2}$

$y_3 = 5 - x^2$

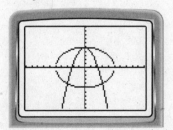

Pre-AP Copymasters

| CHAPTER 9 | **Systems of Equations with at Least One Nonlinear Equation** *continued* |

There appears to be three intersection points. Use the intersection option in the CALC menu of the graphing calculator to find the intersection points. This system has three solutions: $(0, 5)$, $(-3, -4)$, $(3, -4)$. ■

Practice

Draw an example of the situation. If the situation is not possible, then write "not possible."

1. A line and a circle that have 1 intersection point.

2. Two circles that intersect in 4 places.

3. A parabola and a circle that have 4 intersection points.

4. A line and a circle that intersect in 3 places.

Solve the system algebraically. Do not use a graphing calculator.

5. $\begin{cases} y = 7x \\ x^2 + y = 0 \end{cases}$

6. $\begin{cases} x^2 + y^2 = 100 \\ y + 6 = 0 \end{cases}$

7. $\begin{cases} x^2 + y = 9 \\ x + y = -3 \end{cases}$

8. $\begin{cases} y = 2 - x^2 \\ y = x^2 - 4x + 4 \end{cases}$

Solve the system graphically. You may use a graphing calculator. Round your answer to the nearest hundredth.

9. $\begin{cases} x^2 + 6y = 12 \\ 4 - x^2 = y \end{cases}$

10. $\begin{cases} x^2 + y = 5.2 \\ y - x = 20 \end{cases}$

11. $\begin{cases} y = x^2 + 2x + 1 \\ y + 1 = -x^2 - 2x \end{cases}$

12. $\begin{cases} x^2 + y^2 = 4 \\ x^2 + y^2 = 7 \end{cases}$

13. $\begin{cases} y = \frac{1}{2}x - x^2 \\ x - y = 2 \end{cases}$

14. $\begin{cases} y - 2x^2 = 0.1x \\ y + x^2 = 1.5 \end{cases}$

CHAPTER 9

Compare Linear, Exponential and Quadratic Graphs

It is interesting to compare and contrast some additional features of the graphs of linear, exponential and quadratic functions.

KEY CONCEPT

Increasing and Decreasing Functions

A function is said to be **always increasing** if given any two x-values a and b where $b > a$, the corresponding y-value at b is greater than the corresponding y-value at a. A function is said to be **increasing over an interval** if given any two x-values a and b in the interval where $b > a$, the corresponding y-value at b is greater than the corresponding y-value at a.

A function is said to be **always decreasing** if given any two x-values a and b where $b > a$, the corresponding y-value at b is less than the corresponding y-value at a. A function is said to be **decreasing over an interval** if given any two x-values a and b in the interval where $b > a$, the corresponding y-value at b is less than the corresponding y-value at a.

EXAMPLE 1

Features of $y = mx + b$

Show that the function $y = -2x + 1$ has a constant rate of change. Then determine where the function is decreasing and/or increasing.

Solution:

The rate of change between any two real numbers a and b ($b > a$) is:

$$\frac{(-2b + 1) - (-2a + 1)}{b - a} = \frac{-2b + 2a}{b - a} = \frac{-2(b - a)}{b - a} = -2.$$

This shows that the rate of change is constant for all values of x. The graph of the function confirms that the rate of change is constant.

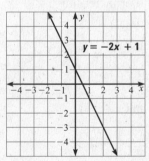

The graph is *always decreasing*. ■

If a function is increasing over an interval, then rates of change within that interval will always be positive. Similarly, if a function is decreasing over an interval, rates of change within that interval will always be negative. Portions of a graph that are straight lines will have a constant rate of change.

CHAPTER 9

Compare Linear, Exponential and Quadratic Graphs *continued*

EXAMPLE 2 ## Features of $y = ab^x$

Show that the exponential function $y = 2 \cdot 3^x$ has a variable rate of change. Then determine where the function is decreasing and/or increasing.

Solution:

Compute the rate of change from $x = 0$ to $x = 1$:

$$\frac{2 \cdot 3^1 - 2 \cdot 3^0}{1 - 0} = \frac{6 - 2}{1} = 4$$

Now, compute the rate of change from $x = 1$ to $x = 2$:

$$\frac{2 \cdot 3^2 - 2 \cdot 3^1}{2 - 1} = \frac{18 - 6}{1} = 12$$

This shows that the rate of change is variable. The graph of the function confirms that the rate of change is variable.

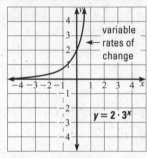

The graph is *always increasing.* ■

EXAMPLE 3 ## Features of $y = ax^2 + bx + c$

Show that the quadratic function $y = x^2 + 4x + 4$ has a variable rate of change. Then determine where the function is decreasing and/or increasing.

Solution:

Compute the rate of change between $x = -3$ and $x = -2$:

$$\frac{\left[(-2)^2 + 4(-2) + 4\right] - \left[(-3)^2 + 4(-3) + 4\right]}{-2 - (-3)} = \frac{0 - 1}{1} = -1$$

Compute the rate of change between $x = -2$ and $x = -1$.

$$\frac{\left[(-1)^2 + 4(-1) + 4\right] - \left[(-2)^2 + 4(-2) + 4\right]}{-1 - (-2)} = \frac{1 - 0}{1} = 1$$

CHAPTER 9 Compare Linear, Exponential and Quadratic Graphs *continued*

This shows that the rate of change is variable. The graph of the function confirms that the rate of change is variable.

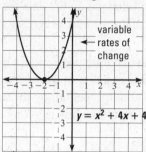

$y = x^2 + 4x + 4$

Notice that the graph is both *decreasing* and *increasing*. The vertex $(-2, 0)$ is where the graph changes from decreasing to increasing. The graph is decreasing on the interval $x < -2$, and increasing on the interval $x > 2$. ■

Practice

Use the graphs below to answer Exercises 1–3.

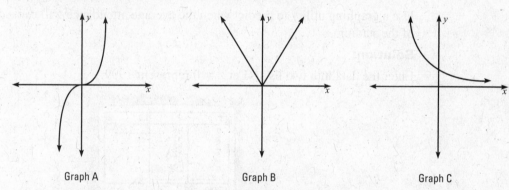

Graph A   Graph B   Graph C

1. Compare the graph of $y = x^2$ to Graph B. Compare in terms of increasing and/or decreasing, symmetry, rates of change, extreme points, and other features. Be specific.

2. Compare the graph of $y = 2x$ to graph A. Compare in terms of increasing and/or decreasing, symmetry, rates of change, extreme points, and other features.. Be specific.

3. Compare the graph of $y = 2^x$ to graph C. Compare in terms of increasing and/or decreasing, symmetry, rates of change, extreme points, and other features. Be specific.

CHAPTER 9

Using Regression Models

A regression model can be a useful tool in making future predictions about a set of data. In statistics, such a prediction is called an **extrapolation**.

There are three regression models that you will need to be familiar with: linear, exponential, and quadratic. The use of each will depend on the data that you are working with. You will use your graphing calculator to find a regression model given a set of data.

A regression model does not always provide an accurate prediction. For example, if a young boy is 48 inches tall and is now growing at a rate of about 2 inches per year, a linear model would predict that he would be about 9 feet tall by the time he was 24 years old! The linear model is accurate only when the boy is young and growing.

EXAMPLE 1 ## Use a model to predict

A sports stadium was designed to hold up to 46,000 fans at a time. The table below shows the average attendance at the stadium from the year 1999 to the year 2004.

Year	1999	2000	2001	2002	2003	2004
Average Attendance (Thousands)	41	41.5	42	42.4	43.2	43.8

Use a graphing utility to predict when the average attendance will exceed the capacity of the stadium.

Solution:

Enter the data into two lists. (Let $x = 0$ represent 1999.)

Next, make a scatter plot. The scatter plot shows a linear trend.

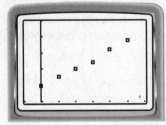

Use the linear regression feature to obtain the model $y = 0.56x + 40.9$. According to this model, the average attendance at the stadium will exceed capacity by the year 2009. ∎

CHAPTER
9

Using Regression Models *continued*

EXAMPLE 2 Choose an appropriate regression model

The population of a colony of insects is decreasing due to consumption of an insecticide.

Day	1	2	3	4	5	6
Number of Insects	1280	670	310	140	70	20

Find a quadratic model and an exponential model for this data using a graphing utility. Which model best fits the data?

Solution:

Use a graphing calculator to create a scatter plot of the data. From the scatter plot, you may think that either an exponential model or a quadratic model could fit the data.

The quadratic model $y = 71x^2 - 731x + 1902$ fits the data fairly well for the first few days, but shows a population increase after about day 5.

The exponential model $y = 3297(0.44)^x$ also fits the data well. Unlike the quadratic model, the exponential model shows a continued population decrease over time.

The exponential model best fits the data, since it predicts a continued decline in population. ■

Practice

Use a graphing utility to answer questions 1–3.

1. The table shows the value of a property over a four year period.

Year	2000	2001	2002	2003
Value (in dollars)	98,000	104,000	112,500	147,000

   a. Find an exponential model for the data in the table. (Let $x = 0$ represent the year 2000.)

   b. Use the model from part a) to predict the value of the property in the year 2020.

   c. How reasonable is your prediction from part b)?

2. The table shows the height of a palm tree for the first 5 years since it was planted.

Year	1	2	3	4	5
Height (in feet)	4	6.5	8.2	11	13.4

   a. Find a linear model for the data in the table.

   b. Use the model from part a) to predict the height of the tree in 30 years.

   c. How reasonable is your prediction from part b)?

3. The table shows the height of an airplane taking off from a runway. The height of the airplane is recorded in terms of its time (in minutes) from the runway.

Minutes from Runway	0.5	1	1.5	2
Height (in meters)	75	200	400	650

   a. Find an exponential model for the data in the table.

   b. Use the model from part a) to predict the height of the plane when it is 5.5 minutes after take off.

   c. How reasonable is your prediction from part b)?

CHAPTER 9 Describing Regions Bounded by Graphs

It is important to be able to describe regions that are bounded by two or more graphs. Specifically, you should be able to describe the region using appropriate inequalities. You should also be able to identify and label significant points of the region such as vertices (where the graphs intersect), as well other extreme points of the region.

EXAMPLE 1 ### Describe a region using a system of inequalities

Describe the region bounded by the graphs of $y = 3^x$ and $y = 4 - x^2$ using appropriate inequalities.

Solution:

Begin by graphing both equations.

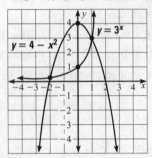

The region consists of

- All points above the graph of : $y = 3^x$: $(y \geq 3^x)$
- All points below the graph of : $y = 4 - x^2$: $(y \leq 4 - x^2)$

So, the region is described by the following system of inequalities:

$$y \geq 3^x$$
$$y \leq 4 - x^2 \quad \blacksquare$$

When a region is enclosed by the intersection of two graphs that are functions, there will be a left and a right intersection point. These intersection points are called **vertices**.

EXAMPLE 2 ### Find vertices of an enclosed region algebraically

Find the two vertices of the region bounded by the graphs of $y = x^2$ and $y = x + 2$ algebraically.

Solution:

Using algebraic methods, we can substitute $y = x^2$ into $y = x + 2$ to obtain the following:
$x^2 = x + 2$

Next, solve for x:

$$x^2 - x - 2 = 0$$
$$(x + 1)(x - 2) = 0$$
$$x + 1 = 0 \quad \text{or} \quad x - 2 = 0$$
$$x = -1 \quad \text{or} \quad x = 2$$

CHAPTER 9 ## Describing Regions Bounded by Graphs *continued*

Substitute the values of x into either function to find the corresponding values of y. If $x = -1$, $y = 1$ and if $x = 2$, $y = 4$.

So, the left vertex is $(-1, 1)$ and the right vertex is $(2, 4)$.

Check this result by sketching a graph of the two equations.

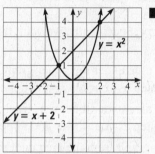

A graphing utility can also be used to find the vertices.

EXAMPLE 3 ## Find vertices using a graphing utility

Find the vertices of the region bounded by the graphs of $y = 2(0.5)^x$ and $y = -x^2 + x + 2$.

Solution:

Begin by graphing the two equations.

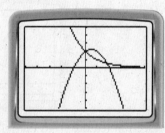

Looking at the region formed, you can see that there are two vertices. Use the intersection feature from the CALC menu of a graphing utility to locate the vertices. The left vertex is $(0, 2)$ and the right vertex is approximately $(1.79, 0.58)$. ■

Describing Regions Bounded by Graphs *continued*

With the aid of a graphing utility, we can find the approximate area of a region enclosed by two graphs.

For example, suppose a region is enclosed by two graphs above the *x*-axis. The approximate area of the region can be found by using a graphing calculator as follows.

- Draw the graph of the region.

- Find the coordinates of each vertex. Specifically, we want the *x*-coordinates of each vertex.

- Use a graphing utility to find the area under the upper graph. Use the *x*-coordinates from the previous step as your lower and upper limits.

- Use a graphing utility to find the area under the lower graph. Use the *x*-coordinates from the previous step as your lower and upper limits.

- Subtract the area under the lower graph from the area under the upper graph.

EXAMPLE 4
Find the area of a region

Find the approximate area of the region bounded by the graphs of $y = 3x^2 + 6x + 5$ and $y = -2x + 3.5$.

Solution:

Begin by graphing the region.

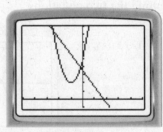

Using the intersection feature from the CALC menu of a graphing utility, the coordinates of the left vertex are approximately $(-2.5, 8.4)$ and the coordinates of the right vertex are approximately $(-0.2, 3.9)$. After finding the coordinates of each vertex, use the *x*-coordinates for the lower and upper limits. The lower limit is $x = -2.5$ and the upper limit is $x = -0.2$. Note that these are approximate values.

The upper graph comes from the equation $y = -2x + 3.5$. Using the $\int f(x)dx$ command from the CALC menu, enter the lower and upper limits and find the approximate area under the upper region to be 14.3. The lower graph comes from the equation $y = 3x^2 + 6x + 5$. Again using the $\int f(x)dx$ command, enter the lower and upper limits and find the approximate area of the lower region to be 8.5.

So, the approximate area of the region is $14.3 - 8.5 = 5.8$. ■

When you study calculus, you will learn exactly what $\int f(x)dx$ means. For now, think of it as the area under the curve for a given interval provided that the curve lies above the *x*-axis.

Describing Regions Bounded by Graphs *continued*

Another important calculation that you will need to understand in further studies of mathematics is the vertical distance between two curves given a specific x-coordinate. This can be called the *vertical distance* across a region at $x = a$.

EXAMPLE 5 ### Find the vertical distance across a region at $x = a$

Find the vertical distance across the region bounded by the graphs of $y = 5 - x^2$ and $y = x^2 - 2x + 2$ at $x = 1$.

Solution:

Begin by graphing the region.

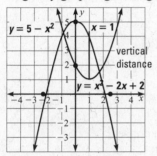

We obtain the vertical distance by subtracting the y-coordinate of the upper graph $y = 5 - x^2$ from the y-coordinate of the lower graph $y = x^2 - 2x + 2$.

y-coordinate of upper graph: $y = 5 - (1)^2 = 4$

y-coordinate of lower graph: $y = (1)^2 - 2(1) + 2 = 1$

So, the vertical distance is $4 - 1 = 3$. ∎

Practice

For the pair of curves, (a) use appropriate inequalities to describe the region enclosed by the equations and (b) use appropriate methods to find the vertices.

1. $y = \frac{1}{2}(3)^x$ and $y = -x^2 + 2x + 6$

2. $y = 1 - x^2$ and $y = x^2 - 1$

3. $y = 18 - x$ and $y = \frac{1}{2}x^2 + 14$

4. $y = 2^x - 1$ and $y = \frac{x}{10}$

5. $y = 0.25x^2 + 9$ and $y = 3x^2 - 2x + 1$

6. $y = 4x^2 - x + 0.5$ and $y = \left(\frac{1}{4}\right)^x$

Pre–AP Copymasters

Describing Regions Bounded by Graphs *continued*

Find the vertical distance between the graphs at the indicated value of x.

7. $y = 2^x + 1$ and $y = -x^2 - 4x + 2$ at $x = -2$

8. $y = 5$ and $y = 0.6x^2 - 1$ at $x = 2$

9. $y = x + 12$ and $y = (1 - x)^2$ at $x = -1$

10. $y = -x$ and $y = x^2 + 2x - 9$ at $x = -3$

Use a graphing calculator to find the approximate area to the nearest hundredths of a decimal place.

11. The region described in Exercise 1

12. The region described in Exercise 3

13. The region described in Exercise 5

14. The region described in Exercise 6

15. **Challenge** The region described in Exercise 2

More Examples of Bias

CHAPTER 10

A random sample is a sample where each member of the population has an equal chance of being in the sample. When members of a population do not have an equal chance of being in the population, then the sampling method is said to be **biased**.

EXAMPLE 1 A biased sample

A grocery store wants to know if costumers are satisfied with the new delicatessen. The grocery store places a survey on their website. Is this sampling method biased?

Yes. This question is biased towards those who have computer access. ■

The wording of a question on a survey can greatly influence the answers given. When a survey question directly or indirectly forces a certain response, then the question is biased. Extra care should be given to the wording of a question.

EXAMPLE 2 Forcing a response

John is running for class president. He gives out a survey to see how he compares with his competitor. He puts the following question on the survey: "Do you want to vote for me because I am the better candidate". Is this question biased?

Yes. This is a bad question because it tries to influence the respondent. ■

Every effort should be made to respect the privacy of survey respondents. If a survey question causes embarrassment or forces dishonesty on the part of the respondent, then it is a bad survey question.

EXAMPLE 3 Identifying respondents

The student government wants to survey the student body to see how many students have overdue library books. On the survey, the respondents are asked to write their names at the top of the survey, and indicate if they have any overdue library books. Is this question biased?

Yes. Here, a respondent who has an overdue library book might be tempted to answer dishonestly to avoid embarrassment. Asking for a name on a survey is rarely a good idea. ■

EXAMPLE 4 Oral questions versus written questions

Suppose you want to take a survey of adults to see how much they earn annually. Is this an appropriate oral question?

No. Issues of personal income are considered personal matters, so an oral question would not be appropriate.

This kind of survey question is best in written form, where the respondent can answer anonymously. ■

CHAPTER 10 **More Examples of Bias** *continued*

Good questions are mutually exclusive.

EXAMPLE 5 **Mutually exclusive questions**

Is this a good question: "Did you grow up on a farm, in the country, or in the city?"

No. This question is not mutually exclusive because most farms are in the country. Therefore, this is not a good question. ■

EXAMPLE 6 **Good questions should not make assumptions**

Is this a good question: "What kind of car do you drive?"

No. This is not a good question because it assumes that the respondent owns or has access to a car.

Survey questions should avoid unfamiliar words and abbreviations. A survey question such as "Do you believe the AGC excise should be semiannual?" is confusing. What does AGC represent? Will all respondents know the meanings of the words in the question?

Here is a possible improvement on the wording of the question: "Do you believe that the American General Contractors' dues should be collected twice a year?" ■

Practice

Describe if each situation represents bias or a poor question. Explain your reasoning.

1. Carl is handing out surveys at lunch. On the survey, he asks respondents to write their names and then write their favorite sport.

2. "Candidate *A* should be elected because she has more experience. Are you going to vote for candidate *A* or candidate *B*?"

3. Mrs. Chang has 30 students in her English class. She selects 4 of the students by blindly drawing names from a hat.

4. "Do you prefer salad or vegetables with your dinner?"

5. Amy wants to know the political preferences of the people at her school. She walks up to 10 of her classmates and asks them what their political preference is.

6. "Do you play soccer, football, or another sport?"

7. "Painting the school library would be very expensive for the school. Do you think the school library should be painted?"

8. "How many hours of TV do you watch per day?"

CHAPTER 10 Interpreting More Graphs

You have learned how to interpret data from stem-and-leaf plots, frequency tables, box-and-whisker plots, and histograms. Now you will learn to interpret data from line graphs, double line graphs, and double bar graphs.

Line graphs are used to show how data changes over a period of time.

EXAMPLE 1 **The graph below shows the sales of homes throughout the year for a certain city. Answer each question, or explain why you cannot answer the question.**

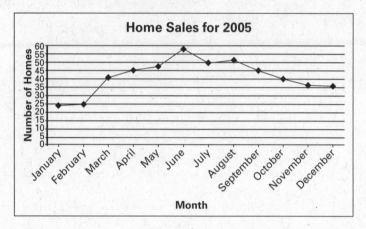

a. Exactly how many homes were sold in May?

b. Which month had the greatest number of home sales?

c. Between which two consecutive months do you see the greatest increase in the number of homes sold?

Solution

a. Look for the point above May: it lies between 45 and 50 homes. An exact number cannot be determined from this graph.

b. Look for the highest point on the graph. June had the greatest number of home sales.

c. Look for the steepest increasing line segment. The greatest increase in the number of homes sold occurred between February and March. ■

Checkpoint for Example 1

Use the graph from Example 1 to answer each exercise, or explain why you cannot answer the exercise.

1. Between which two consecutive months did the number of homes sold change the most?

2. Approximately how many homes were sold in July and August?

3. Exactly how many homes were sold in 2005?

Interpreting More Graphs *continued*

Double line graphs show how data changes over time for two sets of data. A key will show which graph belongs to which category.

EXAMPLE 2 **The graph below compares the number of ice-cream and frozen yogurt cones sold at a stand for a period of six weeks. Answer each question, or explain why you cannot answer the question.**

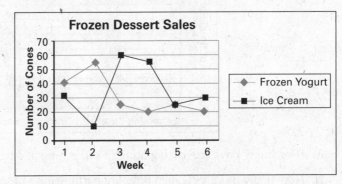

a. In week 1, which type of cone was sold the most?

b. Which dessert had the greatest increase between any two consecutive weeks? Between which two weeks was this increase?

c. During which week was the sale of ice cream and frozen yogurt the same? How much of each was sold?

Solution

a. Look for the higher symbol above week 1. Frozen yogurt had the most sales during week 1.

b. Look for the steepest increasing line segment. Ice cream had the largest increase between two consecutive weeks. This happened between weeks 2 and 3.

c. Look for the point where the graphs intersect. The sale of ice cream and frozen yogurt was the same during week 5. The exact amount of the sales cannot be determined because of the scale of this graph. ■

Checkpoint for Example 2

Use the graph from Example 2 to answer each exercise, or explain why you cannot answer the exercise.

4. Which type of cone was sold the most over the first 3 weeks?

5. Were more ice-cream cones or more frozen yogurt cones sold during week 4? Approximately how many more?

6. During which week do you see the greatest difference between the types of cones sold? What is this difference?

CHAPTER 10 **Interpreting More Graphs** *continued*

Double bar graphs are used to compare two sets of data by category.

EXAMPLE 3 **The graph below shows the number of students participating in four types of sports at a middle school. Answer each question, or explain why you cannot answer the question.**

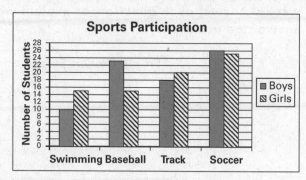

a. How many boys are participating in swimming and baseball?

b. How many more girls than boys are participating in track?

c. In which sport is there the greatest difference between the participation of boys and girls?

Solution

a. Look at the bars for boys' swimming and boys' baseball. Notice that the number of boys who participate in baseball is between 22 and 24. Since the number of boys has to be a whole number we know that 23 boys participate in baseball. Add the number of boys who participate in swimming to the number of boys who participate in baseball. 33 boys participate in swimming and baseball.

b. Look at the height of each bar above track. There are 18 boys and 20 girls who participate in track. Subtract the number of boys from the number of girls who participate. Two more girls participate in track than boys.

c. Look at the heights of each pair of bars and look for the pair with the greatest difference. The sport with the greatest difference between the participation of boys and girls is baseball. ∎

Checkpoint for Example 3

Use the graph from Example 3 to answer each exercise, or explain why you cannot answer the exercise.

7. Which sport shows the smallest difference in participation between boys and girls?

8. What is the total number of students participating in soccer at this school?

9. Which sports have the same number of girls participating? How many girls participate in each?

CHAPTER 10 | # Interpreting More Graphs *continued*

Practice

Use each graph to answer Exercises 1–3. Answer each exercise, or explain why you cannot answer the exercise.

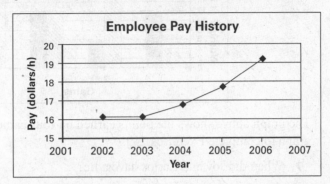

The graph above shows the pay, in dollars per hour, of an employee who worked for the same company for a period of five years.

1. Between which two years did the employee not receive a raise?

2. Between which two years did the employee receive the biggest raise? How much was the raise?

3. Approximately how much more per hour was the employee making in 2006 than in 2002?

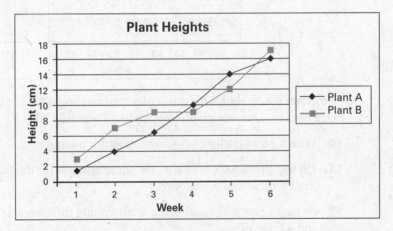

The graph above shows the heights of two plants, to the nearest centimeter, recorded for a period of 6 weeks that were grown under different conditions. Use this graph to complete Exercises 4–6.

4. When was plant A taller than plant B?

5. Which plant had a week with no growth?

6. Between which two weeks did plant B have its greatest growth? How many centimeters did it grow during that time?

CHAPTER 10 **Interpreting More Graphs** *continued*

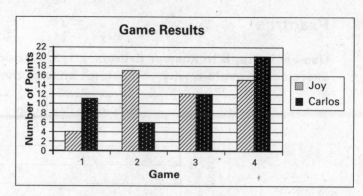

The graph above shows the points earned on four games by Joy and Carlos. Use this graph to complete Exercises 7–9.

7. When did Joy and Carlos have a tie?

8. On what game was the biggest difference in the number of points? How much was the difference?

9. What is Joy's total number of points for all four games?

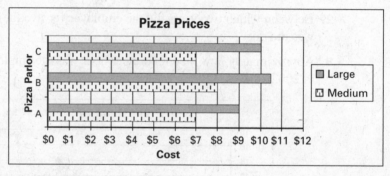

The graph above shows the costs of a medium and a large pizza at three different pizza parlors. Use this graph to complete Exercises 10–13.

10. Which pizza parlor charges the most for a large pizza?

11. Do any pizza parlors charge the same amount for the same size pizza? Which pizza parlors and which size?

12. At pizza parlor B, what is the approximate difference in price between a medium and a large pizza?

13. Suppose you want to order two medium pizzas and one large pizza. About how much would you save by going to pizza parlor A instead of pizza parlor B?

CHAPTER 10 **Introduction to Standard Deviation**

Box-and-whisker plots provide a visual representation of how varied, or spread out, a set of data is. Just as there are different measures that can be used to describe the *average* of a data set, so there are also different measures that can be used to describe the *spread* of a set of data. You are already familiar with one measure of spread called the *range*, or the difference between the greatest and least data values.

Another measure of spread that is commonly used in statistics is called the **standard deviation**. The standard deviation measures the average distance of a data value from the mean.

EXAMPLE 1 ## Understanding Standard Deviation

Two students' test scores on five tests are shown below.

> **Student A: 81, 84, 85, 87, 88**
> **Student B: 62, 76, 88, 95, 99**

a. Find the mean test score for each student.

To find the mean, find the sum of the test scores and then divide by the number of test scores:

$$\text{Mean for Student A:} \quad \frac{81 + 84 + 85 + 87 + 88}{5} = \frac{425}{5} = 85$$

$$\text{Mean for Student B:} \quad \frac{62 + 76 + 88 + 95 + 99}{5} = \frac{420}{5} = 84$$

b. Which set of scores would you expect to have the *greater* standard deviation? Why?

Standard deviation is a measure of average distance from the mean.

Student A's test scores are all clustered very close to the mean of 85. In fact, the furthest score from the mean, 81, is only 4 points away.

Student B's scores are much more spread out, with all scores *at least* 4 points away from the mean of 84. The furthest score from the mean, 62, is 22 points away.

So, you can expect the standard deviation of Student B's test scores to be greater than that for Student A. ■

Checkpoint for Example 1

The numbers of runs scored in six games by two baseball teams is shown below.

> **Red Team: 2, 3, 12, 0, 10, 0**
> **Blue Team: 4, 4, 2, 3, 6, 2**

1. Find the mean number of runs scored for each team.

2. Which set of scores can you expect to have the greater standard deviation? Explain.

Introduction to Standard Deviation *continued*

Finding the standard deviation for a set of data requires several steps. The reasoning behind some of the steps can be quite complex. These reasons will be discussed in a later course.

KEY CONCEPT

To find the standard deviation of a set of data:

Step 1: Find the difference between each value and the mean.
Step 2: Square each difference.
Step 3: Find the mean of the squared differences.
Step 4: Take the square root of the mean found in Step 3.

EXAMPLE 2 ## Finding the Standard Deviation of a Data Set

Find the standard deviation for Student A's test scores from Example 1. Round your answer to the nearest hundredth.

STEP 1 Find the difference between each value and the mean.

In Example 1, the mean of Student A's test scores was found to be 85. Subtract 85 from each data value.

Data Value	81	84	85	87	88
Difference from the Mean	−4	−1	0	2	3

STEP 2 Square each difference.

Data Value	81	84	85	87	88
Difference from the Mean	−4	−1	0	2	3
Square of the Difference	16	1	0	4	9

STEP 3 Find the mean of the squared differences.

$$\text{Mean} = \frac{16 + 1 + 0 + 4 + 9}{5} = \frac{30}{5} = 6$$

STEP 4 Take the square root of the mean found in Step 3.

$$\sqrt{6} \approx 2.45$$

So, the standard deviation of Student A's test scores is approximately 2.45. ■

Checkpoint for Example 2

3. Find the standard deviation for Student B's test scores from Example 1.

4. How do the actual standard deviations for each students' test scores compare to your prediction from Example 1, part (b)?

5. Find the standard deviation for the runs scored for each of the following teams. Round your answers to the nearest hundredth.
   Red Team: 2, 3, 12, 0, 10, 0
   Blue Team: 4, 4, 2, 3, 6, 2

| CHAPTER 10 | Introduction to Standard Deviation *continued* |

EXAMPLE 3 ## Using Standard Deviation

Dana and Steve each conducted an experiment to find the average respiration rate (in breaths per minute) of goldfish at a certain temperature. The results of their trials are shown in the table.

Dana's Trials	Steve's Trials
85, 90, 91, 91, 91, 91, 92, 92, 93, 93, 93, 95, 96, 96, 97	85, 85, 86, 86, 87, 90, 91, 92, 93, 94, 95, 95, 96, 96, 97

a. Which measure of spread would be better to use to compare the data sets to find how they are different: range or standard deviation?

The minimum and maximum values in each set are the same, so the sets have the same range: $97 - 85 = 12$.

Since the *values* in the data sets differ, it is likely that the standard deviations are different, so it would be better to use the standard deviation to compare the data sets.

b. Find the mean of each data set.

Mean for Dana's trials: $\frac{1386}{15} = 92.4$ Mean for Steve's trials: $\frac{1368}{15} = 91.2$

c. The standard deviation for Dana's trials is approximately 2.87. How many of Dana's trials are within one standard deviation of the mean?

A value that is within one standard deviation of the mean falls within the range of values from one standard deviation *below* the mean, to one standard deviation *above* the mean. For Dana's trials, these are any values between $92.4 - 2.87 = 89.53$ and $92.4 + 2.87 = 95.27$. Of her fifteen trials, 11 of them fall within one standard deviation of the mean.

d. The standard deviation for Steve's trials is about 4.25. How many of Steve's trials are within one standard deviation of the mean?

For Steve's trials, these are any values between $91.2 - 4.25 = 86.95$ and $91.2 + 4.25 = 95.45$. Of his fifteen trials, 8 of them fall within one standard deviation of the mean.

e. Which set of data is more tightly clustered about the mean?

Dana's data set has a lower standard deviation and a greater number of data values falling within one standard deviation of the mean. So, the results from Dana's trials are more tightly clustered about the mean than those from Steve's trials. ■

Checkpoint for Example 3

6. Amy repeated Dana and Steve's experiment and obtained the data shown.

Amy's Trials
86, 89, 90, 90, 91, 91, 91, 92, 93, 94, 97, 98, 98, 99, 99

   a. What is the mean of this data set?

   b. The standard deviation for Amy's trials is approximately 3.95. How many of Amy's trials are within one standard deviation of the mean?

   c. How do Amy's results compare to those of Dana and Steve?

Pre-AP Copymasters

CHAPTER 10	**Introduction to Standard Deviation** *continued*

Practice

For each set of data, calculate the mean and standard deviation. Round your answers to the nearest hundredth.

1. 10, 10, 11, 12, 12, 13

2. 3, 5, 7, 7, 7, 7, 7, 7, 7, 7, 7

3. 24, 30, 31, 34, 29, 23

4. 1, 2, 3, 4, 5, 6, 7, 8, 9, 10

5. 90, 95, 96, 92, 90, 93, 92

6. **Challenge** x, $2x$, x, $3x$, x, $4x$, x, $5x$

7. **Writing** Calculate the mean and standard deviation of the data set: 0, 0, 0, 0, 0, 0, 0, 0. Now calculate the mean and standard deviation of the data set: 1, 1, 1, 1, 1, 1, 1, 1, 1, 1. Can you generate a data set whose standard deviation is zero even though not every entry is the same number? Explain.

8. **Multiple Choice** Which of the following sets of data do you expect to have the largest standard deviation?

   A. 1, 3, 5   **B.** 24, 25, 26   **C.** 100, 100, 100   **D.** 10, 20, 30

Problem Solving

9. A college lacrosse team scored 9, 9, 11, 12, 9, 17, 9, 11, 10, and 8 times in their first 10 games. What is the mean and standard deviation of this team's goals?

10. A woman's lacrosse team scored 12, 8, 17, 17, 15, 21, 16, 12, 10, and 9 times in their first 10 games. What is the mean and standard deviation of this team's goals? How does it compare with your answer to Exercise 9?

11. Using a chemical assay, a scientist found that the concentration of proteins in a series of test tubes was 30, 35, 34, 36, 34, 33, 34, 35, 34 mg/mL. Using a light assay, the concentrations were read as 30, 34, 39, 26, 31, 32, 35, 37, 40 mg/mL. Calculate the mean concentration of the test tubes for each of the assay methods. Calculate the standard deviation for each data set. Which method was a more precise measurement technique?

12. **Open-Ended Math** Toss a coin 20 times. Record 0 if it lands on heads and 1 if it lands on tails. Calculate the mean and standard deviation of your data set.

Introduction to Standard Deviation *continued*

Using statistics, it can be shown that the average of all sets of data tends to a *normal distribution* as the experimenter makes more and more observations. The normal distribution is a mathematical function that describes the probability of observing any given event during the experiment. An especially nice property of normally distributed data sets is that approximately 68% of the observed trials will fall within one standard deviation of the mean, approximately 95% of the observed trials will fall within two standard deviations of the mean and approximately 99.7% of the observed trials will fall within three standard deviations of the mean.

For each set of data, determine the mean and standard deviation, and then determine how many values fall within the first standard deviation.

13. 15, 16, 18, 21, 25, 29, 31

14. 10, 20, 30, 40, 50, 60

15. Most statisticians consider any trial that falls outside the third standard deviation to be an outlier.

   a. Calculate the mean and standard deviation for this set of data: 9, 5, 6, 8, 8, 6.

   b. Draw a box-and-whisker plot for the data.

   c. An extreme outlier is defined to be greater than 3 standard deviations from the mean. Use your answer from part (a) and the given definition to find an extreme outlier larger than the mean.

   d. Now recalculate the standard deviation of the data set, including the extreme outlier from part (c). What happens to the mean and standard deviation?

CHAPTER 11 Probability Distributions and Expected Value

Probability is defined as the number of favorable outcomes divided by the total number of outcomes. The number of favorable outcomes will always be less than or equal to the total number of outcomes, which makes the value of any probability less than or equal to 1.

KEY CONCEPT

Laws of Probability

There are two important laws to become familiar with when working with probabilities:

Law #1: The probability that a certain outcome will occur is a number greater than or equal to 0, and less than or equal to 1.

Law #2: The sum of the probabilities of all possible individual outcomes is equal to 1.

EXAMPLE 1 ## Demonstrate Law #1 and Law #2

A small bookshelf has 50 books: 20 fiction and 30 non-fiction. A book is randomly selected from the shelf. What is the probability that the book is non-fiction?

Solution:

The probability that the book selected is non-fiction is equal to 30 (number of favorable outcomes) divided by 50 (total number of outcomes), which is equal to 0.6. This demonstrates Law #1.

There are two outcomes in this experiment: selecting a fiction book or selecting a non-fiction book. The probability of selecting a fiction book is equal to 0.4 and the probability of selecting a non-fiction book is equal to 0.6. Notice that the sum of these probabilities is equal to 1, which demonstrates Law #2. ∎

An **experiment** is a situation that involves a probability that leads to certain outcomes. Rolling a number cube is considered an experiment. The outcome of the experiment is the number that the cube lands on (1, 2, 3, 4, 5, or 6). The probability of each individual outcome is $\frac{1}{6}$, which is approximately equal to 0.17.

A **probability distribution** is a table, chart, or graph that shows the probability for each outcome.

EXAMPLE 2 ## Find a probability distribution with equal outcomes

Consider again the experiment of rolling a number cube. What is the probability distribution for this experiment?

Solution:

We want to make a probability distribution table for this situation. We know that there are a total of 6 outcomes, and that the probability of each outcome is $\frac{1}{6}$.

Algebra 1
Pre-AP

| CHAPTER 11 | **Probability Distributions and Expected Value** *continued* |

Below is a probability distribution table for this situation.

Outcome	Probability of Outcome
1	$\frac{1}{6}$
2	$\frac{1}{6}$
3	$\frac{1}{6}$
4	$\frac{1}{6}$
5	$\frac{1}{6}$
6	$\frac{1}{6}$

Notice that the sum of all 6 probabilities is equal to 1 (Law #2) ■

In the last example, all of the outcomes had an equal chance of occurring. In the next example, the outcomes do not have an equal chance of happening.

EXAMPLE 3 **Find a probability distribution with unequal outcomes**

Consider another experiment using the spinner shown below:

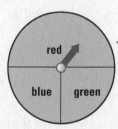

What is the probability distribution for this experiment?

Solution:

Spinning the spinner is an experiment with the following outcomes: red, blue, and green. After spinning, the spinner has an equal chance of landing on either the blue or the green sections. However, the spinner has twice the likelihood of landing in the red section because of its relative size (50% of the spinner outcome space).

| CHAPTER 11 | **Probability Distributions and Expected Value** *continued* |

Below is a probability distribution for this situation.

Section	Probability of Outcome
blue	$\frac{1}{4}$
green	$\frac{1}{4}$
red	$\frac{1}{2}$

Again, notice that the sum of the probabilities is equal to 1. ■

Law #2 is useful when finding missing probabilities in a probability distribution.

EXAMPLE 4 ## Find missing probabilities in a distribution

A deck of cards used for a game contains blue, yellow and orange cards. The probability distribution for randomly selecting each of the cards from the deck is shown below:

Card Color	Probability of Randomly Selecting the Card
blue	0.2
yellow	?
orange	0.3

What is the probability of randomly selecting a yellow card from the deck?

Solution:

Law #2 ensures that the sum of the probabilities is equal to 1. So, the probability of randomly selecting a yellow card is equal to 0.5. ■

The **expected value** of an experiment can be calculated when the outcomes are numerical. Numerical outcomes, such as dollar amounts or points, vary depending on the outcome, but the expected value gives us an "average" that weighs all of the outcomes.

Expected value is calculated by multiplying each outcome by its probability, then adding all of the products.

CHAPTER 11 Probability Distributions and Expected Value *continued*

EXAMPLE 5 Calculate expected value

A bag contains 10 quarters, 14 dimes, and 16 nickels. We want to calculate the expected value if a coin is randomly chosen from the bag.

The chart below shows the outcomes, the probabilities of each outcome, and the product of the outcome and its probability.

Outcome	Probability of Outcome	Product
Quarter ($0.25)	$\frac{10}{40} = \frac{1}{4}$	$\frac{1}{4} \cdot (\$0.25)$
Dime ($0.10)	$\frac{14}{40} = \frac{7}{20}$	$\frac{7}{20} \cdot (\$0.10)$
Nickel ($0.05)	$\frac{16}{40} = \frac{2}{5}$	$\frac{2}{5} \cdot (\$0.05)$

The expected value is calculated by adding up the three products:

$$\frac{1}{4} \cdot (\$0.25) + \frac{7}{20} \cdot (\$0.10) + \frac{2}{5} \cdot (\$0.05) \approx \$0.1175$$

So, the expected value is approximately equal to *12 cents*. ■

It is important to remember that the expected value is unlikely to be equal to the actual outcome. Suppose a quarter was blindly chosen in the last example. Here, the actual value (25 cents) differs from the expected value by 13 cents. However, if 5 coins were randomly selected from the bag, their average value is likely to be close to the expected value.

Practice

A bag contains 20 red, 40 blue, 15 white, and 5 green marbles. A marble is selected at random from the bag. Find the probability of the outcome.

1. A blue marble is selected.

2. A green marble is selected.

3. A white marble is not selected.

4. A red, blue, white, or green marble is selected.

5. An orange marble is selected.

Make a table that shows the distribution of probabilities for each possible outcome of the experiment.

6. A coin is tossed.

7. Two coins are tossed.

Probability Distributions and Expected Value *continued*

8. The spinner shown below is spun.

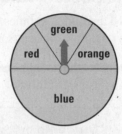

9. A student is randomly chosen from a class that has 6 ninth graders, 8 tenth graders, and 5 eleventh graders.

Problem Solving

10. An experiment has four possible outcomes: *A*, *B*, *C*, and *D*. The probability that outcome *A* will occur is 0.24 and the probability that outcome *D* will occur is 0.46. If the probability of outcomes *B* and *C* are equal, what is the probability that outcome *C* will occur?

11. Valerie can be assigned one of three jobs by a temporary-worker agency. The table below shows the probability that she will get each job, along with the hourly wage for each job.

Job	Probability of getting the job each day	Hourly Wage
Filing	0.6	$6.60
Receptionist	0.1	$8.40
Typing	0.3	$7.80

What is the expected value for Valerie's hourly wage?

12. A card game involves a deck containing 20 red, 10 blue, 18 green, and 6 yellow cards. The table below shows the number of points that a player will get for randomly selecting each card color.

Card Color	Number of Points
Red	40
Blue	25
Green	35
Yellow	60

What is the expected value for the number of points earned from a card that is chosen at random?

Name _____ Date _____

CHAPTER 11 · Permutations

A permutation is an arrangement of objects in a certain order.

EXAMPLE 1 List the permutations: set of three

List all of the possible permutations of the letters *X*, *Y*, and *Z*.

Solution:

XYZ   XZY   YXZ   YZX   ZXY   ZYX

Notice that there are exactly 6 permutations. There are a total of 3 letters to choose from for the first letter, 2 letters to choose from for the second letter, and 1 letter to choose from for the third letter. The counting principle (page 931 in the textbook) allows us to multiply these numbers to obtain our answer of 3 • 2 • 1 = 6 permutations. ■

We can now see that a formula for finding the number of permutations of *n* objects is obtained by multiplying *n* by $(n-1) \cdot (n-2) \cdot \ldots$ until we reach the number 1. The product of the numbers 1 to *n* is called *n* **factorial**, and is written *n*!.

EXAMPLE 2 Find the number of permutations: set of four

In how many ways can you arrange the letters *X*, *Y*, *Z*, and *W*?

Solution:

Here, there are *n* = 4 elements in the set. There are a total of *n*! = 4! = 4 • 3 • 2 • 1 = 24 permutations of the letters *X*, *Y*, *Z*, and *W*. ■

EXAMPLE 3 List the permutations: subset of a set of four

List the permutations of the letters *X*, *Y*, *Z*, and *W* using only 2 of these letters at a time.

Solution:

XY   XZ   XW   YX   YZ   YW   ZX   ZY   ZW   WX   WY   WZ

Notice that there exactly 12 such permutations. There are a total of 4 letters to choose from for the first letter and 3 letters to choose from for the second letter. So, the answer is obtained by multiplying 4 • 3 to obtain the answer of 12. ■

From the last example, notice that $12 = 4 \cdot 3 = \frac{4 \cdot 3 \cdot 2 \cdot 1}{2 \cdot 1} = \frac{4!}{2!} = \frac{4!}{(4-2)!}$. This observation leads us to the following formula:

KEY CONCEPT

Permutations

Consider a set with *n* objects, and a subset of this set with *r* objects. The number of permutations of *n* objects taken *r* at a time is given by:

$$\frac{n!}{(n-r)!}$$

Permutations *continued*

EXAMPLE 4 ## Use the permutation formula

Find the number of permutations of the word FOREST taken 4 letters at a time.

Solution:

Here, $n = 6$ and $r = 4$. Substituting into the formula, we have:

$$\frac{n!}{(n-r)!} = \frac{6!}{(6-4)!} = \frac{6!}{2!} = \frac{6 \cdot 5 \cdot 4 \cdot 3 \cdot 2 \cdot 1}{2 \cdot 1} = 6 \cdot 5 \cdot 4 \cdot 3 = 360$$

So, there are 360 permutations of the word FOREST, taken 4 letters at a time. ■

Practice

List all of the possible permutations for the situation.

1. The letters of the word RED.

2. Two of the letters of the word BOY.

3. Two of the letters of the word READ.

Find the number of permutations of a) all of the letters in the given word, b) 3 of the letters of the word, and c) 2 of the letters of the word.

4. SPACE   5. NUMBER

6. FIND   7. FIGURES

CHAPTER 11

Combinations

A combination is a grouping of objects in which the order of the objects does not matter.

EXAMPLE 1 ## Compare permutations and combinations

Find the permutations and combinations of the letters X, Y, and Z taken 2 at a time.

Solution:

The *permutations* of these letters taken 2 at a time are:

XY YX YZ ZY XZ ZX

The *combinations* of these letters taken 2 at a time are:

XY or YX YZ or ZY ZX or XZ

There are a total of 6 permutations, but only 3 combinations. This is because the order does not matter in a combination. In other words, XY and YX are considered to be the same in a combination. ■

Notice in the last example that the number of combinations is equal to the number of permutations, divided by 2. This is because we are dividing 6 (the number of permutations of 3 objects taken 2 at a time) by the number of permutations of 2 letters, which is equal to $2! = 2$.

In general, the number of combinations of n objects taken r at a time is equal to the number of permutations of n objects taken r at a time, divided by $r!$. This can be written as follows:

$$\frac{n!}{(n-r)!} \div r! = \frac{n!}{(n-r)!} \cdot \frac{1}{r!} = \frac{n!}{r!(n-r)!}$$

KEY CONCEPT

Combinations

Consider a set with n objects, and a subset of this set containing r objects. The number of combinations of n objects taken r at a time is given by:

$$\frac{n!}{r!(n-r)!}$$

EXAMPLE 2 ## Find the combination of 5 objects taken 3 at a time

Find the number of combinations of the letters A, B, C, D, and E taken 3 at a time.

Solution:

Using the formula, we have $n = 5$ and $r = 3$. Substitute these values into the formula.

$$\frac{5!}{3!(5-3)!} = \frac{5!}{3! \cdot 2!} = 10$$

So, there are a total of 10 combinations of 5 objects taken 3 at a time. ■

| CHAPTER 11 | **Combinations** *continued* |

Practice

Simplify.

1. $\dfrac{4!}{2! \cdot 2!}$

2. $\dfrac{8!}{3! \cdot 5!}$

3. $\dfrac{10!}{3! \cdot 7!}$

4. $\dfrac{15!}{2 \cdot 3! \cdot 9!}$

In Exercises 5–8, solve each problem.

5. Given the letters S, T, A, M, and P.

   a. Find the number of permutations of these letters.

   b. Find the number of combinations of these letters.

   c. Find the number of permutations of these letters taken 2 at a time.

   d. Find the number of combinations of these letters taken 2 at a time.

6. Given the letters W, H, I, S, P, E, and R.

   a. Find the number of permutations of these letters.

   b. Find the number of combinations of these letters.

   c. Find the number of permutations of these letters taken 4 at a time.

   d. Find the number of combinations of these letters taken 4 at a time.

7. Given the letters P, E, N, C, I, and L.

   a. Find the number of permutations of these letters.

   b. Find the number of combinations of these letters.

   c. Find the number of permutations of these letters taken 3 at a time.

   d. Find the number of combinations of these letters taken 3 at a time.

8. The number of combinations of the letters of the word CAKE taken r times is equal to 4. What is the value of r.

Name _____   Date _____

CHAPTER 11 · More Compound Events

Probabilities often involve 2 events, called **compound events**. When we want to calculate the probability that 2 events will occur, we are calculating a **compound probability**.

Sometimes, the two events have nothing in common (no common elements), or the two events do have common elements. When two events have no common elements, then they are called **mutually exclusive**.

EXAMPLE 1 Find the probability of mutually exclusive events

A bookshelf contains 40 books. Ten of the books are fiction, and 15 of the books are nonfiction. The remaining books are encyclopedias. A book is randomly selected from the shelf. Find the probability that the book selected is fiction or nonfiction.

Solution:

The Venn diagram shows the two events.

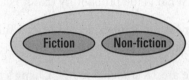

These events are mutually exclusive because a book cannot be both fiction and nonfiction. We add to find the probability that a fiction or nonfiction book is randomly selected:

$$P(\text{fiction or nonfiction}) = P(\text{fiction}) + P(\text{nonfiction}) = \frac{10}{40} + \frac{15}{40} = \frac{25}{40} = \frac{5}{8} \blacksquare$$

Notice that when two events A and B are mutually exclusive, then $P(A \text{ and } B) = 0$. This is because there is no chance that both outcomes could occur at the same time. When two events do have common elements, then they are **inclusive events**.

EXAMPLE 2 Find the probability of inclusive events

A full deck contains 52 cards. Find the probability of randomly selecting an ace or a black card from a full deck.

Solution:

The Venn diagram shows the two events.

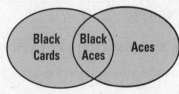

There are 4 aces and 26 black cards in a full deck of cards. As shown in the Venn diagram, these are inclusive events because some aces are black (there are 2 black aces). Begin by calculating the following:

Probability of selecting an ace: $\frac{4}{52}$

More Compound Events *continued*

Probability of selecting a black card: $\frac{26}{52}$

Probability of selecting a black ace: $\frac{2}{52}$

We will need to subtract the probability of selecting a black ace from the sum of the other two probabilities, so that the black aces are not counted twice.

$$P(\text{Ace or Black}) = \frac{4}{52} + \frac{26}{52} - \frac{2}{52} = \frac{28}{52} = \frac{7}{13} \blacksquare$$

Practice

In Exercises 1–4, a) identify the following as exclusive or inclusive, and b) find the probability.

1. Brenda has 4 nickels, 2 pennies, and 8 dimes in her pocket. She randomly selects one. What is the probability that it is a penny or a dime?

2. A card is randomly selected from a full deck of cards. What is the probability that it is a red card or a face card?

3. There are 18 students in Ms. Chang's art class. Four of the students are 15 years old, twelve of the students are 16 years old, and two of the students are 17 years old. What is the probability that a randomly selected student is age 15 or 17?

4. Of the 26 employees at the Electro Company, 8 of the employees use PC computers, 14 of the employees use Mac computers, and 4 of the employees use both. What is the probability that an employee uses a PC or a Mac computer, but not both?

The table below shows the number of male and female freshman, sophomore, junior, and senior students at Valley High School.

	Freshman	Sophomore	Junior	Senior
Male	120	118	108	102
Female	134	100	102	110

Determine the probability of each situation.

5. A randomly chosen student is a freshman or a female junior.

6. A randomly chosen student is a female or a freshman.

7. A randomly chosen student is a female sophomore or a male.

8. A randomly chosen student is a female or a sophomore or junior.

CHAPTER 11 **Distinguishing Between Mutually Exclusive and Independent Events**

Distinguishing between mutually exclusive events and independent events is useful when solving problems that involve probability.

KEY CONCEPT

Mutually Exclusive Events

Mutually exclusive events are subsets of the same sample space as shown in the Venn diagram.

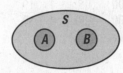

For example, let the sample space S be all of the students that attend a school. Then let subset A be all male students who have brown eyes, and subset B be all female students with green eyes. Both A and B are subsets of S, but have no common elements. A and B are mutually exclusive events.

KEY CONCEPT

Independent Events

Independent events have different sample spaces as shown in the Venn diagram.

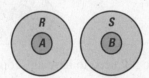

For example let the sample space R be the 6 outcomes when a die is tossed, and subset A be the desired outcome. Similarly, let sample space S be the 2 outcomes when a coin is tossed, and subset B be the desired outcome. Both A and B are independent because they have different sample spaces. If event A occurs, it does not affect event B and vice versa.

EXAMPLE 1 ## Compare mutually exclusive and independent events

The table below shows the number of 9th, 10th, 11th, and 12th grade boys and girls at a certain high school.

	9th	10th	11th	12th
Girls	90	115	100	95
Boys	110	85	100	105

CHAPTER 11

Distinguishing Between Mutually Exclusive and Independent Events *continued*

a. Out of all of the boys at the school, a boy is selected at random. Out of all of the girls at the school, a girl is selected at random. Find the probability that the boy is in 11th grade and the girl is in 12th grade.

Solution:

These events are independent because they have different sample spaces (boys and girls).

The probability is $\underbrace{\dfrac{100}{400}}_{P(\text{boy})} \cdot \underbrace{\dfrac{95}{400}}_{P(\text{girl})} = \dfrac{1}{4} \cdot \dfrac{19}{80} = \dfrac{19}{320} \approx 0.059$

b. A student is selected from the student body at random. Find the probability that the student is in 9th grade and 11th grade.

Solution:

Although each event is part of the same sample space (the student body), these events are mutually exclusive because there is no way a student could be in both grades.

The probability is 0. ■

It is important to note that mutually exclusive events are never independent. Look at the diagram below, which shows two mutually exclusive events A and B:

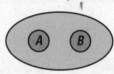

Events A and B do not need to have any common elements for us to calculate $P(A \text{ or } B)$. However, it is impossible to calculate $P(A \text{ and } B)$, because events A and B cannot happen at the same time.

EXAMPLE 2 ## Find probabilities

A drawer contains 6 red paper clips, 10 blue paper clips, and 2 yellow paper clips. Selecting a red or yellow paper clip are mutually exclusive events (e.g. a paper clip cannot be red and yellow). A paper clip is chosen at random.

a. Find the probability that the paper clip is red or yellow:

$$P(\text{Red or Yellow}) = \dfrac{6}{18} + \dfrac{2}{18} = \dfrac{8}{18} = \dfrac{4}{9}$$

b. Find the probability that the paper clip is red and yellow:

$$P(\text{Red and Yellow}) = 0 \quad ■$$

Distinguishing Between Mutually Exclusive and Independent Events *continued*

The information above is also useful in finding probabilities that involve inclusive compound events A and B, where knowing $P(A)$ and $P(B)$ is necessary in order to calculate $P(A \text{ or } B)$.

KEY CONCEPT

Probability of Inclusive Events

If two events A and B are inclusive, then the probability that event A or event B will occur can be calculated as follows:

$$P(A \text{ or } B) = P(A) + P(B) - P(A) \cdot P(B)$$

EXAMPLE 3

Use the formula for inclusive events

Suppose the probability that it will rain on Saturday is 0.5, and the probability that it will rain on Sunday is 0.7. Find the probability that it will rain on Saturday or Sunday, but not both days.

Solution:

$P(A \text{ or } B) = P(A) + P(B) - P(A \text{ and } B) = 0.5 + 0.7 - (0.5) \cdot (0.7) = 0.85$

There is an 85% chance of rain on Saturday or Sunday. ■

Practice

1. **Challenge** Give an example of a situation that involves mutually exclusive events. Draw a Venn diagram that illustrates the situation.

2. **Challenge** Give an example of a situation that involves independent events. Draw a Venn diagram that illustrates the situation.

Identify the events as either *mutually exclusive* or *independent*.

3. A number cube and a coin are tossed. The events are: getting a 4 on the die and a tails on the coin.

4. Mr. Wong's class has 28 students. A student leaves the room for a music lesson, then returns. A second student does the same thing. The events are: the first student is a boy and the second student is a girl.

5. Two number cubes are tossed. The events are: the sum of the numbers is 7 and each die has the same number.

6. A bag contains red and blue marbles. A marble is selected, and then it is replaced. A second marble is selected, and then it is replaced. The events are: both marbles are red.

Binomial Probabilities

When a coin is tossed, the outcome is either heads or tails. Each outcome (heads or tails) has the same chance of occurring, $\frac{1}{2}$. A probability distribution that involves a number of independent trials that has only two possible outcomes (success or failure), with each trial having the same chance of success, is a **binomial distributions**.

EXAMPLE 1 **Two coin toss**

Two coins are tossed at the same time. Graph the binomial distribution.

Solution:

The outcomes are listed in the table below.

1ˢᵗ toss	Tails	Tails	Heads	Heads
2ⁿᵈ toss	Tails	Heads	Tails	Heads

Notice that there are a total of $2^2 = 4$ outcomes. If "tails" is the desired outcome, then the probabilities of these outcomes are shown in the table below.

Number of Tails	Probability
0	$\frac{1}{4}$
1	$\frac{1}{2}$
2	$\frac{1}{4}$

The graph of this binomial distribution is:

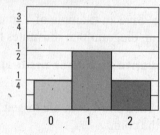

EXAMPLE 2 **Three coin toss**

Three coins are tossed at the same time. Graph the binomial distribution.

Solution:

All of the outcomes are listed in the table below.

1ˢᵗ coin	Tails	Tails	Tails	Heads	Heads	Heads	Tails	Heads
2ⁿᵈ coin	Tails	Tails	Heads	Heads	Heads	Tails	Heads	Tails
3ʳᵈ coin	Tails	Heads	Heads	Heads	Tails	Tails	Tails	Heads

Notice that there are a total of $2^3 = 8$ outcomes. Given that "tails" is the desired outcome, then the probabilities can be shown in a table.

CHAPTER 11 **Binomial Probabilities** *continued*

Number of Tails	Probability
0	$\frac{1}{8}$
1	$\frac{3}{8}$
2	$\frac{3}{8}$
3	$\frac{1}{8}$

The graph of this binomial distribution is:

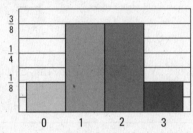

A probability calculated from a binomial distribution is called a **binomial probability**. Calculating a binomial probability from a binomial distribution like the one in the last example is fairly simple. We can answer simple probability questions by looking at the distribution in Example 2.

If three coins are tossed:

- the probability that one of the coins will show "tails" is $\frac{3}{8}$.

- the probability that 1 *or more* of the coins will show "tails" is $\frac{3}{8} + \frac{3}{8} + \frac{1}{8} = \frac{7}{8}$.

- the probability of getting 0 or 1 tails is $\frac{1}{8} + \frac{3}{8} = \frac{1}{2}$.

The first two examples listed the outcomes for 2 coins and 3 coins. As the number of trials increase, however, the need for a formula becomes necessary. This is due to the fact that the sample space grows exponentially with each new trial, depending on the number of outcomes in each trial.

CHAPTER 11

Binomial Probabilities *continued*

In general, we want to know the probability of *n* successes out of *m* trials in a binomial distribution, and will assume that the probability of success in a given trial is *p*.

Consider the example of the three coin toss from Example 2. Let's say that we want to know the probability of getting two heads. Here, $n = 2$ and $m = 3$. Also, the probability of getting a heads (success) is 0.5.

The probability of getting two heads in a three coin toss is obtained by multiplying the number of combinations of 2 out of 3 by the product of each independent event.

$P(\text{2 out of 3 heads}) = (\text{number of combinations of 2 out of 3}) \cdot$
$(P(\text{success})) \cdot (P(\text{failure}))$

$$= \underbrace{\frac{3!}{2!(3-2)!}}_{\text{number of combinations}} \cdot \underbrace{(0.5)(0.5)}_{\text{success}}\underbrace{(0.5)}_{\text{failure}}$$

$$= 0.375 = \frac{3}{8}$$

So, the answer is $\frac{3}{8}$. We can generalize this calculation for any *m*, *n* and *p* with this formula.

KEY CONCEPT

Binomial Distribution

The probability of *n* successes out of *m* trials in a binomial distribution is given by:

$$P(n \text{ out of } m) = \frac{m!}{n!(m-n)!} \cdot p^n \cdot (1-p)^{m-n}$$

where *p* represents the probability of success in a given trial.

EXAMPLE 3

Use the Binomial Distribution formula

Consider a number cube rolled four times. There are a total of $6^4 = 1296$ outcomes! We want to calculate the probability that we will get a 3 on two of the rolls. Here, there are $n = 2$ successes out of $m = 4$ trials. The probability of success is $p = \frac{1}{6}$. Substituting into our formula, we have:

$$P(\text{2 out of 4}) = \frac{4!}{2!(4-2)!} \cdot \left(\frac{1}{6}\right)^2 \cdot \left(1 - \frac{1}{6}\right)^2$$

$$= \frac{4!}{2! \cdot 2!} \cdot \left(\frac{1}{6}\right)^2 \left(\frac{5}{6}\right)^2$$

$$= \frac{25}{216} \approx 0.1157 \blacksquare$$

CHAPTER 11

Binomial Probabilities *continued*

EXAMPLE 4 Find expected value

Two coins are tossed at the same time. Find the expected value for the number of heads that result.

Solution:

$$0 \cdot \frac{1}{4} + 1 \cdot \frac{1}{2} + 2 \cdot \frac{1}{4} = \frac{1}{2} + \frac{1}{2} = 1$$

$\underbrace{\phantom{0 \cdot \frac{1}{4}}}$ probability of getting 0 head $\underbrace{\phantom{1 \cdot \frac{1}{2}}}$ probability of getting 1 head $\underbrace{\phantom{2 \cdot \frac{1}{4}}}$ probability of getting 2 heads

So, the expected value for the number of heads in a 2 coin toss is 1. ■

Practice

Round each answer to the nearest thousandths of a decimal place.

1. Two coins are tossed. Calculate the probability that both coins show heads.

2. Six number cubes are tossed. Calculate the probability of getting a 5 on 4 of the number cubes.

3. Four coins are tossed. Calculate the probability that three of the coins show tails.

4. Four number cubes are tossed. Calculate the probability that 2 or more of the cubes show a 1.

Use the dial shown below to answer Exercises 5–6.

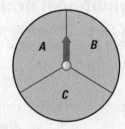

5. The dial is spun three times in a row. Calculate the probability that the dial lands on section *B* two of the times.

6. The dial is spun four times in a row. Calculate the probability that the dial lands on section *A* or section *B*, three of the times.

Find the expected value in Exercises 7–8.

7. Calculate the expected value for the number of tails in a 4 coin toss.

8. Three number cubes are tossed. Calculate the expected value for getting a 4.

CHAPTER 11 **Conditional Probabilities**

The probability that an event B will occur, given that another event A has already occurred is called a **conditional probability**, and is written $P(B|A)$. The Venn diagram below illustrates the situation.

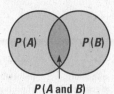

$P(A \text{ and } B)$

We can see that it is necessary to divide $P(A \text{ and } B)$ by $P(A)$ in order to find $P(B|A)$.

The formula for conditional probability can also be derived from the formula for dependent events:

$P(A \text{ and } B) = P(A) \cdot P(B|A)$ (probability of dependent events)

We want to solve this equation for $P(B|A)$, as this is the conditional probability. If we divide both sides of the equation by $P(A)$, we obtain this result:

KEY CONCEPT

Conditional Probability

When two events A and B are dependent, then the probability of event B, given that event A has already occurred is given by:

$$P(B|A) = \frac{P(A \text{ and } B)}{P(A)}$$

EXAMPLE 1 **Find the conditional probability**

At Franklin High School, 50% of the student body is female. Also, 30% of the students ride a bicycle. What is the probability that a student rides a bicycle, given that she is female?

Solution:

The Venn diagram below represents this situation.

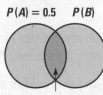

$P(A) = 0.5$ $P(B)$

$P(A \text{ and } B) = 0.3$

Let A represent the number of females at Franklin High School, and let B represent the number of students who ride a bicycle to school. It follows that $P(A) = 0.5$ and $P(A \text{ and } B) = 0.3$. Substituting into the formula, we have the following result:

$$P(B|A) = \frac{P(A \text{ and } B)}{P(A)} = \frac{0.3}{0.5} = 0.6$$

So, the probability that a student rides a bicycle, given that she is female, is 0.6 ∎

CHAPTER 11 | **Conditional Probabilities** *continued*

EXAMPLE 2 Find the conditional probability

The local Weather Service office reports that there is a probability of 0.84 that it will rain on Saturday, and a probability of 0.77 that it will rain on Saturday and Sunday. What is the probability that it will rain on Sunday, given that it rained on Saturday?

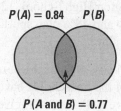

$P(A) = 0.84$ $P(B)$

$P(A \text{ and } B) = 0.77$

Let A represent rain on Saturday and B represent rain on Sunday. It follows that $P(A) = 0.84$ and $P(A \text{ and } B) = 0.77$. Substituting into the formula, we have the following result:

$$P(B|A) = \frac{P(A \text{ and } B)}{P(A)} = \frac{0.77}{0.84} \approx 0.92$$

The probability that it rains on Sunday, given that it rained on Saturday, is about 0.92. ■

The next example looks at another way to calculate a conditional probability.

EXAMPLE 3 An alternate solution

The table below shows the number of 6th, 7th, and 8th grade boys and girls at Lincoln Middle School.

	6th grade	7th grade	8th grade
Boys	46	42	46
Girls	50	38	45

What is the probability that a student is a girl, given that the student is in 8th grade?

Solution:

Let A represent the set of 8th graders, and let B represent the set of girls at Lincoln Middle School. It follows that $P(A) = \frac{91}{267}$ and $P(A \text{ and } B) = \frac{45}{267}$. Substituting into the formula, we have the following result:

$$P(B|A) = \frac{P(A \text{ and } B)}{P(A)} = \frac{45}{267} \div \frac{91}{267} = \frac{45}{91} \approx 0.49$$

Because of the way the data is presented in this problem, we can calculate this result by dividing the number of 8th grade girls (45) by the total number of 8th graders (133).

So, the probability that a student is a girl, given that she is in 8th grade is $\frac{45}{133}$ or about 0.34. ■

Pre-AP Copymasters

CHAPTER
11

Conditional Probabilities *continued*

Practice

1. The probability that it is Monday and that it is a School holiday is 0.01. The probability that it is Monday is 0.2 (1 out of 5 school days). What is the probability that it is a school holiday, given that it is Monday?

2. At Washington High School, 12% of the student body play sports and are in the school play and 48% play sports. What percent of students who play sports are in the school play?

3. In a certain city, 60% of the households have a television set and a DVD player and 90% of the households have a television set. What percent of households in the city have a DVD player, given that they have a television set?

4. Ms. Weller gave two tests so far this semester. The probability that a student passed the first and the second test is 0.85 and the probability that a student passed the first test is 0.9. What is the probability that a student passed the second test, given that they passed the first test?

The table below shows the number of ninth grade boys and girls who are on the soccer and tennis teams. Use the table to answer Exercises 5–8.

	Boys	Girls
Soccer	18	12
Tennis	12	16

5. What is the probability that a student is on the soccer team, given that the student is a boy?

6. What is the probability that a student is on the tennis team, given that the student is a girl?

Answers

Blackline—Chapter 1

Extended Problem Solving

1. b **2.** 0, 1, 2, 3, 4, 5, 6, 7 **3.** 0 **4.** 71 **5.** 16
6. 72 **7.** 23 **8.** 3, 17, 51 **9.** 4, 6, or 12 friends
10. 58 cards **11.** 78 **12.** 54 baseball cards
13. 5 employees **14.** 24 boxes **15.** math: 24;
Spanish: 23 **16.** 119

Identifying Functions

1. Domain: the set of Mr. Brown's employees;
Range: {$1,000, $2,000} **2.** Domain: the set of
Candace's friends; Range: {video game, CD}
3. Domain: the set of students at Woodruff High
School; Range: {gymnasium, auditorium, cafeteria, football field} **4.** Domain: the set of students
in Mrs. Childress's art classes; Range: {van Gogh,
Rodin} **5.** Yes, the rule describes a function; each
customer is assigned exactly one price. Jared will
pay $12.95. **6.** Yes, the rule describes a function;
each student is assigned to exactly one group.
7. No, the rule does not describe a function; a
person who weighs more than 150 pounds will be
prescribed two different dosages according to this
rule. **8.** Yes, the rule describes a function; each
taxpayer is assigned exactly one date to file his or
her annual return. **9.** No, the rule does not describe a function; customers who drive more than
10,000 miles are not assigned a rebate. **10.** Yes,
the rule describes a function; each football player
is assigned to exactly one group.

Real-World Functions

1. the weight of the apples and the price per pound
2. the number of hours he works and his hourly
wage **3.** the distance between her home and her
friend's house and the speed at which she drives
4. the number of days and the cost per day **5.** the
base and the height of the triangle **6.** the length
and the width of the rectangle **7.** the radius
and the height of the cylinder **8.** the radius and
the height of the cone **9.** the length, the width,
and the height of the rectangular prism **10.** the
amount deposited, the interest rate, and the time of
the investment **11.** Answers will vary.

Blackline—Chapter 2

Counting Sets of Rationale Numbers

1. 4 **2.** 6 **3.** 6 **4.** 5 **5.** 26 **6.** 8
7. 1, 2, 3, 4; 4 **8.** 1, 2, 3, 4, 5, 6, 7, 8; 8

9. 1, 2, 3, 4, 5, 6, 7, 8, 9, 10, 11, 12, 13, 14; 14
10. 5, 6, 7, 8, 9, 10, 11, 12, 13, 14, 15; 11
11. $-9, -8, -7, -6, -5, -4, -3, -2$; 8
12. $-4, -3, -2, -1, 0, 1, 2, 3, 4$; 9
13. 21 **14.** 201 **15.** 1000 **16.** 500
17. infinite **18.** 11 **19.** 8 **20.** infinite
21. unbounded **22.** bounded **23.** bounded
24. unbounded **25.** No; the number of students
in Greg's Algebra class can be counted, so the set
is not infinite. **26.** Answers will vary. Sample
answer: 0 years; 150 years

Building a Number System

1a. When you add any two numbers in the set, the
answer is in the set. **b.** When you subtract any
two numbers in the set, the answer is in the set.
c. When you multiply any two numbers in the set,
the answer is in the set. **d.** When you divide any
two numbers in the set, the answer is in the set.
2. Division by zero is undefined. **3.** 13; yes
4. 51; yes **5.** -3; no **6.** -19; no **7.** 40; yes
8. 245; yes **9.** $\frac{8}{5}$; no **10.** 5; yes **11.** 1; yes
12. $\frac{1}{3}$; no **13.** 3; yes **14.** $\frac{5}{2}$; no **15.** 3; yes
16. -9; yes **17.** -18; yes **18.** $-\frac{1}{2}$; no
19. -10; yes **20.** 0; yes **21.** 25; yes **22.** 1; yes
23. 10; yes **24.** 30; yes **25.** -200; yes
26. -2; yes **27.** 0; yes **28.** -1; yes
29. $-\frac{1}{4}$; yes **30.** -1; yes **31.** $\frac{8}{9}$; yes
32. $-\frac{8}{9}$; yes **33.** 0; yes **34.** 0; yes
35. 38.4; yes **36.** 36; yes **37.** 44.64; yes
38. 31; yes **39.** yes **40.** no **41.** yes **42.** no
43. closed under multiplication and division; not
closed under addition or subtraction; answers will
vary, sample answer: $1 + 1 = 2, 1 - 1 = 0$
44. closed under multiplication; closed under
division with the exception of division by zero;
not closed under addition or subtraction; answers
will vary, sample answer: $1 + 1 = 2$,
$1 - (-1) = 2$ **45.** not closed under addition,
subtraction, multiplication, or division; answers
will vary, sample answer: $2 + 2 = 4, 2 - 2 = 0$,
$2 \times 2 = 4, 2 \div 2 = 1$ **46.** not closed under addition, subtraction, multiplication, or division;
answers will vary, sample answer: $2 + 2 = 4$,
$2 - (-2) = 4, 2 \times 2 = 4, 2 \div 2 = 1$ **47.** closed
under addition and multiplication; not closed
under subtraction or division; answers will vary,
sample answer: $5 - 9 = -4, 8 \div 12 = \frac{2}{3}$

48. closed under addition; not closed under subtraction, multiplication, or division; answers will vary, sample answer:
$-5 - (-9) = 4, -3 \times (-6) = 18, -8 \div (-2) = 4$
49. closed under multiplication; not closed under addition, subtraction, or division; answers will vary, sample answer:
$7 + 7 = 14, 19 - 11 = 8, 9 \div 5 = \frac{9}{5}$

50. closed under addition, subtraction, and multiplication; not closed under division; answers will vary, sample answer: $14 \div 2 = 7$ **51.** not closed under addition, subtraction, multiplication, or division; answers will vary, sample answer:
$3 + 7 = 10, 7 - 3 = 4, 3 \times 7 = 21, 7 \div 3 = \frac{7}{3}$

52. closed under multiplication; not closed under addition, subtraction, or division; answers will vary, sample answer:
$25 + 9 = 34, 49 - 9 = 40, 25 \div 4 = \frac{25}{4}$

53. No; the total number of cars and the number of cars washed by each team will be whole numbers. The total number of cars divided by three may not be a whole number. **54.** Yes; the even integers are closed under subtraction. **55.** No; the set of odd numbers is not closed under addition. The sum of two odd numbers is always even. **56.** No; if each of the books cost a whole number of dollars, then the total would also be a whole number of dollars since the whole numbers are closed under addition. **57.** No; though the total of the test scores will be a whole number, when you divide it by 3, the result may not be a whole number, because the set of whole numbers is not closed under division. **58.** Yes; the rational numbers are closed under multiplication.

The Need for Irrational Numbers

1. Answers will vary. **2.** Answers will vary. Sample answer: cube roots or other roots.
3. No; for every rational number r, the number $r\sqrt{2}$ is irrational, so there are at least as many irrational numbers as rational numbers. **4.** The irrational numbers are not closed under any of these operations. Answers will vary. Sample answer:
$\pi + (-\pi) = 0, \pi - \pi = 0, \sqrt{2} \times \sqrt{2} = 2,$
$\pi \div \pi = 1$

More Logical Reasoning

1. The Grand Canyon is not in Minnesota.; false; true **2.** Niagara Falls is not in Alabama.; false; true **3.** One inch is not longer than one centimeter.; true; false **4.** One pound is not heavier than one kilogram.; false; true **5.** A triangle does not have five sides.; false; true **6.** A trapezoid does not have four sides.; true; false **7.** The day after Monday is not Thursday.; false; true **8.** The day before Wednesday is not Tuesday.; true; false **9.** Apples do not grow on trees.; true; false **10.** Strawberries are not blue.; false; true
11. $5 + 6 \neq 13$; false; true **12.** $4 + 8 \neq 12$; true; false **13.** $5 \times 6 \neq 11$; false; true **14.** $5 + 6 \geq 13$; true; false **15.** $4 + 8 \leq 12$; false; true **16.** $5 \times 6 < 13$; true; false **17.** $3.2 > \pi$; false; true **18.** $\sqrt{3} \leq 1.7$; true; false **19.** $\sqrt{2} < 2$; false; true **20.** $0.11 \geq 0.101$; false; true **21.** $0.303 > 0.033$; false; true **22.** $0.818 \leq 0.188$; true; false **23.** Some cars are not red.; false; true **24.** Some trucks are not green.; false; true **25.** Some squares are not rectangles.; true; false **26.** Some rectangles are not squares.; false; true **27.** Some whole numbers are not integers.; true; false **28.** Some negative numbers are not less than zero.; true; false **29.** Some cars are red.; false; true **30.** Some trucks are green.; false; true **31.** Some squares are triangles.; true; false **32.** Some rectangles are squares.; false; true **33.** Some integers are irrational.; true; false **34.** Some positive numbers are less than zero.; true; false **35.** No cars are red.; true; false **36.** No trucks are green.; true; false **37.** No squares are triangles.; false; true **38.** No rectangles are squares.; true; false **39.** No integers are positive.; true; false **40.** No rational numbers are irrational.; false; true **41.** Some integers are not whole numbers.; false; true; answers will vary, sample answer: -1 **42.** Some whole numbers are not greater than zero.; false; true; answers will vary, sample answer: 0 **43.** Some even numbers are not prime.; false; true; answers will vary, sample answer: 4 **44.** Some odd numbers are not prime.; false; true; answers will vary, sample answer: 9 **45.** Some integers are whole numbers.; false; true; answers will vary, sample answer: 1 **46.** Some odd numbers are prime.; false; true; answers will vary, sample answer: 3 **47.** Some odd numbers are positive.; false; true; answers will vary, sample answer: 3 **48.** Some rational numbers are whole numbers.; false; true; answers will vary, sample answer: 1 **49.** No integers are whole numbers.; true; false; answers will vary, sample answer: 1 **50.** No odd numbers are prime.; true; false; answers will vary, sample answer: 3

Algebra 1

Answers, *continued*

51. No positive real numbers are irrational.; true; false; answers will vary, sample answer: π
52. No negative real numbers are rational.; true; false; answers will vary, sample answer: -1
53a. All pianists are singers. **b.** All birds fly. **c.** No authors are poets. **d.** No athletes are millionaires. **e.** All books are novels. **f.** All cars are red.

Writing Repeating Decimals as Fractions

1. $\frac{2}{9}$ **2.** $\frac{4}{9}$ **3.** $\frac{7}{9}$ **4.** $\frac{8}{9}$ **5.** $\frac{17}{99}$ **6.** $\frac{59}{99}$ **7.** $\frac{26}{99}$ **8.** $\frac{71}{99}$

9. $\frac{7}{11}$ **10.** $\frac{9}{11}$ **11.** $\frac{205}{999}$ **12.** $\frac{53}{111}$ **13.** $5\frac{1}{9}$ **14.** $3\frac{5}{9}$

15. $6\frac{2}{3}$ **16.** $7\frac{92}{99}$ **17.** $4\frac{23}{99}$ **18.** $9\frac{19}{99}$ **19.** $6\frac{172}{333}$

20. $9\frac{755}{999}$ **21.** 1; Answers will vary.

22. $8\frac{17}{33}$; $8\frac{17}{33}$; yes; Answers will vary. **23.** Yes; the method works because 6 is a multiple of 3.
24. No; since π is an irrational number, it is impossible to rewrite it as a fraction where both the numerator and denominator are integers.

Unit Rates and Dimensional Analysis

1. $0.105 per ounce **2.** $0.795 per liter
3. $3.60 per pound **4.** $5.95 per pound
5. $3750 per day **6.** 1240 customers per week
7. 53.75 miles per hour **8.** 64.75 kilometers per hour **9.** 36 pages per hour **10.** 52 words per minute **11.** $1.50 per liter **12.** $14 per hour
13. Mia: $0.79; Allison: $0.75; Mia paid the higher price per candy bar. **14.** Nat: $0.095; Chi: $0.09; Nat paid the higher price per minute.
15. Mr. Lighthorse: 58 miles per hour; Mr. Lopez: 55 miles per hour; On average, Mr. Lighthorse was driving faster. **16.** Plane traveling west: 400 miles per hour; plane traveling east: 450 miles per hour; The plane traveling east had the greater average speed. **17.** Renate: $0.08 per ounce; Dean: $0.07 per ounce; Dean paid less per ounce.
18. Keisha: $0.07 per ounce; Jules: $0.08; Keisha paid less per ounce. **19.** Mrs. Billings: 64 miles per hour; Mr. Lucas: 70 miles per hour; Mr. Lucas was driving faster. **20.** Dena: 30 pages per hour; Jamison: 32 pages per hour; Jamison was reading at the faster rate. **21.** $2.00 per foot
22. $0.19 per ounce **23.** $26.91 per square yard

24. $16.11 per square yard **25.** $0.02 per square inch **26.** $3.78 per square foot **27.** $4.76 per square foot **28.** $3.44 per square foot
29. 17 miles per hour **30.** 24 miles per hour
31. 11 miles per hour **32.** 16 miles per hour
33. 17 miles per hour **34.** 85 miles per hour
35. 27 miles per hour **36.** 34 miles per hour
37. First pipe: 4500 gallons per hour; second pipe: 4350 gallons per hour; The first pipe had water flowing through it at the faster rate.
38. First swimming pool: 5700 gallons per hour; second swimming pool: 6100 gallons per hour; The second swimming pool is filling at the faster rate. **39.** First store: $2.28 per foot; second store: $2.29 per foot; The first store has the lower price.
40. Flooring store: $22.41 per square yard; home improvement store: $17.99 per square yard; The home improvement store has the lower price.

Deciding When to Use Cross Products

1. No **2.** No **3.** No **4.** No **5.** Yes **6.** Yes **7.** No **8.** No

9. $\frac{x}{8} = \frac{3}{4}$; $x = 6$ **10.** $\frac{c}{14} = \frac{-5}{7}$; $c = -10$

11. $\frac{3}{5} = \frac{-d}{25}$; $d = -15$ **12.** $\frac{1}{6} = \frac{w}{24}$; $w = 4$

13. $\frac{10}{y} = \frac{-5}{16}$; $y = -32$ **14.** $\frac{9}{v} = \frac{3}{7}$; $v = 21$

15. $\frac{6}{11} = \frac{12}{b}$; $b = 22$ **16.** $\frac{7}{13} = \frac{-63}{g}$; $g = -117$

17. $\frac{z}{4} = \frac{5}{2}$; $z = 10$ **18.** $\frac{m}{6} = \frac{5}{3}$; $m = 10$

19. $\frac{1}{y} = \frac{1}{56}$; $y = 56$ **20.** $\frac{1}{d} = \frac{1}{72}$; $d = 72$

21. $\frac{x+1}{2} = \frac{8}{1}$; $x = 15$ **22.** $\frac{x+2}{5} = \frac{3}{1}$; $x = 13$

23. $\frac{10}{h+2} = \frac{2}{1}$; $h = 3$ **24.** $\frac{25}{n-9} = \frac{5}{1}$; $n = 14$

25. $\frac{y}{3} = \frac{y}{1}$; $y = 0$ **26.** $\frac{m}{5} = \frac{m}{1}$; $m = 0$

27. $\frac{k+2}{3} = \frac{k}{1}$; $k = 1$ **28.** $\frac{\ell-3}{4} = \frac{\ell}{1}$; $\ell = -1$

29. $\frac{z-1}{3} = \frac{z+1}{2}$; $z = -5$

30. $\frac{r+1}{5} = \frac{r-1}{4}$; $r = 9$

31. $\frac{m+2}{3} = \frac{-(m-5)}{2}$; $m = \frac{11}{5}$

32. $\frac{b-5}{2} = \frac{-(b+1)}{5}$; $b = \frac{23}{7}$

33. $\dfrac{p-5}{p-6} = \dfrac{1}{2}$; $p = 4$

34. $\dfrac{x+1}{x+2} = \dfrac{-2}{3}$; $x = -\dfrac{7}{5}$

35. $\dfrac{1}{y-5} = \dfrac{1}{2y-4}$; $y = -1$

36. $\dfrac{1}{t-4} = \dfrac{1}{2t+5}$; $t = -9$

37. $\dfrac{x}{4} + \dfrac{2}{3} = 0$; $\dfrac{x}{4} = \dfrac{-2}{3}$; $x = -\dfrac{8}{3}$

38. $\dfrac{y}{5} + \dfrac{3}{4} = 0$; $\dfrac{y}{5} = \dfrac{-3}{4}$; $y = -\dfrac{15}{4}$

39. $\dfrac{a}{2} - \dfrac{4}{5} = 0$; $\dfrac{a}{2} = \dfrac{4}{5}$; $a = \dfrac{8}{5}$

40. $\dfrac{b}{6} - \dfrac{1}{7} = 0$; $\dfrac{b}{6} = \dfrac{1}{7}$; $b = \dfrac{6}{7}$

41. $\dfrac{x+5}{8} = \dfrac{1}{2}$; $x = -1$ **42.** $\dfrac{y-1}{10} = \dfrac{2}{5}$; $y = 5$

43. $\dfrac{4}{d+2} = -\dfrac{1}{3}$, $\dfrac{4}{d+2} = \dfrac{-1}{3}$; $d = -14$

44. $\dfrac{5}{n+1} = -\dfrac{1}{4}$, $\dfrac{5}{n+1} = \dfrac{-1}{4}$; $n = -21$

Interpreting Percents

1. 40%   **2.** 84%   **3.** $263.76   **4.** $4375
5. $2250   **6.** $37.40   **7.** 43,421   **8.** $54,600
9. $200   **10.** $71.43   **11a.** Hamilton High School
b. Greene High School; Greene: 60%; Hamilton: about 53%   **12a.** $26.64   **b.** $26.42   **c.** Greg
13a. $2.10   **b.** 6.5%   **c.** $36.60   **d.** $36.74
e. By the same percentage; each share is worth $0.14 more.   **14a.** Comparing numbers of votes may not be fair because Bay County may have a much larger population.   **b.** The candidate is actually more popular in Marion County where about 58% of the population voted for him. Only about 24% of the population of Bay County voted for him.   **15a.** $361,000   **b.** $385,000   **16.** Answers will vary.   **17.** The number of students only increased by about 33%; the previous year the number increased by 100%.

Identifying the Domain of a Variable in a Formula

1. The set of all positive real numbers   **2.** The set of all positive real numbers   **3.** The set of all positive real numbers   **4.** The set of all positive real numbers   **5.** The set of all positive real numbers
6. The set of all positive real numbers   **7.** Domain of r: the set of all positive real numbers less than or equal to 10; domain of A: the set of all positive real numbers less than or equal to 100π

8. Domain of g: the set of all nonnegative real numbers less than or equal to 14; domain of d: the set of all nonnegative real numbers less than or equal to 280.   **9.** The set of whole numbers
10. The set of whole numbers less than or equal to 14   **11.** The set of nonnegative multiples of 8.50 ({0, 8.50, 17.00, 25.50,...})   **12.** The set of nonnegative multiples of 30 ({0, 30, 60, 90,...})
13. The set of numbers 30, 35, 40, 45, ..., 95, 100

Solving Linear Equations with a Graphing Calculator

3. −2   **4.** 1   **5.** −4   **6.** 3
7. −7   **8.** −6   **9.** 8   **10.** 3
11. −4   **12.** 5   **13.** −3   **14.** 7

Blackline—Chapter 3

Scatter Plots

1. a. Answers vill vary. Sample answer: Temperature of a glass of hot water on a table, related to time. The temperature of a glass of hot water on a table decreases as the amount of time increases.
b. Answers vill vary. Sample answer: Winning time in Kentucky Derby, related to inches of rain in Seattle on Derby Day. There is no connection between how fast a horse runs in one part of the U.S. and how much it rains in another part far away on the same day.   **2.** Scatter plots relate two quantitative variables, and ice cream flavor is not quantitative.
3a.

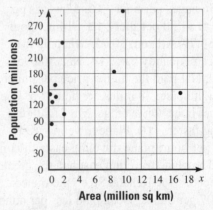

Area (million sq km)

b. There is a fairly tight cluster of six countries whose area ranges up to 2 million square kilometers and whose population falls roughly in the 100−150 million range. Outside that cluster, four more countries with larger area and/or population are widely distributed across the plot. The correlation between area and population is overall

Answers, continued

not very strong except for countries with area less than 2 million square kilometers.   **c.** In the scatter plot, the slope of the line between each country's data point and the origin represents the density. The steeper the line, the denser the population.
d. The first reason is that the scatter plot shows the world's ten most populous countries, and therefore does not give reliable information about countries generally. But even if the plot were accepted as applicable, the distribution of points suggests wide variation in population for countries with more than 2 million square kilometers. A country with 5 million square kilometers could have a population anywhere between 100 million and 250 million people.   **4.** The weight at 3 months is likely to be more accurate. For one thing, 3 months is within the range $1-12$ months, which is covered by the given data. The pattern might change past 12 months. For another thing, common sense suggests (and the graph seems to confirm) that as babies grow older and heavier, there is more room for variation in individual weights.   **5.** Answers will vary.

Distinguishing Between Discrete and Continuous Variables

1. discrete   **2.** continuous   **3.** discrete
4. discrete   **5.** continous   **6.** discrete   **7.** discrete
8. Values of continuous variables are very commonly recorded with rounding to set number of places. Even though the values being rounded to are discrete, the true range of possible values is continous.

Intercepts of Horizontal and Vertical Lines

1. x-intercept: none, y-intercept: 5
2. x-intercept: -4, y-intercept: none
3. x-intercept: none, y-intercept: $-\frac{3}{4}$
4. x-intercept: 0, y-intercept: all real numbers
5. x-intercept: none, y-intercept: 9
6. x-intercept: all real numbers, y-intercept: 0
7. $x = -2$ **8.** $y = 7$ **9.** $x = 0$

Integer Solutions of Linear Equations

1. $x = -1 + 2n, y = 3 - 5n$
2. $x = -1 + 3n, y = 1 + 4n$
3. $x = 2 + 7n, y = -2 - 2n$

4. $x = n, y = -7 + 4n$
5. $x = 9 + 3n, y = n$ **6.** $x = 8n, y = -n$
7. no solutions   **8.** $x = -5 - 3n, y = n$
9. no solutions   **10.** $x = -1 + 6n, y = 1 + 11n$
11. $x = 1 + 7n, y = -2 - 5n$ **12.** no solutions
13. 9 ranchhands and 1 horse; 7 ranchhands and 2 horses, 5 ranchhands and 3 horses, or 3 ranchhands and 4 horses.   **14.** C_4O_7, C_8O_4, or $C_{12}O_1$.
15. There are no integer solutions to the equation $12x + 16y = 162$.

Interpreting the Slope and y-Intercept

1. 1842 is the town's population in 2003, and 15.6 is the annual rate of increase.   **2.** 40 points is the base score; a student gets that much credit just for turning the test in. 2 is the number of points awarded per correct answer.   **3.** $800 is the fixed portion of the charges; it doesn't depend on the size of the house. $3.30 is the charge per square foot of living space.   **4.** -10 is the initial temperature; at 6:00 A.M. the temperature was ten degrees below zero Celsius. 0.15 is the rate at which the temperature rises: 0.15 degree per minute, or 1 degree every 6.67 minutes.   **5.** $V = 150 + 7t$, where V is water volume and t is minutes.
6. $C = 450 + \frac{1}{4}x$, where C is each roommate's cost and x is the total amount of the phone bill.
7. $v = 55 + 2t$, where v is the speed and t is seconds of acceleration.   **8.** $C = 48 + 0.15d$, where C is the cost and d is miles traveled.
9. When a constant term does not appear, it means the constant term is zero. In the equation $v(t) = 9.81t$, a constant term would be the speed at $t = 0$. The fact that the constant term is 0 means that the object was released from rest.

Distinguishing Between Direct Variation and Other Linear Models

1. linear but not direct variation   **2.** linear but not direct variation   **3.** linear, direct variation
4. not linear   **5.** not linear   **6.** linear, direct variation   **7.** $C = 2.78x$, where C is cost and x is gallons of gas. Direct variation.   **8.** $C = 178 + 65t$, where C is cost and t is hours of labor; not direct variation   **9.** $N = 9216A$, where N is total number of pixels and A is area in square inches; direct variation   **10.** $I = \frac{1}{120}p + 0.5$, where I is current and p is power; not direct variation.

Blackline—Chapter 4

Representations of Lines

1. $y - 4 = 3x$ **2.** $y - 2 = \frac{1}{3}(x - 3)$

3. $y + 1 = \frac{4}{3}(x + 1)$ **4.** $y = -5(x - 6)$

5. $y - 2 = -\frac{5}{2}(x + 4)$ **6.** $y + 4 = -(x - 4)$

7. $y = x + 3$ **8.** $y = \frac{3}{2}x - 3$ **9.** $y = -\frac{3}{5}x + 3$

10. $y = -\frac{4}{5}x - \frac{7}{5}$ **11.** $y = -\frac{3}{2}x + \frac{1}{2}$

12. $y = \frac{1}{2}x - \frac{3}{2}$ **13.** $y = \frac{2}{3}x + 2$

14. $y = -2x$ **15.** $y = \frac{3}{2}x - 1$

16. 1 hour: $70; 2 hours: $90; 3 hours: $110; 4 hours: $130; $y - 70 = 20(x - 1)$; $y - 90 = 20(x - 2)$; $y - 110 = 20(x - 3)$; $y - 130 = 20(x - 4)$

Unique Representations

1. Answers may vary.

Sample answers: $\frac{2}{7}$ and $\frac{100}{350}$

2. Answers may vary.

Sample answers: $\frac{18}{32}$ and $\frac{90}{160}$

3. Answers may vary.

Sample answers: $-\frac{2}{3}$ and $-\frac{80}{120}$

4. Answers may vary.

Sample answers: $-\frac{4}{3}$ and $-\frac{240}{180}$

5. Answers may vary. Sample answers: 2×12 and 3×8

6. Answers may vary. Sample answers: 4×9 and 6×6

7. Answers may vary. Sample answers: 3×50 and 10×15

8. Answers may vary. Sample answers: 2×38 and 4×19

9. $\frac{2}{5}$ **10.** $\frac{5}{2}$ **11.** $\frac{4}{9}$ **12.** $-\frac{14}{25}$

13. $3 \times 3 \times 5$ **14.** $2 \times 2 \times 3 \times 5$

15. $2 \times 2 \times 2 \times 5 \times 5$ **16.** $3 \times 3 \times 11$

17. Answer will vary. Possible answers: $3x + 5y = 750$; $6x + 10y = 1500$; $12x + 20y = 3000$

18. $12; Answer will vary. Possible answers: $y - 41 = 12(x - 3)$; $y - 29 = 12(x - 2)$; $y - 17 = 12(x - 1)$

19. $y = 12x - 60$

20. Answer will vary. Possible answers: $40x + 25y = 1000$; $8x + 5y = 200$; $80x + 50y = 2000$

21. Answer will vary. Possible answers: $50x + 30y = 300$; $5x + 3y = 30$; $25x + 15y = 150$

22. $y = -\frac{2}{5}x + 40$

Sequences as Discrete Functions

1. A sequence is a discrete function whose domain is the set of positive integers. A linear function is continuous with the domain being the set of real numbers.   **2.** The graph of a sequence represents a function since each member of the domain maps to exactly one member of the range. Scatter plots, however, are not necessarily functions since their domains could map to more than one range value.

3.

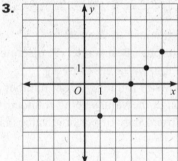

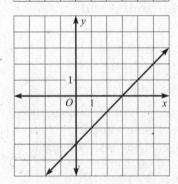

Answers, continued

4.

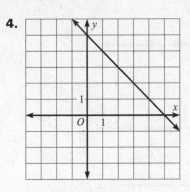

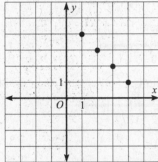

5. Answers will vary. Sample answer:

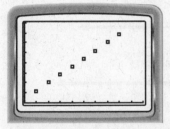

6. Answers will vary. Sample answer:

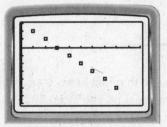

7. Answers will vary. Sample answer:

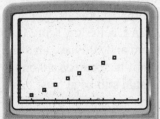

8. Answers will vary. Sample answer:

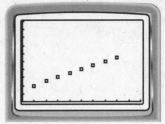

9.

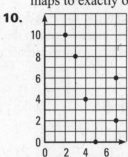

This is a function since every domain value maps to exactly one range value.

10.

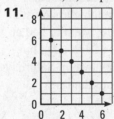

This is not a function since one domain value, 7, maps to more than one range value.

11.

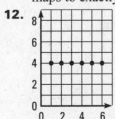

This is a function since every domain value maps to exactly one range value.

12.

This is a function since every domain value maps to exactly one range value.

13.

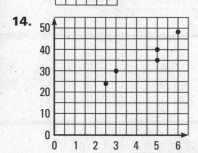

14.

This is not a function since one domain value, 5, maps to more than one range value.

15. The graph cannot be used to represent the number of pages read because it shows a domain with continuous data. Days represent the domain of this situation, and days are discrete.

16. Answers will vary.

Blackline—Chapter 5

The Meanings of *And* and *Or* in Logic

1. true **2.** true **3.** false **4.** true **5.** true **6.** true
7. false **8.** false **9.** All students in math class must be girls, or all students in math class must be boys, but not both. **10.** Ashley went to bed at 9:00 P.M., or Ashley read a book at 9:00 P.M., but not both. **11.** Adam mowed the lawn on Saturday and he also cleaned the garage on Sunday.
12. $q = 3$ or $q = -13$ **13.** $a \geq -7$ and $a \leq -2$

14. $m < \frac{5}{9}$, or $n < 2$, or $m < \frac{5}{9}$ and $n < 2$

Compound Inequalities with No Solution or All Real Numbers as Solutions

1. $-11 < k < -6$

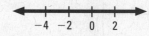

2. $\varnothing$

3. $5 \leq m < -2$

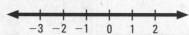

4. All real numbers

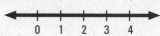

5. $\varnothing$

6. All real numbers

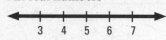

7. $a < -4$ or $a > 4$

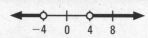

8. All real numbers

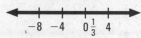

9. All real numbers

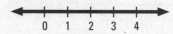

10. $\varnothing$

11. $\varnothing$

12. $j \geq -1$ or $j \leq -4$

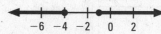

13. All real numbers

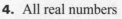

14. $\varnothing$

15. $\varnothing$

16. All real numbers

17. It is not possible for Gina to work any hours according to this inequality. The inequality gives the hours ≤ 24 *and* ≥ 34, which is impossible.
18. This is not possible. Solving the inequality shows that each block's weight is less than 4 pounds *and* greater than 5 pounds, which cannot be true. **19.** Scott can receive any score from 0 to 100 on his last exam and still have an average greater than 70. Even if he received a 0 on the last exam, his average would still be at least 72.
20. The garden can be any width physically possible since the inequality solution shows the width ≥ 10 feet *or* ≤ 25 feet. **21.** It is not likely at all that Carina earns this profit since the inequality solution shows the pieces of jewelry ≤ 25 *and* > 75, which is impossible.

Answers, *continued*

Graphing Calculators and Logic

1. False   **2.** False   **3.** False   **4.** True   **5.** False
6. False   **7.** True   **8.** False   **9.** False   **10.** True
11. False for $x = -3, -2, -1, 0, 1, 2, 3$
12. True for $x = -3, -1, 0, 1, 2, 3$, false for
$x = -2$ **13.** True for $x = -3, -1, 0, 1, 2, 3$,
false for $x = -2$ **14.** True for $x = 0, 1, 2, 3$, false
for $x = -1, 4, 5$ **15.** True for $x = 1$, false for
$x = -1, 0, 2, 3, 4, 5$ **16.** True for $x = -2, -1$,
$0, 1, 3$, false for $x = -3, 2$

A Closer Look at Absolute Value

1. 18   **2.** 50   **3.** 9   **4.** 1   **5.** -46

6. $y = |-x| = \begin{cases} x, & \text{when } x \geq 0 \\ -x, & \text{when } x < 0 \end{cases}$

7. $y = -|x| = \begin{cases} -x, & \text{when } x > 0 \\ x, & \text{when } x \leq 0 \end{cases}$

8. $y = -|-x| = \begin{cases} -x, & \text{when } x > 0 \\ x, & \text{when } x \leq 0 \end{cases}$

9. $y = |4x| = \begin{cases} 4x, & \text{when } x \geq 0 \\ -4x, & \text{when } x < 0 \end{cases}$

10. $y = |2 - x| = \begin{cases} 2 - x, & \text{when } x \leq 2 \\ -(2 - x), & \text{when } x > 2 \end{cases}$

11. $y = |2x + 3| = \begin{cases} 2x + 3, & \text{when } x \geq -\dfrac{3}{2} \\ -(2x + 3), & \text{when } x < -\dfrac{3}{2} \end{cases}$

12. $y = |-5x| = \begin{cases} 5x, & \text{when } x \geq 0 \\ -5x, & \text{when } x < 0 \end{cases}$

13. $y = -|7 + x| = \begin{cases} -(7 + x), & \text{when } x > -7 \\ 7 + x, & \text{when } x \leq -7 \end{cases}$

14. $y = |-(x - 6)| = \begin{cases} x - 6, & \text{when } x \geq 6 \\ -(x - 6), & \text{when } x < 6 \end{cases}$

15. $y = -|3 - 6x| = \begin{cases} 3 - 6x, & \text{when } x > \dfrac{1}{2} \\ -(3 - 6x), & \text{when } x \leq \dfrac{1}{2} \end{cases}$

16. $y = |x - 0.75| = \begin{cases} x - 0.75, & \text{when } x \geq 0.75 \\ -(x - 0.75), & \text{when } x < 0.75 \end{cases}$

17. $y = |x - 25| = \begin{cases} x - 25, & \text{when } x \geq 25 \\ -(x - 25), & \text{when } x < 25 \end{cases}$

18. $y = |x - 12| = \begin{cases} x - 12, & \text{when } x \geq 12 \\ -(x - 12), & \text{when } x < 12 \end{cases}$

19. $y = |x - 530{,}000|$
$= \begin{cases} x - 530{,}000, & \text{when } x \geq 530{,}000 \\ -(x - 530{,}000), & \text{when } x < 530{,}000 \end{cases}$

20. $y = |x - 45| = \begin{cases} x - 45, & \text{when } x \geq 45 \\ -(x - 45), & \text{when } x < 45 \end{cases}$

21. $y = |x - 86| = \begin{cases} x - 86, & \text{when } x \geq 86 \\ -(x - 86), & \text{when } x < 86 \end{cases}$

22. $y = |x - 1| + |x + 3| = $
$\begin{cases} -(2x + 2), & \text{when } x < -3 \\ 4, & \text{when } -3 \leq x < 1 \\ 2x + 2, & \text{when } x \geq 1 \end{cases}$

Solving Absolute Value Equations by Graphing

1. 1   **2.** 2   **3.** 1   **4.** 2   **5.** 0   **6.** 2
7. $x = -3$ **8.** $x = -2$ **9.** $x = 0$
10. No solution   **11.** $x = -8, x = -4$
12. $x = -1.5, x = 0$ **13.** $x = 7$
14. No solution   **15.** No solution
16. The solutions to both sets of graphed
equations are the same.   **17.** The two equations
Alesha graphed do not intersect. There is no
solution to the absolute value equation.
18. Answers will vary. Check students' graphs.
19. Answers will vary. Check students' equations.
20. Mattie could use any value for a and b, but c
must be a negative number.   **21.** Dave could use
any value for a and b, but c must be a positive
number.   **22.** Taylor could use any value for a and
b, but c must be 0.

Margins of Error

1. $|x - 14| < 1$ **2.** $|x - 28| \leq 4$
3. $|x - 40| \leq 5$ **4.** The starting salary of
employees at a retail shop is within $1500 of
$24,500. The margin of error is $1500.
5. To the nearest 5 pounds, the average tensile
strength of a spring is 35 pounds. The margin of
error is 2.5 pounds.   **6.** To the nearest tenth of a
centimeter, a measurement is 9.6 centimeters. The
margin of error is 0.05 centimeters.   **7.** Malcolm
can run a mile within 0.25 minutes of 7.75 minutes. The margin of error is 0.25 minutes.

8. $72 \le x \le 88$ or $|x - 80| \le 8$

9. $2025 \le A \le 3025$

10. $37 \le d \le 53$ or $|x - 45| \le 8$

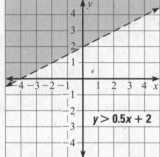

Problem Solving with Linear Equations in Two Variables

1. < **2.** = **3.** ≤ **4.** > **5.** ≥ **6.** ≥

7. All points on the line $y = 4x - 3$.

8. All points on or above the line $y = 4x - 3$.

9. All points below the line $y = 4x - 3$.

10. All points below the line $y = \frac{2}{3}x + 1$.

11. All points on or above the line $y = \frac{2}{3}x + 1$.

12. All points on the line $y = \frac{2}{3}x + 1$.

13.

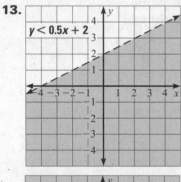

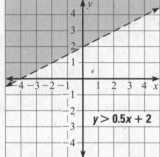

The solution to $y < 0.5x + 2$ is all points below the line $y = 0.5x + 2$, not including the line. The solution to $y > 0.5x + 2$ is all points above the line $y = 0.5x + 2$, not including the line.

14.

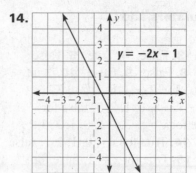

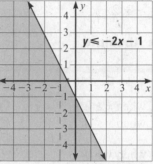

The solution to $y = -2x - 1$ is all points on the line. The solution to $y \le -2x - 1$ is all points on or below the line $y = -2x - 1$.

15.

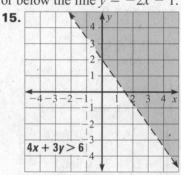

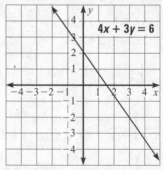

The solution to $4x + 3y > 6$ is all points above the line $y = -\frac{4}{3}x + 2$, not including the line. The solution to $4x + 3y = 6$ is all points on the line.

16.

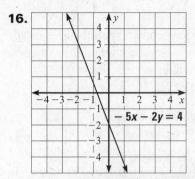

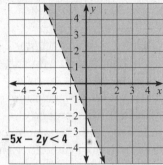

$-5x - 2y = 4$

$-5x - 2y < 4$

The solution to $-5x - 2y = 4$ is all points on the line. The solution to $-5x - 2y < 4$ is all points above the line $y = -\frac{5}{2}x - 2$, not including the line.

17. $3x + 4y = 4x + y$ **18.** $1.50h + 2.50 \le 10$
19. $3x + 5y \ge 30$

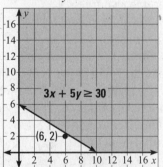

$3x + 5y \ge 30$

$(6, 2)$

No, Lyle could not have answered that number of questions correctly since the point (6, 2) is not part of the solution to this inequality.

Blackline—Chapter 6

Graph Systems of Two Equations and Three Equations

1.

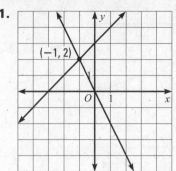

$(-1, 2)$

A point

2.

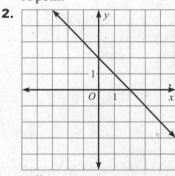

A line

3.

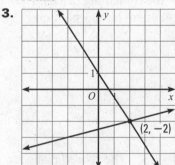

$(2, -2)$

A point

4.

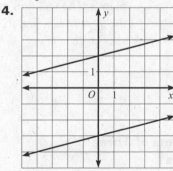

The empty graph

Answers, continued

5.

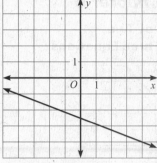

A line

6.

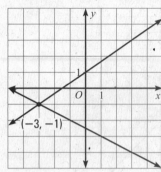

$(-3, -1)$

A point

7. The solution is empty.

8. The solution is empty.

9.

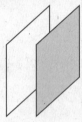

No intersection

The shaded plane represents the coinciding planes. The system has no solution.

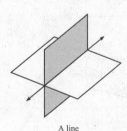

A line

The shaded plane represents the coinciding planes. The solution to the system is a line in *xyz*-space.

Exploring Systems of Three Linear Equations

1. $(-1, 1)$

2. $(-1.5, 2.5)$

3. $(-0.2, -1.44)$

4. $(6.43, -16.79)$

5. $(-2, 2, 3)$

6. $(1.5, -1.2, 3.5)$

7. $(-2, 1, 0, 4)$

8. Advantages are speed and precision. A disadvantage is that when the method fails, it does not tell whether the system has many solutions or no solution.

The Symmetric, Reflexive, and Transitive Properties of Equality

1. $-6y = -6y$ **2.** $12 = 7x$ **3.** $3x - 11 = 2y$
4. $2x + 9 = 8y$ **5.** $5 = 3x$ **6.** $(2y)^2 = 8$
7. $5 + 9b = 2z$ **8.** Since it is given that $x = y$, by the symmetric property, $y = x$. Since it is also given that $x = z$, by the transitive property, $y = z$. **9.** Since it is given that $a = b$ and $b = c$, by the transitive property, $a = c$. Since it is also given that $c = d$, by the transitive property, $a = d$.
10a. No, $>$ is not reflexive. There is no number a such that $a > a$. **b.** No, $>$ is not symmetric. There is are no numbers a and b, with $a > b$, such that $b > a$ is also true. **c.** Yes, $>$ is transitive. For any numbers a, b, and c, if $a > b$ and $b > c$ then $a > c$ must also be true. **11a.** No, $<$ is not reflexive. There is no number a such that $a < a$. **b.** No, $<$ is not symmetric. There is are no numbers a and b, with $a < b$, such that $b < a$ is also true. **c.** Yes, $<$ is transitive. For any numbers a, b, and c, if $a < b$ and $b < c$ then $a < c$ must also be true.
12a. Yes, $\geq$ is reflexive. Since $a = a$ is always true, $a \geq a$ is always true. **b.** No, $\geq$ is not symmetric. If $a = b$, then $a \geq b$ and $b \geq a$. But if $a > b$, then $a \geq b$ but $b \geq a$ is not true. **c.** Yes, $\geq$ is transitive. For any numbers a, b, and c, if $a \geq b$ and $b \geq c$ then $a \geq c$ must also be true. **13a.** Yes, $\leq$ is reflexive. Since $a = a$ is always true, $a \leq a$ is always true. **b.** No, $\leq$ is not symmetric. If $a = b$, then $a \leq b$ and $b \leq a$. But if $a < b$, then $a \leq b$ but $b \leq a$ is not true. **c.** Yes, $\leq$ is transitive. For any numbers a, b, and c, if $a \leq b$ and $b \leq c$ then $a \leq c$ must also be true. **14.** The relation is not transitive. If a is 1 more than b, and b is 1 more than c, then a is 2 more than c, not 1 more.

Adding Equals to Equals

1a. Let $x =$ number of adults and $y =$ number of students. Then $x + y = 1395$ and $3x + y = 2867$.
b. The resulting equation is $2x = 1472$. It has no interesting interpretation, because "dollars minus people" is not a meaningful quantity. All the equation says is that 2 times the number of adults equals 1472. But this information leads to a solution of the problem. **c.** 736 adults and

Answers, *continued*

659 students. **2.** It would not be successful, because the resulting equation, $3x + 14y = 31$, would still have two variables, and the point of the elimination method is to eliminate a variable. **3.** The resulting equation, $-3x + 4y - 10 = 7x + 4y - 2$, would still have two variables, but y would drop out during simplification and then the equation could be solved for x. So this method would be successful, although not as efficient as simply subtracting the original equations. **4.** Since $-1 = -1$ (by the reflexive property), we know from the multiplication property that if $c = d$, then $-c = -d$. Then from the addition property, if $a = b$, it follows that $a + (-c) = b + (-d)$ or $a - c = b - d$. This allow us to subtract $c = d$ from $a = b$.

Solving Systems of Linear Equations Using Cramer's Rule

1. -24 **2.** 0 **3.** -2 **4.** -16 **5.** 4 **6.** 1
7. $x = 2, y = -3$ **8.** $x = -1, y = 2$
9. Infinitely many solutions **10.** No solutions
11. $x = 2, y = 5$ **12.** $x = -4, y = -1$
13. $x = 0, y = 7$ **14.** $x = 9, y = 0$
15. $x = -3, y = -3$ **16.** $x = 4, y = 4$
17. No solutions **18.** Infinitely many solutions
19. $x = 2, y = \frac{1}{2}$ **20.** $x = \frac{1}{3}, y = 5$
21. $x = -\frac{2}{3}, y = 7$ **22.** $x = 2, y = -\frac{2}{5}$
23. No solutions **24.** Infinitely many solutions
25. $x = \frac{2}{5}, y = -3$ **26.** No solutions
27. $x = -\frac{7}{2}, y = \frac{2}{3}$ **28.** $x = -5, y = \frac{3}{4}$
29. No solutions **30.** $x = \frac{4}{5}, y = -\frac{3}{2}$

31. Answers will vary. Sample answer: The elimination method requires making decisions, such as which variable to eliminate and whether to add or subtract the equations. With Cramer's Rule, once the coefficients and constants are identified, there is a direct formula for x and a direct formula for y. **32.** With a, b, c, d, e and f as in Cramer's rule, the assumption means that $ae - db = 0$, $ce - fb = 0$, and $af - dc = 0$. The first equation implies that $\frac{a}{d} = \frac{b}{e}$, and the second equation implies that $\frac{b}{e} = \frac{c}{f}$. Let $k = \frac{a}{d} = \frac{b}{e} = \frac{c}{f}$. Then k times equation $dx + ey = f$ gives equation $ax + by = c$.

Describing Polygons with Systems of Inequalities

1.
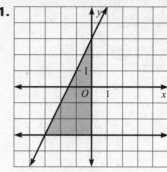

2.
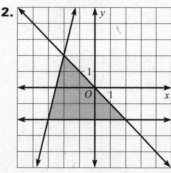

3.
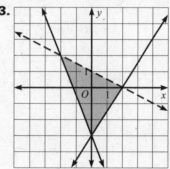

4.
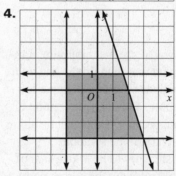

5.
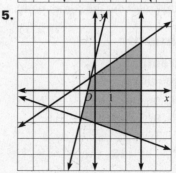

Answers, *continued*

6.

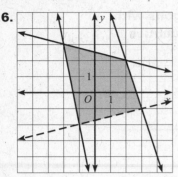

7. $x \geq -1$
$y \geq -1$
$y \leq -x + 2y$

8. $x \leq 1$
$y \leq \frac{3}{2}x + \frac{3}{2}$
$y \geq \frac{x}{2} - \frac{3}{2}$

9. $y \leq -\frac{x}{6} + \frac{3}{2}$
$y \geq \frac{3}{5}x - \frac{4}{5}$
$y > -4x - 10$

10. $x \leq 2$
$y \geq -1$
$y \leq x + 2$
$y \leq -2x + 5$

11. $y \leq 3$
$y \geq -\frac{3}{2}x - 3$
$y \geq \frac{x}{3} - 3$
$y \leq -5x + 13$

12. $y \leq -\frac{x}{3} + 3$
$y \geq 3x - 7$
$y \geq \frac{x}{2} - 2$
$y < 3x + 3$

13. The optimal mix would use the minimum number of peanuts, 0.5 pound, and then fill the bag up to the limit with 1.875 pounds of cashews (upper left corner of solution graph). **14.** The corner point is not part of the solution, because points that lie along the dashed line are not part of the solution. Any solution to the system has to lie *to one side* of the dashed line, and that rules out the corner point.

Blackline—Chapter 7

Adding and Subtracting Exponential Expressions

1. $16a^3$ **2.** $5h^2 + 3h$ **3.** $18g^4$ **4.** $7j^3$ **5.** $2p^4$
6. $2x^3 + 6x$ **7.** $-u^2$ **8.** $2y^3$ **9.** $9w + 8y^2$
10. $2b^2$ **11.** $-3w^2 + 3v$ **12.** $16q^2 + 8q$
13. $24n^5$ **14.** $-3y^2 + 4z^2$ **15.** $-a^2 - b^3 + 4$

16. $5x^4 - 2x^3 + 4x^5 - 3x^2$
17. Perimeter: $20x^2$ units; Area: $25x^4$ units^2
18. $12x - 4$ inches **19.** $x^2 - 8x + 3$ centimeters
20. $2x - 3$ yards

Simplifying Exponential Expressions

1. $19c^6$ **2.** $-8s^6$ **3.** $24v^2w^2$
4. $16x^2y^4 + 3x^4y^2$ **5.** $32a^5b^{10}$ **6.** $10u^{12}v^{24}$
7. $\frac{10h^6}{k^{12}}$ **8.** $\frac{55x^{12}}{4y^4}$ **9.** $\frac{28n^3}{p^3}$ **10.** $\frac{-5y^6}{z^2}$ **11.** $\frac{-9q^6}{8r^6}$
12. $\frac{45r^{10}s^6}{32t^8}$ **13.** $\frac{10a^8c^4}{b^6}$ **14.** $\frac{j^7 - 3j^{12}}{k^4}$
15. $\frac{8x^{12}z^6}{y^9} - \frac{8x^{12}z^6}{y^6}$
16. $(5xy)(3xy) - (2xy)(xy)$; $13x^2y^2$ square units
17. $(6x^4)(4y^2) - (3x^2y)^2$; $15x^4y^2$ square feet

Exploring Non-Integer Exponents with a Graphing Calculator

1. 243 **2.** 16 **3.** 0.037037037 **4.** 27 **5.** 128
6. 64 **7–12.** Check students' keystrokes.
7. 3125 **8.** 0.1428571429 **9.** 32 **10.** 32
11. 3 **12.** 0.0617283951

Average Rates of Change

1. The average rate of change is not constant. Answers will vary. Sample answer: The average rate of change over the interval $0 \leq x \leq 1$ is -1, and the average rate of change over the interval $1 \leq x \leq 2$ is -2. **2.** The average rate of change is constant. This is a linear function with a slope of $\frac{1}{2}$. All linear functions have a constant average rate of change. **3.** The average rate of change is not constant. Answers will vary. Sample answer: The average rate of change over the interval $0 \leq x \leq 1$ is 2, and average rate of change over the interval $1 \leq x \leq 2$ is 4. **4.** The average rate of change is not constant. Answers will vary. Sample answer: The average rate of change over the interval $0 \leq x \leq 1$ is 1, and the average rate of change over the interval $1 \leq x \leq 4$ is $\frac{1}{3}$. **5.** Answers will vary. Function will be a linear function, since all linear functions have a constant average rate of change. **6.** Answers will vary. Function will not be linear, so the average rate of change will not be constant. **7.** All average rates of change over these intervals are equal to 1. This is typical of

Answers, *continued*

linear functions with a constant rate of change, but $y = x^3$ is not linear. If other intervals are checked, it can be shown that the average rates of change are not equal to 1. The function does not have a constant average rate of change. **8.** -4
9. $2.40; $5.97

Exponential Functions: Continuous or Noncontinuous

1. A noncontinuous graph has holes, breaks, jumps, or sharp turns in it. A continuous graph does not. **2.** All exponential functions are continuous because they are defined for all real numbers with no holes, breaks, jumps, or sharp turns.

3. 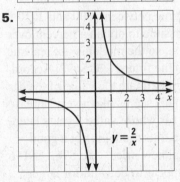 The graph is noncontinuous.

4. 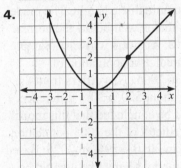 The graph is noncontinuous.

5. The graph is noncontinuous.

6. 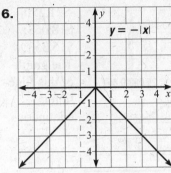 The graph is noncontinuous.

7. 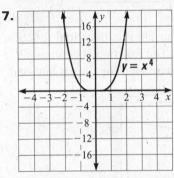 The graph is continuous.

8. 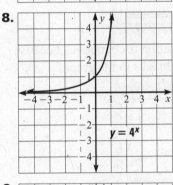 The graph is continuous.

9. 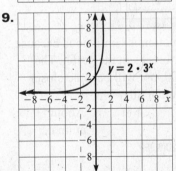 The graph is continuous.

10. 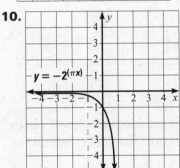 The graph is continuous.

11.

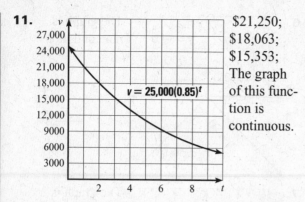

$21,250;
$18,063;
$15,353;
The graph of this function is continuous.

12. No values of *x* cause this exponential function to be noncontinuous. The function is continuous everywhere since it is defined for all real numbers.

13.

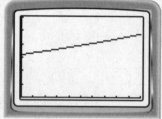

The graph of this function is continuous because there are no holes or breaks in the graph.

14.

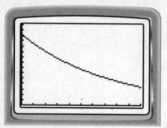

The graph of this function is continuous because there are no holes or breaks in the graph. The value will never be $0, but will become closer and closer to the value of $0.

15.

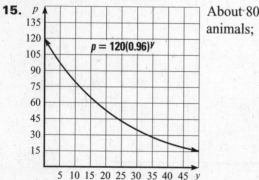

About 80 animals;

16. This function is continuous for all real values of *m* since the exponential function is defined for all real values of *m*.

17.

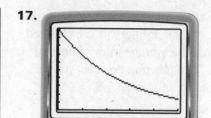

The graph of this function is continuous.

Model Limitations

1. Answers will vary. Sample answer: The amount of defoliation could actually be much higher or lower in any given year than the model predicts, based on factors such as whether or not the gypsy moths die off. Also, other natural disasters may occur to affect the amount of defoliation that the model may not account for. The model may also predict an unrealistic amount of defoliation in years far into the future. **2.** Answers will vary. Sample answer: The model could probably be used to predict the height of the child at 48 months since this age is close to the range of ages shown in the model. However, at 480 months, the model will probably give an unrealistic height. The model levels off at a height that is well below the normal height for an adult. **3.** Answers will vary. Sample answer: The model predicts a population of approximately 1280 in 2005. This differs from the actual population by about 520, a 30% difference. For this reason, it can be concluded that this model is not a very good predictor of the 2005 population. **4.** 9% in 2000; 56% in 2010; 859% in 2025; Based on these results, the model seems like it could be valid for periods of time between 2000 and 2010. However, it is not possible to obtain a percent over 100% in this situation, so the model is not realistic for years farther into the future. **5.** $692; According to this model, approximate the value of the car in 1997 is $71,399. This seems like a very unrealistic price for a new car whose value 5 years later is $12,000. Therefore, this model is not a good predictor of the actual new price. **6.** $96; −$156; The model doesn't appear to be valid for larger quantities of sunglasses since it is not realistic to sell them for negative dollar amounts. This model is probably most valid for smaller quantities of sunglasses.

Solving Exponential Equations

1. 2^5 **2.** 5^4 **3.** 2^6 **4.** 3^5 **5.** 6^{-2} **6.** 10^{-3} **7.** 2^{-2}

8. 2^{-8} **9.** $x = 7$ **10.** $x = 5$ **11.** $x = \dfrac{5}{2}$

12. $x = -3$ **13.** $x = -\dfrac{3}{5}$ **14.** $x = \dfrac{1}{2}$

15. $x = \dfrac{1}{4}$ **16.** $x = -\dfrac{3}{4}$ **17.** $x = \dfrac{8}{3}$

18. $x = -2$ **19.** $x = -5$ **20.** $x = \dfrac{2}{3}$

21. $x = \dfrac{2}{3}$ **22.** $x = \dfrac{1}{6}$ **23.** $x = -11$

Blackline—Chapter 8

A Multiplication Strategy

1. 3 **2.** 6 **3.** 8 **4.** 9 **5.** 4 **6.** 6 **7.** 4 **8.** 8

9. $2u^6 - 5u^5 + 3u^4 + u^3 - 2u^2$

10. $-10b^8 + 25b^7 - 7b^5 - 15b^4 - b^2 - 4b$

11. $4p^8 + p^6 + n^4p^3 + 7n^2p^3 + 12n^2p^5 + 3n^6 + 15n^4 + 12p^5 + 3p^3 + 12n^2$ **12.** $7v^4 - 7z^4 - 48v^2z^2 + 9v^3 + 7z^3 - v^2z - 13vz^2 - 12v^2 - 2z^2 - vz - 4v + 2z$ **13.** $2x \times (30 - 4x) \times (50 - 4x)$; $32x^3 - 640x^2 + 3000x$ **14.** $(x + 4y + z + 4)$ by $(2x + 4y + z)$; $2x^2 + 12xy + 3xz + 16y^2 + 8yz + z^2 + 8x + 16y + 4z$

More Special Products

1. $(x + 3)^2 = x^2 + 6x + 9 \neq x^2 + 9$

2. $(3x - 2y)^3 = 27x^3 - 54x^2y + 36xy^2 - 8y^3 \neq 9x^3 - 4y^3$

3. $(x + y + z)^2 \neq x^2 + y^2 + z^2$ since $(x + y + z)^2 = (x + y + z)(x + y + z) = x^2 + 2xy + y^2 + 2yz + z^2 + 2xz$

4. $m^3 + 6m^2 + 12m + 8$

5. $t^3 - 21t^2 + 147t - 343$

6. $125k^3 + 450k^2 + 540k + 216$

7. $8q^3 - 12q^2 + 6q - 1$

8. $c^3 + 3c^2d + 3cd^2 + d^3$

9. $f^3 - 3f^2g + 3fg^2 - g^3$

10. $w^3 + 6w^2z + 12wz^2 + 8z^3$

11. $64r^3 - 144r^2s + 108rs^2 - 27s^3$

12. $-343v^3 - 294v^2w - 84vw^2 - 8w^3$

13. $x^4 + 12x^3 + 44x^2 + 48x + 16$

14. $h^4 - 4h^3 + 18h^2 - 28h + 49$

15. $9j^4 - 6j^3 + 25j^2 - 8j + 16$

16. $x^2 - 6xy - 4x + 9y^2 + 12y + 4$

17. $16y^2 + 24wy - 16yz + 9w^2 - 12wz + 4z^2$

18. $25m^2 - 30mr - 20mq + 9r^2 + 12qr + 4q^2$

19. $64x^3 - 144x^2 + 108x - 27$

20. $4x^4 + 20x^3 + 13x^2 - 30x + 9$

Prime Trinomials of the Form $x^2 + bx + c$

1.

Factors of 4	Sum of Factors
1, 4	$1 + 4 = 5$
2, 2	$2 + 2 = 4$

No two positive factors of 4 sum to 3.

2.

Factors of 9	Sum of Factors
1, 9	$1 + 9 = 10$
3, 3	$3 + 3 = 6$

No two positive factors of 9 sum to 8.

3.

Factors of 4	Sum of Factors
−1, −4	$-1 + (-4) = -5$
−2, −2	$-2 + (-2) = -4$

No two negative factors of 4 sum to −6.

4.

Factors of −12	Sum of Factors
1, −12	$1 + (-12) = -11$
−1, 12	$-1 + 12 = 11$
2, −6	$2 + (-6) = -4$
−2, 6	$-2 + 6 = 4$
3, −4	$3 + (-4) = -1$
−3, 4	$-3 + 4 = 1$

No two factors of −12 sum to 7.

5.

Factors of −28	Sum of Factors
1, −28	$1 + (-28) = -27$
−1, 28	$-1 + 28 = 27$
2, −14	$2 + (-14) = -12$
−2, 14	$-2 + 14 = 12$
4, −7	$4 + (-7) = -3$
−4, 7	$-4 + 7 = 3$

No two factors of −28 sum to 15.

6.

Factors of 16	Sum of Factors
−1, −16	$-1 + (-16) = -17$
−2, −8	$-2 + (-8) = -10$
−4, −4	$-4 + (-4) = -8$

No two negative factors of 16 sum to −12.

7.

Factors of −15	Sum of Factors
1, −15	$1 + (-15) = -14$
−1, 15	$-1 + 15 = 14$
3, −5	$3 + (-5) = -2$
−3, 5	$-3 + 5 = 2$

No two factors of −15 sum to −8.

Answers, continued

8.

Factors of -20	Sum of Factors
$1, -20$	$1 + (-20) = -19$
$-1, 20$	$-1 + (20) = 19$
$2, -10$	$2 + (-10) = -8$
$-2, 10$	$-2 + 10 = 8$
$4, -5$	$4 + (-5) = -1$
$-4, 5$	$-4 + 5 = 1$

No two factors of -20 sum to -10.

9.

Factors of 45	Sum of Factors
$1, 45$	$1 + 45 = 46$
$3, 15$	$3 + 15 = 18$
$5, 9$	$5 + 9 = 14$

No two positive factors of 45 sum to 28.

10. prime **11.** prime **12.** prime
13. $(z - 3)(z - 9)$ **14.** prime
15. $(g + 3)(g - 14)$ **16.** prime
17. $(h + 4)(h - 19)$ **18.** prime

Prime Trinomials of the Form $ax^2 + bx + c$

1.

Factors of 2	Factors of 7	Possible factorization	Middle term when multiplied
$1, 2$	$1, 7$	$(x + 1)(2x + 7)$	$7x + 2x = 9x$
$1, 2$	$7, 1$	$(x + 7)(2x + 1)$	$x + 14x = 15x$

Since no combination of the factors of $2x^2$ and 7 sum to a middle term of $14x$, the trinomial is prime.

2.

Factors of 3	Factors of 6	Possible factorization	Middle term when multiplied
$1, 3$	$1, 6$	$(g + 1)(3g + 6)$	$6g + 3g = 9g$
$1, 3$	$6, 1$	$(g + 6)(3g + 1)$	$g + 18g = 19g$
$1, 3$	$2, 3$	$(g + 2)(3g + 3)$	$3g + 6g = 9g$
$1, 3$	$3, 2$	$(g + 3)(3g + 2)$	$2g + 9g = 11g$

Since no combination of the factors of $3g^2$ and 6 sum to a middle term of $15g$, the trinomial is prime.

3.

Factors of 5	Factors of 9	Possible factorization	Middle term when multiplied
$1, 5$	$-1, -9$	$(y - 1)(5y - 9)$	$-9y + (-5y) = -14y$
$1, 5$	$-9, -1$	$(y - 9)(5y - 1)$	$-y + (-45y) = -46y$
$1, 5$	$-3, -3$	$(y - 3)(5y - 3)$	$-3y + (-15y) = -18y$

Since no combination of the factors of $5y^2$ and 9 sum to a middle term of $-11y$, the trinomial is prime.

4.

Factors of 4	Factors of -1	Possible factorization	Middle term when multiplied
$1, 4$	$1, -1$	$(s + 1)(4s - 1)$	$-s + 4s = 3s$
$1, 4$	$-1, 1$	$(s - 1)(4s + 1)$	$s + (-4s) = -3s$
$2, 2$	$1, -1$	$(2s + 1)(2s - 1)$	$-2s + 2s = 0$

Since no combination of the factors of $4s^2$ and -1 sum to a middle term of $-6s$, the trinomial is prime.

Answers, continued

5. If $3p^2 - 8p + 8$ is prime, then $-3p^2 + 8p - 8$ is prime. Check $3p^2 - 8p + 8$.

Factors of 3	Factors of 8	Possible factorization	Middle term when multiplied
1, 3	−1, −8	$(p - 1)(3p - 8)$	$-8p + (-3p) = -11p$
1, 3	−8, −1	$(p - 8)(3p - 1)$	$-p + (-24p) = -25p$
1, 3	−2, −4	$(p - 2)(3p - 4)$	$-4p + (-6p) = -10p$
1, 3	−4, −2	$(p - 4)(3p - 2)$	$-2p + (-12p) = -14p$

Since no combination of the factors of $3p^2$ and 8 sum to a middle term of $-8p$, the trinomial is prime.

6. If $2q^2 - 9q - 10$ is prime, then $-2q^2 - 9q + 10$ is prime. Check $2q^2 + 9q - 10$.

Factors of 2	Factors of −10	Possible factorization	Middle term when multiplied
1, 2	1, −10	$(q + 1)(2q - 10)$	$-10q + 2q = -8q$
1, 2	2, −5	$(q + 2)(2q - 5)$	$-5q + 4q = -q$
1, 2	5, −2	$(q + 5)(2q - 2)$	$-2q + 10q = 8q$
1, 2	10, −1	$(q + 10)(2q - 1)$	$-q + 20q = 19q$
1, 2	−1, 10	$(q - 1)(2q + 10)$	$10q + (-2q) = 8q$
1, 2	−2, 5	$(q - 2)(2q + 5)$	$5q + (-4q) = q$
1, 2	−5, 2	$(q - 5)(2q + 2)$	$2q + (-10q) = -8q$
1, 2	−10, 1	$(q - 10)(2q + 1)$	$q + (-20q) = -19q$

Since no combinations of factors of $2q^2$ and -10 sum to a middle term of $9q$, the trinomial is prime.

7. prime **8.** prime **9.** prime **10.** prime
11. prime **12.** $-(w + 3)(4w - 5)$
13. prime **14.** prime **15.** $(2j - 3)(3j + 1)$

Blackline—Chapter 9

Features of the Graph of $y = x^2$

Answers will vary. Check students' work.

Average Rates of Change of Quadratic Functions

1. 1 **2.** $\frac{26}{9}$ **3.** $-\frac{1}{2}$ **4.** -1 **5.** $-\frac{7}{12}$ **6.** 2
7. -10 **8.** -9 **9.** 13 **10.** -11 **11.** 4 **12.** 0
13. $\frac{1}{2}$ **14.** 4 **15.** 1 **16.** 14 **17.** $-\frac{1}{4}$ **18.** $-\frac{3}{2}$
19. $-\frac{5}{2}$ **20.** $-\frac{1}{2}$ **21.** $\frac{1}{2}$ **22.** -2

Area Under a Graph

1. 6 **2.** 10 **3.** 100 **4.** 580
5a. 19.50 **b.** 23.50 **c.** 21.33
6a. 2.21 **b.** 2.64 **c.** 3.12
7a. 2.75 **b.** 2.70 **c.** 3.08
d. 3.38; The smaller base length results in a more accurate estimate. **8a.** 3.75 **b.** 3.92
c. 4.28 **d.** 4.67; The smaller base length results in a more accurate estimate.

Solving Quadratic Inequalities by Graphing

1. $x < 0$ or $x > 2$ **2.** $1 \leq x \leq 3$
3. $x < -3$ or $x > 3$ **4.** $x < -1$ or $x > 0$
5. $x < 0$ or $x > 24$ **6.** No solution
7. $x \leq -10$ or $x \geq 0$ **8.** $-4 \leq x \leq 2$
9. $k \geq 0$ **10.** $k > 0$ **11.** $0 < x < 0.80$
12. $x < -2.87$ or $x > 2.87$
13. $x \leq -6.65$ or $x \geq 1.10$ **14.** $-4 < x < 0$

Systems of Equations with at Least One Nonlinear Equation

1. Answers will vary.   **2.** Not possible
3. Answers will vary.   **4.** Not possible
5. $(0, 0)$, $(-7, -49)$ **6.** $(8, -6)$, $(-8, -6)$
7. $(4, -7)$, $(-3, 0)$ **8.** $(1, 1)$
9. $(-1.55, 1.6)$, $(1.55, 1.6)$ **10.** No solution
11. $(-1, 0)$ **12.** No solution
13. $(-1.69, -3.69)$, $(1.19, -0.81)$
14. $(-0.72, 0.98)$, $(0.69, 1.02)$

Compare Linear, Exponential, and Quadratic Graphs

1. Both graphs are increasing and decreasing and have y-axis symmetry. Both have an extreme point at the origin. The graph of $y = x^2$ has a variable rate of change. Graph B has two rates of change: one when $x < 0$ and another when $x > 0$.   **2.** Both graphs are always increasing. Neither has y-axis symmetry or any extreme points. The graph of $y = 2x$ has a constant rate of change. Graph A has a variable rate of change.   **3.** The graph of $y = 2^x$ is always increasing while Graph C is always decreasing. Neither has y-axis symmetry or any extreme points. Both graphs have a variable rate of change.

Using Regressions Models

1a. $y = 7125x^2 - 5825x + 99175$ **b.** \$2,832,675
c. Not an accurate long term model
2a. $y = 2.33x + 1.63$ **b.** 71.5 feet
c. Not an accurate long term model
3a. $y = 41.6(4.2)^x$ **b.** 111,420 meters
c. Not an accurate long term model

Describing Regions Bounded by Graphs

1a. $\begin{cases} y \geq \frac{1}{2}(3)^x \\ y \leq -x^2 + 2x + 6 \end{cases}$ **b.** $(2.19, 5.57)$ and $(-1.63, 0.08)$

2a. $\begin{cases} y \leq 1 - x^2 \\ y \geq x^2 - 1 \end{cases}$ **b.** $(-1, 0)$ and $(1, 0)$

3a. $\begin{cases} y \leq 18 - x \\ y \geq \frac{1}{2}x^2 + 14 \end{cases}$ **b.** $(2, 16)$ and $(-4, 22)$

4a. $\begin{cases} y \leq \frac{x}{10} \\ y \geq 2^x - 1 \end{cases}$ **b.** $(0, 0)$ and $(-9.99, -0.99)$

5a. $\begin{cases} y \leq 0.25x^2 + 9 \\ y \geq 3x^2 - 2x + 1 \end{cases}$ **b.** $(2.11, 10.11)$ and $(-1.38, 9.48)$

6a. $\begin{cases} y \leq \left(\frac{1}{4}\right)^x \\ y \geq 4x^2 - x + 0.5 \end{cases}$ **b.** $(0.34, 0.62)$ and $(-0.5, 2)$

7. 4.75   **8.** 3.6   **9.** 7   **10.** 9   **11.** 15.14   **12.** 18
13. 19.81   **14.** 0.28   **15.** 2.67

Blackline—Chapter 10

More Examples of Bias

1. Asking for a name is not necessary.   **2.** This question forces a response.   **3.** This is a random sample and is not biased.   **4.** Not mutually exclusive   **5.** Violates privacy/potentially embarrassing question   **6.** Little or no variability   **7.** This question forces a response.   **8.** Makes assumptions

Interpreting More Graphs

Checkpoint

1. February and March   **2.** approximately 100
3. An *exact* number cannot be determined from this graph, but a fair estimate would be 500.
4. frozen yogurt   **5.** ice cream, approximately 35 more   **6.** week 2, approximately 45 cones
7. soccer   **8.** 51   **9.** swimming and baseball, 15

Practice

1. 2002 and 2003   **2.** 2005 and 2006; An exact amount cannot be determined from this graph (approximately \$1.50/h).   **3.** approximately \$3/h
4. weeks 4 and 5   **5.** plant B   **6.** weeks 5 and 6; approximately 5 cm   **7.** game 3   **8.** game 2; 11 pts   **9.** 48 pts   **10.** B   **11.** yes, a medium at pizza parlors A and C   **12.** approximately \$2.50   **13.** approximately \$3.50

Introduction to Standard Deviation

Checkpoint

1. Mean for the Red Team: 4.5; Mean for the Blue Team: 3.5

2. Red Team; The Red Team's scores are much more spread out from the mean than are the Blue Team's scores.

3. about 13.49

Answers, *continued*

4. The actual standard deviations match the prediction; the standard deviation for Student B (13.49) is greater than that for Student A (2.45)

5. Red Team's standard deviation ≈ 4.75; Blue Team's standard deviation ≈ 1.38

6. a. 93.2
   b. 9
   c. Amy's data is more clustered about the mean than Steve's data, but less clustered about the mean than Dana's data.

Practice

1. Mean = 11.33; S.D. = 1.11   **2.** Mean = 6.45; S.D. = 1.23   **3.** Mean = 28.5; S.D. = 3.86   **4.** Mean = 5.5; S.D. = 2.88   **5.** Mean = 92.57; S.D. = 2.13   **6.** Mean = 2.25x; S.D. = 1.48x **7.** Mean = 0; S.D. = 0 Mean = 1; S.D. = 0; Any set containing a group of identical elements will have an S.D. equal to 0. Although a mean can equal 0 if the set's positive and negative numbers cancel out, this will never be the case with a standard deviation since one must add a group of squares, and squares are never negative.   **8.** D   **9.** Mean = 10.5; S.D. = 2.46   **10.** Mean = 13.7; S.D. = 3.95; The mean and standard deviation in problem 10 exceed those in problem 9.

11. Chemical assay/Mean = 33.89; S.D. = 1.59; Light assay/Mean = 33.78; S.D. = 4.26; The chemical assay.

12. Results will vary.

13. Mean = 22.14; S.D. = 5.87; 3 values fall within the first S.D.

14. Mean = 35; S.D. = 17.08; 4 values fall within the first S.D.

15. a. Mean = 7; S.D. = 1.41

   b.

   c. It will have to be greater than 11.23
   d. Answers will vary. The mean and standard deviation will both increase.

Blackline—Chapter 11

Probability Distributions and Expected Value

1. $\frac{1}{2}$ **2.** $\frac{1}{16}$ **3.** $\frac{13}{16}$ **4.** 1   **5.** 0

6.

head	0.5
tails	0.5

7.

heads and tails	0.25
tails and heads	0.25
tails and tails	0.25
heads and heads	0.25

8.

red	$\frac{1}{6}$
green	$\frac{1}{6}$
orange	$\frac{1}{6}$
blue	$\frac{1}{2}$

9.

ninth	$\frac{6}{19}$
tenth	$\frac{8}{19}$
eleventh	$\frac{5}{19}$

10. 0.15   **11.** $7.14   **12.** 38 points

Permutations

1. RED, RDE, ERD, EDR, DRE, DER
2. BO, BY, OB, OY, YB, YO   **3.** RE, RA, RD, ER, EA, ED, AR, AE, AD, DR, DE, DA
4. a) 120   **b)** 60   **c)** 20   **5. a)** 720   **b)** 120   **c)** 30
6. a) 24   **b)** 24   **c)** 12   **7. a)** 5040   **b)** 210   **c)** 42

Combinations

1. 6   **2.** 56   **3.** 120   **4.** 300,300
5. a) 120   **b)** 1   **c)** 20   **d)** 10
6. a) 5040   **b)** 1   **c)** 840   **d)** 35
7. a) 720   **b)** 1   **c)** 120   **d)** 20
8. 3

More Compound Events

1. a) exclusive   **b)** $\frac{5}{7}$ **2. a)** inclusive   **b)** $\frac{8}{13}$
3. a) exclusive   **b)** $\frac{1}{3}$ **4. a)** inclusive   **b)** $\frac{9}{13}$
5. $\frac{178}{447}$ **6.** $\frac{283}{447}$ **7.** $\frac{274}{447}$ **8.** $\frac{112}{149}$

Distinguishing Between Mutually Exclusive and Independent Events

1. answer will vary   **2.** answers will vary
3. mutually exclusive   **4.** independent
5. mutually exclusive   **6.** independent

Binomial Probabilities

1. 0.25   **2.** 0.008   **3.** 0.25   **4.** 0.132   **5.** 0.222
6. 0.395   **7.** 2   **8.** 0.5

Conditional Probabilities

1. 0.05   **2.** 25%   **3.** 67%   **4.** 94%
5. 0.6   **6.** 0.57